This timely book challenges theory's critique of literary art. It argues that the institutionalization of theory, particularly in North American universities over the last quarter century, has led to a pervasive intellectual sterility. Theory's institutional triumph induces critics to offer categorical explanations and demystifying analyses that ignore the actual power and scope of literature. Mark Edmundson traces this tendency to systematize and sterilize literature to Plato's famous quarrel, on behalf of philosophy, against the poets. Edmundson goes on to show how contemporary theorists like de Man, Derrida and Bloom have renewed the philosophical drive to demean poetic art, or to subsume it into some "higher" form of thought. This is not an anti-theoretical book: it acknowledges the value of theory and the intellectual prowess of the theorists it treats. But it is also concerned to recognize theory's limits and to establish the responsibility of literary criticism to do more than theorize: to identify those points at which literature *resists* being explained away. This book comes to the defence of poetry – and of literary art overall – at a time when its cultural status is in doubt. Challenging, clear, and controversial, Mark Edmundson's work should be read by all teachers of literature and theory, and by anyone concerned with the future of literary studies.

"By focusing on the condescension with which philosophy has, since Plato, treated poetry, Edmundson has given us a remarkably successful and genuinely original treatment of the relation between contemporary European philosophy and American literary criticism. Though he writes in a spirit of reconciliation, his view is bound to be controversial. Many literary theorists have no wish to be reconciled with the poets." Richard Rorty

LITERATURE AGAINST PHILOSOPHY, PLATO TO DERRIDA

A DEFENCE OF POETRY

LITERATURE AGAINST PHILOSOPHY, PLATO TO DERRIDA

A Defence of Poetry

MARK EDMUNDSON

University of Virginia

CAMBRIDGE
UNIVERSITY PRESS

Published by the Press Syndicate of the University of Cambridge
The Pitt Building, Trumpington Street, Cambridge CB2 1RP
40 West 20th Street, New York, NY 10011–4211, USA
10 Stamford Road, Oakleigh, Melbourne 3166, Australia

First published 1995
Reprinted 1996, 1997

Printed in Great Britain by Athenaeum Press Ltd, Gateshead, Tyne & Wear

A catalogue record for this book is available from the British Library

Library of Congress cataloguing in publication data

Edmundson, Mark, 1952–
Literature against Philosophy, Plato to Derrida: a defence of poetry
/ Mark Edmundson,
p. cm.
Includes index.
ISBN 0-521-41093-2 (hardback) – ISBN 0-521-48532-0 (paperback)
1. Literature – History and criticism – Theory, etc. 2. Poetics.
3. Philosophy and literature. I. Title.
PN81.E25 1995
809.1 – dc20 94-27021 CIP

ISBN 0-521-41093-2 hardback
ISBN 0-521-48532-0 paperback

For Matthew and William

Contents

Acknowledgments

This book began with the pleasurable work of teaching Romantic poetry and literary theory at the University of Virginia. There are many students to whom I am grateful, among them Gayle Wald, Gregory Jones, Pam Burton, Virginia Heffernan, Jennifer Mendelsohn, Susan Schultz, Alice Gambrell, Neil Arditi, and Paul Outka. From classrooms, some of the thoughts that take final form here went into essays. For advice, endorsement, and permission to reprint, thanks to Laurence Goldstein of *Michigan Quarterly Review*, Gordon Hutner of *American Literary History*, Frank Lentricchia of *South Atlantic Quarterly*, and Suzanne Hyman and Richard Poirier of *Raritan*. To Richard Poirier I'm grateful for more than editorial advice: his example as a literary critic who has succeeded in becoming one of America's foremost writers was a continuing source of pleasure and encouragement.

The first complete draft of the book was written at Ralph Cohen's Commonwealth Center for Literary and Cultural Change. Ralph Cohen's support for the project, his suggestions along the way, and his intellectual presence abetted the work in numerous ways.

Once fully formed, the manuscript got generous, comprehensive readings from friends. Chip Tucker, with wit and singular intelligence, pointed out errors, made suggestions for development, and pushed hard on the structure of argument. Jahan Ramazani enlightened me with his energetic, perceptive, and impassioned response. Richard Rorty straightened me out on some philosophical questions, and made numerous valuable comments. The chance to have Richard Rorty as a colleague, and to teach courses with him, has been among the luckiest parts of a fortunate intellectual life.

Thanks too to J. Hillis Miller, Geoffrey Hartman, William Kerrigan, Gordon Braden, Anthony Winner, Viola Winner, and Jason Bell, who read pieces of the book and offered generous responses.

Michael Pollan gave me his warmth, intelligence, humor, and invaluable friendship, as well as his assurance that a book about literary theory that he could read on the New York Subway System might not be all bad.

Kevin Taylor is, in my experience, unique among university press editors, blending as he does calm intelligence with marvelous energy and self-trust. Working with him has been a pleasure.

My wife, Elizabeth Denton, gave me more than I can say. The beauty I find in her and in her work is a continual inspiration. My sons, Matthew and William, to whom I dedicate this book, slowed its composition down and made it better than it would otherwise have been, for which I'm grateful.

Prologue: an ancient quarrel

Literary criticism in the West begins with the wish that literature disappear. Plato's chief objection to Homer is that he exists. For to Plato poetry is a deception: it proffers imitations of imitations when life's purpose is to seek eternal truth; poetry stirs up refractory emotions, challenging reason's rule, making men womanish; it induces us to manipulate language for effect rather than strive for accuracy. The poets deliver many fine speeches, but when you question them about what they've said, their answers are puerile: they don't know what they're talking about. Though Plato can be eloquent about the appeal of literary art, to him poetry has no real place in creating the well-balanced soul or the just state. When he conceives his Utopia, Plato banishes the poets outside its walls.

All this is well known, yet it remains salutary to stop and think how odd it is for literary criticism to begin as it does. Is there any other kind of intellectual inquiry that originates in a wish to do away with its object? Imagine art history beginning in puritan iconoclasm; sociology in a commitment to deep solipsism; history in a wish that we should live always in the present.

I begin this book with reference to the quarrel between the poets and philosophers, which Plato said was already ancient in his time, because I think that, though changed in some important ways, that quarrel continues on into the present.[1] But the balance

---

[1] On the contemporary relevance of the ancient quarrel Richard Rorty and Martha Nussbaum concur. Rorty reflects on the contention throughout his work, but especially in *Contingency, Irony, and Solidarity* (Cambridge: Cambridge University Press, 1989), pp. 23–43 and 73–95; Nussbaum throughout *The Fragility of Goodness: Luck and Ethics in Greek Tragedy and Philosophy* (Cambridge: Cambridge University Press, 1986) and in *Love's Knowledge: Essays on Philosophy and Literature* (New York: Oxford University Press, 1990), especially pp. 3–53.

of power has shifted considerably from the time when Plato, coming on as something of an upstart, protested Homer's godlike standing. Now the philosophical critique of poetry is ascendant. In the provinces of literary criticism, Plato's heirs have apparently won out.

In this book I will offer some speculations about how that victory has come to pass and do my best to defend poetry (with poetry understood here as shorthand for any revitalizing cultural activity) against some of the preeminent analytical methods that have been used, over the past thirty or so years, to discipline it. I will consider deconstruction in two very different guises, influence theory, ideological critique, New Historicism, and a number of other forms. My aim is not to discredit these developments, for most of them are potentially enlivening. This isn't a book in defence of sweet appreciation.

Rather I shall propose a dialectical mode of interpretation – interpretation as mental fight, to cite a phrase of William Blake's that will crop up often here – in which the critic answers back to theory on behalf of poetry. This answering style acknowledges where theory has scored its points, admitting the ways it circumscribes this or that piece of writing. But I mean also to take the side of a number of art works (which as Northrop Frye said are in a certain sense mute) and show how they pass beyond analytical vocabularies and paradigms in valuable ways.

The first chapter will measure Wordsworth's achievement in the "Intimations" ode against a de Manian critique, pointing out what may be a surprising genealogy for de Man's work. I will show how, rather than upending the modes of criticism he inherits from Coleridge and the New Critics, de Man affirmed and augmented them. This chapter will prepare the way for the contention, developed throughout the book, that despite his personal fall from grace, de Man continues to be one of the most influential literary critics in the Anglo-American academic world.

The next chapter will consider Derrida (a writer in many ways unlike de Man), and other polemicists against presence, in the context of the ancient quarrel. Here the argument will take place under the aegis of Emerson's great essay "Compensation": I admit the ascetic appeal of Derrida's hostility to the visual, but it is a matter of calculating costs. What is the price to the literary imagination for turning against presence and affirming the ethos of never-ending textuality? Against Derridean iconoclasm, I pose the Romantic drive to transform the verbal image from a facile to a demanding pleasure. But is anyone afraid of Jacques Derrida any more? Hasn't his form of thinking been displaced? Not, I shall argue, to the degree that uncritical embrace of "reading" and the "text" and a hostility to the visual continue to reign in Anglo-American literary study.

Wordsworth is a central figure in this volume: no poet who wrote in English has come under more negative criticism than he has over the last two decades. The third chapter will consider two critiques of Wordsworth, one informed by Althusserian Marxism, the other by feminism. The objective will be to show what in Wordsworth remains vital – and it is a great deal – after these critical modes have scored their points.

Perhaps the most influential form of criticism currently active descends from Michel Foucault, and chiefly from his great book, *Discipline and Punish.* The fourth chapter will show first how Foucault's way of thinking *can* form a critical background, a hyperbolic, Blakean vision of the worst in contemporary social life. Against Foucault's account of the disciplines, I believe, we can profitably measure the force of literary creations, and see why we need those creations as much as we do. But in work supposedly inspired by Foucault, that of Greenblatt's Berkeley School of New Historicists, Foucault's best possibilities have been largely left untouched.

Harold Bloom seems to me one of the major critics in the Western tradition, yet his best-known book, *The Anxiety of Influence*, turns from what is most valuable about his work overall. The fifth chapter will describe that turning, speculate on how it transpired, then show how useful Bloom has been and can be in the defence of poetry.

In sum, these pages will argue that theory is crucial for a culture of criticism, but that we are doing harm to ourselves and others if we theorize literature and leave it at that. For too long the study of literature has been divided between enthusiastic adherents to this or that theoretical method, and those who feel that any contact between the poetic and the theoretical mind is sacrilege, a fouling of the altars. In such an atmosphere a call for an exchange between poetry and theory can sound almost insurrectionary.

   To begin making my case I need to spend some time describing the form that the philosophical critique of the poets has previously taken, and to suggest how in recent years it has gained added force.[2] Here in the prologue I attempt to make my arguments in accessible summary form. As the book develops, matters will necessarily grow more complex. But I try throughout to write so as to reach as large a readership as possible, among them, perhaps, the many practicing poets and fiction writers whom institutional literary criticism seems to have done all in its power to leave behind.

To Plato – to put it unceremoniously – the poets must lie, for they live among phantoms, at a third remove from reality. There exists, somewhere on high, the form of the bed; the craftsman building a bed draws on the form, imitating it, though imperfectly. Along comes the painter or poet, whose rendering merely imitates the craftsman's imitation. Why can't it be an imitation of the form of the bed? This question Plato handles adroitly. The bed made by the craftsman can be seen from a variety of perspectives: one learns more about what a bed is by looking at it from one side, then from above, then getting beneath it and examining the slat-work. But the painter gives you the bed from only one perspective (just as, presumably, the poet renders it from one point of view, his); thus you learn less about beds from artistic and poetic imitations than from the craftsman's rendering.

   The worldly reception of artistic knowledge – knowledge at the third remove from truth – bears out Plato's judgment. Socrates asks Glaucon if he knows of any rulers who have enlisted poets as counselors, and Glaucon admits that he doesn't. Then too, the poets attract no followers. "Well," Socrates says (to his

---

[2] In *Trials of Desire: Renaissance Defenses of Poetry* (New Haven: Yale University Press, 1983), Margaret Ferguson offers an account of the ways that writers from Tasso to Sidney have defended poetry against various forms of attack. I know of no comparable volume for the modern period from, say, Sidney up through Blake, Shelley, Emerson, and T. S. Eliot.

followers), "if there is no mention of public services, do we hear of Homer in his own lifetime presiding, like Pythagoras, over a band of intimate disciples who loved him for the inspiration of his society and handed down a Homeric way of life . . . ? If Homer had really possessed the knowledge qualifying him to educate people and make them better men, instead of merely giving us a poetical representation of such matters, would he not have attracted a host of disciples to love and revere him?"[3]

It's not only the fact that poetry is of little epistemological worth that should make good men shun it, it also disrupts the soul's balance. The best sort of people are wise and reserved: they aren't easily ruffled; they often don't have much to say. But such people are of little dramatic interest. Tragedies are full of overwrought characters who let their misfortunes push them into florid grief. About such grief they can be beautifully eloquent, and make surrender to passion – and turning from reason – look most attractive.

Plato believes that passion ought always to be controlled: "Instead of behaving like a child who goes on shrieking after a fall and hugging the wounded part, we should accustom the mind to set itself at once to raise up the fallen and cure the hurt, banishing lamentation with a healing touch" (p. 336). Poetic drama unhinges manly character: it makes one behave childishly, or, as Plato says later, like a woman (p. 338). Enjoying a tragedy means pitying the fallen character, identifying with him. But this identification has its costs: "to enter into another's feelings must have an effect on our own: the emotions of pity our sympathy has strengthened will not be easy to restrain when we are suffering ourselves" (p. 338). Plato assumes that we become what we pleasurably behold. He also believes – movingly and outrageously – that no one of truly noble character could suffer as tragic protagonists do, for you cannot harm a person whose soul is in a state of true harmony.

The indictment against the poets is simultaneously psychological and political. Believing that the soul and the commonwealth are mirror images of each other, Plato argues that poetry's

---

[3] *The Republic*, trans. Francis MacDonald Cornford (London: Oxford University Press, 1941), p. 330. Henceforth cited in the text. Other Platonic works that touch on the question of poetry include *Ion*, *Phaedrus*, *Laws*, and *Apology*.

appeal to the passions is also an appeal to the more passionate and thoughtless citizens. "So, we shall be justified in not admitting [the poet] into a well-ordered commonwealth, because he stimulates and strengthens an element which threatens to undermine the reason . . . The dramatic poet sets up a vicious form of government in the individual soul: he gratifies that senseless part which cannot distinguish great and small, but regards the same thing as now one, now the other" (p. 337). The poet represents a form of government that Plato intensely dislikes, the one that affirms the rule of the passions, of the crowd. Poets – on this matter Walt Whitman and Plato superficially concur – are naturally on the side of democracy.

It's probably clear that besides deriding the poets, Plato is offering an implicit portrait of what a philosopher ought to be. For in almost every consequential matter, poets are on the other end of the scale from true philosophers. The two groups define each other reciprocally. The philosopher is a member of an elite; the poet a democrat, a man of the crowd. Unlike the philosopher, who might help a ruler to govern (and this was one of Plato's highest hopes), poets are of no use to heads of state. Philosophers gather many disciples (as Socrates and Plato both succeeded in doing), people who love them and spread their teachings; Homer's friends neglected him in old age. Poets dally with feelings, appealing to what's childish and feminine in their audience; maybe they're immature and womanish themselves. Philosophers eschew grief: they are restrained, judicious, manly. And perhaps most important, philosophers dwell with the truth, or at least move toward it through dialectic. Poets are at the third remove from reality, lost amid figments.

It's quite possible, as John Hollander remarks in an artful essay on the ancient quarrel, that *The Republic* offers a polemic not just against poets, but against the poet within the great myth-maker, Plato.[4] He's turning against the parts of his work that aren't consistent with the way he would like to be conceived. The most poetic of philosophers may be repudiating his own poetic prowess at the end of his major volume, and thus teaching

---

[4] "The Philosopher's Cat: Examples and Fictions," *Melodious Guile: Fictive Pattern in Poetic Language* (New Haven: Yale University Press, 1988), pp. 207–32.

us how to read it, retrospectively: as something reasonable and detached, concerned with eternal forms, masculine and mature, attractive to disciples, the province of an elite.

And this is where literary criticism begins in the West, with the conviction, expressed by the greatest of philosophers, the man who invented philosophy in something of the way Freud invented psychoanalysis, that poetry is a harmful diversion, best repudiated in the self and cast from the state. Effective literary criticism ever after attempts to defend poetry against this heaping Platonic insult.

Plato inaugurates what Arthur Danto, in a brilliant essay, calls "the philosophical disenfranchisement of art."[5] Danto begins by describing a key paradox in Plato's polemic against art and artists. Art is an imitation of an imitation, thus it is far removed from the real; it is ineffectual, impotent. Yet, too, art is dangerous in that it challenges reason's supremacy. The fact that these two charges are, to say the least, inconsistent only makes the assault more telling. Plato has art coming and going. Danto clinches his argument with a shrewd sentence: "And ever since this complex aggression, as profound a victory as philosophy has ever known or ever will know, the history of philosophy has alternated between the analytical effort to ephemeralize and hence defuse art, or, to allow a degree of validity to art by treating it as doing what philosophy itself does, only uncouthly" (p. 7).

Kant, Danto says, participates in the former program. His central insistence about the aesthetic object is that it solicits disinterested appreciation from the observer. It takes us out of the sphere of human beliefs and desires into a still, tranquil world. The art object exhibits, in Kant's famous formulation, "purposiveness without any specific purpose." It gives us a detached sense of what human desire looks like from a godlike position. But that raising up of the subject is also a denigration: it transfers us from life to limbo. One may say that Kant saves art from vulgar appropriation: his theory would defend it from being used by ideologues of various sorts. But it does so at the cost of putting art beyond *any* human use. Kant's aesthetics would,

---

[5] "The Philosophical Disenfranchisement of Art" appears in the volume of the same name (New York: Columbia University Press, 1986), pp. 1–21. Henceforth cited in the text.

at least theoretically speaking, license artists to render foreign and maybe threatening kinds of experience, but with the proviso that such renderings have no bearing whatever on day-to-day life. Art can teach us something about the *forms* of cognition and reason, but that is as close to life as it should come.[6]

More powerful still, Danto indicates, is the attempt, most influentially undertaken by Hegel, to demonstrate that art is philosophy in embryonic form. In the Hegelian philosophy of history, art is one stage in the unfolding of spirit and philosophy the next. Art paves the way for the philosophical, but once that conceptual discipline is possible, once, that is, it is possible for us to be self-conscious about what matters most in aesthetic experience, then art, something like Marx's post-revolutionary state, can simply wither away. "But," comments Danto, "this is a cosmic way of achieving the second stage of the platonic program, which has always been to substitute philosophy for art. And to dignify art, patronizingly, as philosophy in one of its self-alienated forms, thirsting for clarity as to its own nature as all of us thirst for clarity as to our own" (p. 16). From the Hegelian perspective, art must submit itself to a sort of philosophical therapy in which it overcomes its fixation on the merely particular and rises into the world of the evolving idea, the world of spirit. Where artistic id was there philosophical ego shall be.

Unmentioned by Danto is the more complex case of Aristotle. In *The Poetics*, Aristotle concurs with his teacher Plato about poetry's power to stimulate violent emotions, but the true result, if the work in question is a well-made tragedy like *Oedipus Rex*, will be that the feelings are discharged, and the spectators leave in a state of calm, all passions spent.[7] Aristotle also departs from Plato's view that art gives us mere imitations of imitations: "poetry," Aristotle famously observes, "is a more philosophical and a higher thing than history: for poetry tends to express the universal, history the particular" (ch. 9). Aristotle's reflections counter his teacher's two main arguments, the epistemological,

---

[6] Immanuel Kant, *Critique of Judgment*, trans. J. H. Bernard (New York: Hafner Press, 1951).

[7] My translation is that of Samuel H. Butcher in his *Aristotle's Theory of Poetry and Fine Art*, ed. John Gassner (New York: Dover Publications, 1951). *The Poetics* will be cited by chapter number in the text.

and the spiritual or psychological. The emotions that Plato fears will corrupt spectators are actually expelled by the actions of the play; and drama, rather than leading away from truth, can give us access to general knowledge. But for such capable advocacy there is a price.

Aristotle, it has been said, is the first formalist. He breaks tragedy down into what he takes to be its constituent elements: Plot, Character, Diction, Thought, Spectacle, and Song (ch. 6), then proceeds to anatomize them. For Aristotle, a work of dramatic art must be a coherent whole, with a beginning, a middle, and an end. On a few occasions, he gestures toward an analogy that will be central for literary criticism in the West, a comparison between the work of art and a living thing. Here the doctrine of literary organicism begins to develop.

The drawbacks of a criticism that limits itself to matters of form have been described by any number of twentieth-century writers. Using formal categories like Plot, Character, and Diction on a number of works tends to elide the ways they differ from each other. One begins to talk more about *the* novel, and less about *Bleak House*, *Lost Illusions*, and *Libra*. Summary terms interfere with our ability to perceive what is unique, and uniquely valuable in a given work. And stable critical categories, even when they designate poetic actions, tend to devalue dramatic movement and place one imaginatively outside of time. Formal terms are often distancing, rendering one immune to the emotional force in the work. Using the formal vocabulary, you may analyze a work, but it is unlikely that you will afford it the chance to read and interpret you.

Exclusive reliance on formal categories for criticism can lead one to do to literary experience what metaphysical philosophers are prone to do to experience overall: bring it under the control of concepts and so assume a godlike detachment and power. This is what Derrida is getting at when he says that "literary criticism has already been determined, knowingly or not, voluntarily or not, as the philosophy of literature."[8] Aristotle, according to many, starts out trying to defend poetry against Plato, but he ends up engendering modes of formalism that

[8] *Writing and Difference*, trans. Alan Bass (Chicago: University of Chicago Press, 1978), p. 28.

undermine poetry's influence in more sophisticated ways than Plato ever conceived.[9] Plato, Kant, and Hegel with their more overt programs to banish or subdue art have been easier to resist than its apparent defender, who may have spawned the most subtle of philosophical disenfranchisements. For an exclusive emphasis on structure can give rise to the situation that Derrida writes so passionately against and that Harold Bloom evokes when he says that "Aristotle . . . ruined literary criticism almost from the beginning."[10]

Dismissal, subordination, tendentious celebration, costly defence: these are some of the forms in which, beginning with Plato, the ancient quarrel has been joined by philosophy. Danto goes so far as to say that the history of philosophy could be seen as a series of attempts to neutralize art. "And since Plato's theory of art *is* his philosophy, and since philosophy down the ages has consisted in placing codicils to the platonic testament, philosophy itself may just be the disenfranchisement of art – so the problem of separating art from philosophy may be matched by the problem of asking what philosophy would be without art" (p. 7). In this observation Danto seems to concur with Derrida, who says that "Philosophy, during its history, has been determined as the reflection of poetic inauguration."[11]

Both Danto and Derrida come out of Nietzsche's *Birth of Tragedy* and its thesis that Socratic philosophy moves to suppress the Dionysian energies alive in early Greek tragedy. To Socrates, says Nietzsche, the Dionysian abyss was "something quite abstruse and irrational, full of causes without effects and effects seemingly without causes, the whole texture so checkered that it must be repugnant to a sober disposition, while it might act as dangerous

---

[9] For the argument that Aristotle answers his teacher, see William K. Wimsatt, Jr. and Cleanth Brooks, *Literary Criticism: A Short History* (New York: Vintage Books, 1957), pp. 21–34. See also Gerald F. Else, *Plato and Aristotle on Poetry*, ed. Peter Burian (Chapel Hill: University of North Carolina Press, 1986). Else speculates as follows on the genesis of *The Poetics*:

Nothing in Aristotle's previous education or subsequent experience, outside the Akademy, could have impelled him to take up the cudgels in defense of poetry. It was the immediate shock of Plato's attack on all that he held most holy – above all, Homer – that engendered the *Poetics*. He had the materials for a defense ready in his mind; it was only a question of organizing them. (p. 73)

[10] "The Art of Criticism," an interview with Antonio Weiss, *Paris Review*, 118 (Spring 1991), p. 187.   [11] *Writing and Difference*, p. 28.

tinder to a sensitive and impressionable mind."[12] For Nietzsche, Socrates' victory against the pre-Euripidean tragic writers was nearly total, and is at the root of an over-rational, falsely optimistic culture. Derrida sees ours as a comparably misguided civilization: one might say, a touch crudely, that he goes on to rename Socratism as the metaphysics of presence and liberating Dionysus as *différance*. Philosophy, in the dramatic view of Nietzsche, Derrida, and Danto, springs not from wonder, as Aristotle had it, or, as Wittgenstein believed, from the feeling that one has lost one's way, but from the effort to discipline refractory energies, literary energies.

Is it true? Ought we to follow the implication alive in Nietzsche, Derrida, and Danto who, different as they are, suggest that we might see metaphysical philosophy as a reaction against art, and hence as something antithetical to art, as a distinctly different mode of writing and thought? The position I am describing here has recently been rendered with considerable elegance by Bernard Williams, whose *Shame and Necessity* is in many ways a contemporary rewriting of Nietzsche's *Birth of Tragedy*.

In a certain sense, Williams observes, "Plato, Aristotle, Kant [and] Hegel are all on the same side, all believing in one way or another that the universe or history or the structure of human reason can, when properly understood, yield a pattern that makes sense of human life and human aspirations. Sophocles and Thucydides, by contrast, are alike in leaving us with no such sense. Each of them represents human beings as dealing sensibly, foolishly, sometimes catastrophically, sometimes nobly, with a world that is only partially intelligible to human agency and in itself is not necessarily well-adjusted to ethical aspirations."[13] Beautiful and suggestive though this passage is, its division between those who take the world to be fully intelligible and those who don't may be a bit stark, not responsive enough to moods and varieties in the writers at hand. I think there is another, more flexible way to talk about the tensions between poetry and

---

[12] *The Birth of Tragedy & The Genealogy of Morals*, trans. Francis Golffing (New York: Anchor Books, 1956), p. 86.
[13] (Berkeley and Los Angeles: University of California Press, 1993), pp. 163–4.

systematic thought, a way derived from another brilliant
Nietzschean book.

Toward the close of his *Preface to Plato*, Eric Havelock points to
a key gesture that Socrates deploys in prosecuting his case against
the poets.[14] Homer's work, Havelock points out, was commonly
committed to memory. He who recited it was for all purposes lost
in its immediacy, its pure presence. The reciter became the poem.
How then do you break Homer's spell, regather and retract the I
from the flow of images and events? How do you initiate philosophical thought in someone attracted to, in fact substantially
formed by, unselfconscious immersion?

The key, says Havelock, is to arrest the poem's motion by
asking a critical question. Coming upon an event in which, by
the poet's or a character's account, someone acts justly, you
pause and inquire not what is just about this act, but what justice
is per se. The phrase *kath' auto*, "in itself," may, Havelock suggests,
be the crucial verbal turn in Plato's polemic against the poets.
For if you follow through on Plato's question, you are compelled
to put together all of the events in the poem where someone
behaves justly and to find the common denominator. You need
to become abstract, intellectual. You become a knower with an
object of knowledge. "The saga," Havelock says, "will contain
a thousand aphorisms and instances which describe what a proper
and moral person is doing. But they have to be torn out of context,
correlated, systematized, unified and harmonized to provide a
formula for righteousness. The many acts and events must somehow give way and dissolve into a single identity. In short 'the
thing *per se*' is also a 'one'" (p. 218).

The simple turn of phrase – *per se* – is central to the act of
isolation that separates a concept from its diverse instances in
experience or in a poem. This operation removes the particular
event from time and places it in an eternal world. It also makes
the event difficult to visualize, if not impossible. Acquiring the
philosophical habit of mind changes one's identity; to Havelock
it in fact creates our modern sense of selfhood. "Thus the autonomous subject who no longer recalls and feels, but knows, can

---

[14] (Cambridge: Harvard University Press, 1963). Cited in the text.

now be confronted with a thousand abstracted laws, principles, topics, and formulas which become the objects of his knowledge" (p. 219).

It is Havelock's genius, I believe, to see how a, if not the, crucial movement in philosophy may arise from repudiating poetry. Yet I think that Havelock sees more. For he has shown us just how the philosophers' adjuring us to "stop and think" – a talismanic phrase through the metaphysical tradition, says Hannah Arendt – calls for something much more specific than halting in one's steps and abstrusely wondering.[15] Stopping and thinking in this tradition entails pondering the meanings of particular key words. So it is not surprising that to every philosopher of consequence we attach a word list, a central vocabulary. We think of the words and phrases they have invented or those that they have bent themselves over for long periods, minutely shaping and polishing, like expert gem cutters. To think of Kant is to recall words like noumena, phenomena, category, reason, imagination, beautiful, sublime; for Heidegger Being, thrownness, anxiety, care, disclosure, clearing; for Derrida *pharmakon, différance, écriture,* phallogocentrism, metaphysics of presence, hedgehog (my favorite).[16] The arch metaphysician of Königsberg and his two brilliant detractors hold in common a drive to compose lists of exalted words, words that serve as markers for the point at which one is supposed to stop and think. Stop, halt the flow of reading, of experience, of time, and abide with this term; measure your life against it. Just so every mode of theory we shall encounter in this book also has its word list: Bloom's ephebe, precursor, influence anxiety; Foucault's discipline, power, knowledge; Greenblatt's subversion and containment; de Man's blindness and insight, metaphor and metonymy.

Derrida's key words are designed to signify the flow that philosophy would stem. But if he were as committed to the ethos of the interminable text as he says he is, could we so readily recite his master list of incantations? You cannot, I believe, qualify as a

---

[15] *The Life of the Mind* (New York: Harcourt Brace, 1971).
[16] "Hedgehog," which purportedly loses something in being translated from the French *hérisson,* cues Derrida's broodings in "Che cos'è la poesia?" in *A Derrida Reader: Between the Blinds,* ed. Peggy Kamuf (New York: Columbia University Press, 1991), pp. 221–37.

philosopher (or as a major theorist) unless you confer aura, charismatic glow, on particular words. And that process, Havelock teaches us, is at enmity with something that has been part of literature since Homer, the urge to proliferate narrative, to spread before the reader a vast array of incidents that, while they may have much to teach, resist being housed under any given sign or system of signs.

And yet it is manifestly the case that philosophers, even those in the much-maligned metaphysical tradition, aren't always solidifying or deploying key terms. Often, to cite just one alternative, philosophers are propounding myths, fictions that are open to broad interpretation: the parable of the cave, the myth of Er, the noble fiction about human origins, all the flights of imagination in *The Republic* are susceptible to ongoing interpretation. They move away from definitions, from truth. Just so, the writers we call poets can be obsessed with magic words, as Blake and Yeats and Stevens sometimes are.

I suggest we think of the drive to create fixed terminologies and the paradigmatic narratives that arise with them as part of the disciplinary pull of philosophy, as its literal dimension. Thus the urge to propound ultimate or final vocabularies ought to be seen in the same way that we might see the tendencies that Plato, in *Republic* X, calls forth to distinguish philosophers from poets. Philosophers, you will recall, are supposed to be mature, manly, aristocratic, appealing to disciples. But this, one quickly recognizes, is just a description of a stiff, tiresome man. It's a literal-minded version of a Platonic philosopher: Plato is far better.

Except when he gets talking about poetry. When the philosophical mind encounters art, it is disposed to slip into anxiously literal ways of thinking. (What are poetry's corresponding literalizations? Phantasmagoria? Nonsense? Wish-fulfillment?) It's then that the charged vocabularies are likely to come to the fore, then that the thinker is likely to go authoritarian and begin propounding a disenfranchising theory. So Williams' distinction between those who are persuaded that the world is fully intelligible and those who aren't seems to reduce a more fluid relation. There's a strong tendency toward declaring ultimate truths in the metaphysical line, but it's not always ascendant. Poets bow their heads to the mystery, sometimes, but not always.

It is in relation to art that systematic philosophy is most inclined to become harshly disciplinary, but then that isn't always so bad a thing. For reduction to key terms and paradigmatic narratives can entail an intensification of values and commitments. Strong analytical critique can revise our valuations of art in bracing, salutary ways, provided someone is willing to respond to the disenfranchising theory when response is tenable.

This book will argue that as of late literary criticism – egged on by a number of developments both conceptual and material – has taken up a philosophical attitude toward the poets. Now the last thing most of the theorists I consider here would like to be called is heirs of Plato. Yet I think that I can show how in the work of Bloom, de Man, Derrida, and other figures in contemporary theory, there exist drives, analogous to Plato's, to demean literary art, or to subsume it in some higher kind of thought. For at some point – shall we say 1966, the year of the Johns Hopkins Conference on the Sciences of Man; '67, the year of Derrida's three major volumes; 1971, when de Man published *Blindness and Insight?* – at some point that could only be arbitrarily located, the tone of Anglo-American criticism changed. The attitude of criticism to literature became less celebratory, more inquisitive, even inquisitorial (more Platonic). Poets were less often conceived as ideals of maturity or human triumph against odds, and more frequently addressed with a skeptical discerning tone. This book takes that turn toward an intense, nearly pervasive disenfranchising critique as its starting point, examines some of the major figures and works, and attempts to defend poetry against their remarkable strictures.

But, one might respond, all that I have said so far about an ancient quarrel is beside the point. Granted theory goes too far in its claims to offer the analyst total controlling knowledge: we've known that for some time. And we have solved the problem by bringing history to the fore. By historicizing literature we are able to put its particularity into focus. Historicist thought can demonstrate how singular any cultural formation is, and how we are, accordingly, bound to study it in its own terms.[17] In the

---

[17] Erich Auerbach provides a fine compressed discussion of historicism in *Mimesis: The Representation of Reality in Western Literature*, trans. Willard R. Trask (Princeton: Princeton University Press, 1953), pp. 443–4.

view commonly referred to as "strong historicism," our assumptions and values differ so much from those of past eras that no real comprehension is possible.[18] But even "weak historicism" posits a chastening gap between then and now. Awareness of past periods in their true alterity – of the diachronic abyss, breach, line or what you will – can break the drive to assimilate those periods to synchronic theoretical models. Historicist thinking ought to qualify as a cure for theory's epistemological hubris.

Perhaps. In chapters to come I will take up the question of the relations between historiography and literary studies, focusing on contemporary versions of Marxist ideological critique and the New Historicism that takes some of its impetus from Michel Foucault. History is now something of a sacrosanct word in literary criticism; challenging its status can draw professorial bile. For to be historical is to be, almost by definition, responsible, a good citizen of the academy and of the world. The proponent of historical criticism is likely to see the purveyors of close reading, whether they quest for organic form or the breaking of forms, as decadents, self-indulgently removed from real people and events. Not to be resolutely historical is to betray social responsibility.

It will take two chapters to unfold my reservations about currently operative forms of historical critique, but a few preliminary words may be helpful. I have no doubt that texts need, *to a certain degree*, to be read within their historical contexts. One wishes to know whom Pope refers to in *The Dunciad*; it is impossible to read Whitman's "Lilacs" elegy without knowing something about Lincoln and the American Civil War. But how much one contextualizes a work of art is a matter of some delicacy, an issue of taste. It takes considerable poise and intellectual honesty not to use historical context as another way to engage in the philosophical disenfranchisement of art.

One can employ conceptual terms and paradigmatic narratives to pretend to know works of art that, in their breadth, intricacy, and emotive force, actually exceed existing systematic modes. Just so, one can produce and manipulate historical context to

---

[18] For reflections on historicism and radical relativism see Friedrich Meinecke, *Historicism: The Rise of a New Historical Outlook*, trans. J. E. Anderson (London: Routledge, 1972), pp. 339–40, 368–9, 488–91.

give the appearance that the work is merely a symptom of its moment: historical data, piled high, can cover a work as convincingly as well-deployed concepts. What is called historical criticism often adapts extant theoretical moves, clothing them in the language of fact and context. The aggressive historical critic's contextual pilings, cultural grave markers, signify a conviction that the work beneath has, or ought to have, no direct bearing on the present. Yet perhaps it is the currently disruptive force of the work, its strong resistance to being conquered by critical understanding, that makes the historical critic dig so anxiously and hard.

If the proposed analogy between Plato's critique of poetry and current critical practices suggests anything, it is never to underestimate the hostility that literary critics may nurse toward literature.[19] This hostility is in general not a matter of envy: that is usually a facile diagnosis. Rather, it derives from the fact that, in certain ways, the minds of the philosopher and the poet can be at odds. The critic, even when she holds her appointment in an English department, even when she sees herself as a purveyor of historical understanding, will often be devoted to the philosophical side of the ancient quarrel.

Thus an admonition to historical critics, which will not be developed fully until much later in the book: use the past to clarify, but not to contextualize, the work at hand. The only contexts that matter – and I say this aware that few who read these words will concur – are the present and the future. And the only way to know those contexts (this more inflammatory still) is to know yourself. But what a self might comprise: that will be the difficult question.

So history, at least as we now understand it, hardly seems a way to dissolve the philosophy/poetry dispute. Too much has happened. Philosophy's polemic against poetry has been augmented by recent events and in such a way that it has had a fairly easy time enlisting historicism on its side. But what are these critical events? Exactly how has the philosophical critique gained the

---

[19] My thoughts are in line here with one of Nietzsche's most valuable works, *On the Use and Abuse of History*, trans. Adrian Collins (Indianapolis: Bobbs-Merrill, 1949).

upper hand in the contemporary installment of the ancient quarrel? Perhaps the best way to begin answering these questions is with a story.

In 1936 the English department at Columbia University denied reappointment to Lionel Trilling, then a young instructor. A spokesman for the department told him that "as a Freudian, a Marxist, and a Jew," he would probably "be more comfortable elsewhere" – meaning that the department would be more comfortable without a Jew steeped in Freud and Marx. Upon hearing that he'd been let go, Trilling went from office to office, visiting his more influential senior colleagues to inform them that if they fired him they would be losing someone who, in time, would bring the university great distinction. The department reconsidered and renewed his contract.

Trilling's first book, on which he was still at work when Columbia tried to let him go, was on Matthew Arnold, and throughout his long career Trilling sustained an Arnoldian sense of the serious burden that culture in the twentieth century was compelled to take up.[20] "There is not a creed which is not shaken," Arnold writes at the beginning of "The Study of Poetry" (quoting himself), "not an accredited dogma which is not shown to be questionable, not a received tradition which does not threaten to dissolve."[21] With this diagnosis of the modern condition Trilling generally concurred. And when faith in religion, national identity, and historical destiny wanes, then the study of literature – Trilling also agreed with Arnold in this – takes on crucial importance.

"The future of poetry is immense," Arnold writes in the same passage, "because in poetry, where it is worthy of its high destinies, our race, as time goes on, will find an ever surer and surer stay." The study of poetry can be of major value in an age of generalized doubt, but not as an end in itself. Criticism matters most when it helps to sustain a culture that can compensate for waning faith. Arnoldian criticism devotes itself to making art available to the uses of such a culture. Trilling never seems seriously to have doubted these convictions, though he was quite capable of turning

[20] *Matthew Arnold* (New York: Harcourt Brace Jovanovich, 1939).
[21] *Matthew Arnold's Essays in Criticism* (London: Everyman's Library, 1964), p. 235.

against a respectably established literary culture that he believed was no longer serving the needs of the time, as he did against modernism. But always he worked to found some new cultural synthesis, more sustaining because more attuned to contemporary exigencies than the one he was compelled to renounce.

Trilling's Arnoldian sense of the place literature ought to have in creating civilization naturally places a considerable onus on the critic and on the institution of criticism. If the once authoritative centers no longer hold, if it is up to criticism to provide grounds for a humane social life, then critics must take on a high seriousness. Aestheticism, antinomianism, decadence, such excesses may be marginally tolerable in a world where religious and civil institutions seem stable. But in the current crisis, literature has to become a source for knowledge, not a region for sophisticated play and pleasure. Arnold renounced his early allegiance to Keatsian aestheticism and eventually stopped writing poetry: the more fitting task for the hour was disseminating the best that is known and thought. Trilling, for his part, wrote fiction, including a well-received novel, *The Middle of the Journey*, but the fiction is almost as soberly instructive as the critical work.

In the cultural crisis that Arnold identified and Trilling deeply felt, literature mattered in large part because of the guiding truths that one could draw from it. Poets, and even poetry itself, sometimes look almost frivolous beside the burdened critic disinterestedly committed to social betterment. Even the best poets include distracting dross with the pure invaluable essence. Poets are the all too human vehicles for immortal truth: sometimes they seem almost an inconvenience; sometimes, as Plato has it, they don't quite know what they're doing.

Few critics working today will be pleased to acknowledge themselves as Trilling's descendants, much less Arnold's. But I think many of us have inherited their sense of cultural crisis and of criticism's promise to ameliorate, if not overcome, anxieties attendant on living without secure authority. If there are no centers and no generally agreed upon truths to undergird experience, then interpretation becomes the name of the game: in a world without God or god substitutes we compare readings rather than warring over creeds, or at least we should like to. And where better to learn the art of existential interpretation than from the critics, the expert readers of the most complex cultural creations we have? To learn to read poems may be preparation for the ongoing, ungrounded process of interpretation that, it's said, constitutes life in the post-modern West.

With this view of criticism as a central cultural pursuit often comes the conviction that poetry is a marvelous raw matter that cannot be left in its unprocessed state. To assist civilization in its unending war with barbarism, poetry has to be fully exploited, its impurities refined away, and its essential ore salvaged as touchstones, concepts, as guides to life, as philosophy. Thus the notion that we are enmeshed in a general crisis of authority, common to critics as diverse as, say, Trilling, Derrida, Julia Kristeva, and Fredric Jameson, considerably abets the philosophical disenfranchisement of art. When war is on, even cultural war, all able bodies, corporeal and textual, have to be pressed into service and worked into shape.

You'll recall that it was Trilling's interest in Marx and Freud, as well as his Judaism, that piqued the elders. The anti-Semitism and unease about the Red Menace are predictable enough, but why was Freud named in the indictment? Perhaps Trilling's seniors sensed that psychoanalysis contained resources for severely undermining humanistic literary culture: Trilling, perhaps, looked like an early infiltrator, a harbinger of the plague. But actually one of Trilling's major intellectual objectives was to try to draw an Arnoldian circle around Sigmund Freud. Trilling's essay "Freud and Literature," published in 1940, the year after Freud's death, is among his most intense and moving.[22] What makes it so is Trilling's struggle to stage a compressed but thorough encounter with Freud's work that honestly expresses his high regard for its courage and boldness, but that also leaves the Arnoldian cultural project substantially unchanged.[23]

---

[22] Collected in *The Liberal Imagination: Essays on Literature and Society* (New York: Scribners, 1950), pp. 34–57. Hereafter cited in the text.

[23] Norman O. Brown offers a similar view of Trilling in *Life Against Death: The Psychoanalytical Meaning of History* (Hanover, N.H.: Wesleyan University Press, 1959), pp. 55–62. The book's back cover carries a generous endorsement from Trilling.

So Trilling praises Freud for rendering a comprehensive vision of life that places him among the great tragic artists: "Man, as Freud conceives him, is not to be understood by any simple formula (such as sex) but is rather an inextricable tangle of culture and biology. And not being simple, he is not simply good; he has, as Freud says somewhere, a kind of hell within him from which rise everlastingly the impulses which threaten his civilization. He has the faculty of imagining for himself more in the way of pleasure and satisfaction than he can possibly achieve. Everything that he gains he pays for in more than equal coin; compromise and the compounding with defeat constitute his best way of getting through the world. His best qualities are the result of a struggle whose outcome is tragic" (p. 57). This is without doubt eloquent. At the same time it is general enough so that it might apply to any number of other writers who came before Freud: to Sophocles, to Shakespeare, to Goethe, but also to Montaigne, and even, with just a few modifications, to someone as thoroughly unlike Freud as the Alexander Pope of *An Essay on Man*.

Throughout the piece, Trilling is continually struck by this or that apparently novel point in Freud, which he then suavely associates with a prior source. Freud teaches us a good deal about the unconscious, but naturally the Romantics knew more than a little about it beforehand; the Oedipal complex is a striking enough theory, though you'll find it anticipated in a dialogue of Diderot's; for prior emphasis on the determining powers of sexual desire look in Stendhal and Schopenhauer; the Death Drive? – read Novalis. Freud's theory of the repetition compulsion contributes to a Mithridatic theory about the uses of tragedy, yet it's a view that has been in circulation for some time. From Trilling's soft-voiced, encompassing account, Freud emerges as a major original thinker with little new to say.

A stroke of remarkable interpretive subtlety comes when Trilling, anticipating Lacan, identifies condensation and displacement, two major techniques of dream distortion, with metaphor and metonymy. He concludes that Freud is to be commended for teaching us that the mind is, by nature, a poetry-making agency. Thus poetry, at the center of Arnoldian culture, is itself close to the center of the human essence, the unconscious. But by reaching a bit far here, Trilling almost falls. For couldn't one just as well say that if metaphor making resembles a technique of dream censorship, then perhaps metaphors are themselves devices for obscuring certain unpalatable matters?

One surely can, and many in the years to come will. For Freudian thinking does more to change the interpretive game than any other single development. Deploying Freud, and particularly his theory of the unconscious, one is in a position to say things about literary works that their authors could not have said. With a stroke, the standing relations between poet and critic can be reversed. The professor no longer has to accept the role of explicator, editor, or votary. Rather she can stand as an authority, take up the role of physician to patient, finding motives for the creation-symptom that were beyond the ken of the pre-Freudian cultural world.

When he challenges the poets, Plato must show that he commands an alternative, a way of thinking and acting that is conducive to the good. He compares this way of life overtly and indirectly to what the poets have to offer. He can be tendentious; he can set up straw men and enter into dialogue with men who might as well be: but he does carry a burden of persuasion. His attempt to usurp the poets occurs in broad daylight. But the critic with Freud in her arsenal can take a detour around the dialectic, and speak authoritatively about repressed content, interpreting the literary text as a dream text. She can defend herself and her readers against its power to produce fresh meanings and complicate experience by proffering fairly certain knowledge about its origins in a well-comprehended past.

This book will argue that the theory of the unconscious, on which so much contemporary criticism bases its authority, ought to be harshly interrogated before being applied to literary texts. The theory provides access to ultimate truths. It enjoins a sort of descendentalism – not a surge to a region on high, but a quick transport to subterranean bedrock – which should be suspect for a mind bent on staying secular. It is in fact surprising just how pervasive this theory, a sort of Platonism in reverse gear, is in contemporary criticism. When Trilling made his brilliant equation between trope and repression, he didn't cause an immediate interpretive revolution. But once fully in play, the theory of the unconscious would do more than any other intellectual development to shift the power relations within criticism: to sway the balance in the ancient quarrel.

Trilling's Freud essay isn't hard to understand. It appeared for the first time in the *Kenyon Review*, a journal that boasted many readers without academic appointments. Throughout his career, Trilling never wrote anything that couldn't be read by an intelligent doctor or lawyer with some background in literary studies. Trilling was often quite pleased with his status as one of America's foremost public intellectuals. But his journal entries reveal that he was anxious about what his colleagues thought: he wasn't a respectable scholar, didn't have an academic field, didn't know foreign languages; after the Arnold book he confined himself largely to essays (there's a short volume on E. M. Forster); he never wrote a footnote when he could help it (recall the insouciant "Freud says somewhere" in the passage I cited above). By the close of his career in the early 1970s, Trilling, though decked with honors of every sort, began looking to his younger colleagues like a monument to past times.

For American literary studies were becoming more professionalized. There were fewer and fewer English professors who addressed a general reading public. Many professors of literature, like their colleagues in the empirical branches, were becoming specialists: it was enough to focus a lifetime's scholarship on Milton, or Shakespeare, or even Donne. Those poet–critics, generalists without advanced degrees, who made their ways in and out of university appointments, writers like Kenneth Burke, R. P. Blackmur, John Berryman, and Delmore Schwartz, were gradually replaced by bona fide Ph.D.'s. To control the engines, one needed to have gone through the mill. The reasons for this turn to professionalism are too varied and complex to discuss satisfyingly here: one would have to consider the rising prestige of the highly professionalized sciences, and the drive to emulate them throughout the university; the fact that one could no longer support oneself as a public intellectual, writing for publications like the *New Republic*, moving from university to free-lance work then back again; the way the academic job market cramped up in the late '60s, inducing a greater reliance on credentials to help draw distinctions among applicants; the enlarging efficiency of, and popular faith in, administered operations.

In the coming pages I will argue that the university's evolution into virtually the sole source for serious literary critical work augmented criticism's theoretical disposition and undermined its capacity to defend poetry. For one thing philosophy can be taught: it's at home in a university in ways that poetry cannot be. It is central to our conceptions of Socrates, Aristotle, Wittgenstein, and many other philosophers that they were great teachers. (Recall Plato's remarks about the inability of poets to create disciples.) Yet metaphor making, says Aristotle, cannot be learned from others. In his reflections on poetic style, he observes that "the greatest thing by far is to have a command of metaphor. This alone cannot be imparted by another; it is the mark of genius, for to make good metaphors implies an eye for resemblances" (ch. 22).

Metaphor making is surely essential to literary art, but broadly conceived, it is also central to the defence of poetry. For to express what is singular and inassimilable about a writer or artist, one must often turn to metaphor. Figurative language, which at its best gives us new perceptions, adding, as Blackmur liked to say, to the stock of available reality, is often necessary to describe what is surprising and vital in a work of art. Paul de Man is a more difficult critic to read and understand than a responsive, rather impressionistic essayist like Virginia Woolf. But one can teach intelligent students to do what de Man does; it is probably impossible to teach anyone to respond like Woolf if he has little aptitude for it. And how could we sustain the academic study of literature if we were compelled to say that a central aspect of criticism is probably not teachable? When you transfer criticism to the academy, the philosophical impulse gets an extra charge. Along with the theory of the unconscious, and a perceived crisis of authority, the professionalization of literary criticism, its withdrawal into the academy, reinforces the philosophical critique.

My point here about the academy is crude as it stands, and it will be necessary later on to elaborate it. But it is important now to say that this is not an anti-professional book in any simple sense. Granted it can be momentarily satisfying to follow George Bernard Shaw and castigate the professions as conspiracies against the laity. But the professionalization of literary studies has yielded real advantages. For one thing, it allows some equality of access: as Frank Lentricchia brusquely indicates, when you have a profession you've got to let in the pigs.[24] In other words, though social polish, background, connections, and the like do matter in the academy, what other professors perceive as talent and energy matter too. A profession in a democracy is by definition open to anyone who can scrap her way in. One goes as far as abilities take one.

It doesn't always work out that way of course; there is a lot of injured merit in professional literary studies and a few bad eminences, too. Yet without professionalization, Anglo-American literary studies would be more socially homogeneous and considerably duller than they are. Without professionalization, and its commitment to disinterested standards of merit, Trilling would not have had much chance with the elders.

Yet I will be showing how professionalization, along with a perceived cultural crisis, and the turn to various theories of the unconscious, has warped the scale of critical values, reinforcing disenfranchising theory at the expense of poetry. The drawbacks I will be pointing to are not inherent in professionalization per se. More often they are the result of our having overlooked its strong influence upon us. Critics, highly adept at seeing the forces that constrain and shape others, might pay some attention to their own material circumstances. In doing so they will, I trust, be able to take those forces into account in their work. This book isn't an argument for an institutional unconscious that will always, whatever vigilance one applies, shape our thoughts. Rather, proceeding in the critical spirit, I assume that when readers see the limits on their current thinking that institutions and the profession impose they can adjust accordingly.

In the past decade or so there has been considerable work published on professionalization in literary studies: Bruce Robbins,

---

[24] The observation comes in Imre Salusinszky's interview with Lentricchia published in *Criticism in Society* (New York: Methuen, 1987), p. 189.

Evan Watkins, Stanley Fish, Gerald Graff, bell hooks, and many others have offered theoretical reflections on the dialectic between professorial thought and its material context.[25] I have read these studies with interest and learned from them, but in this book I have resisted developing a strong theory of academic professionalism. Rather I have been pragmatic and experiential in approach. The objective has been to call attention to influential aspects of the professional and institutional life of criticism, to speculate on their impact, and to ask, often implicitly, if these observations and analyses tally with the reader's own experiences. On this issue, as on all others, I hope my work has the dialogical tone commended, if not always practiced, by F. R. Leavis. To him a critical observation ought to take the form "This is so, isn't it?" and the speaker should expect a return that begins "Yes, but," with the yes, naturally, flavored by varying measures of irony.[26]

Yes, but: some preliminary questions come to mind about this project. First, one might ask whether the book in hand is a historical work, one that focuses on major critical developments in the '70s and '80s, or a volume that attempts to be contemporary in its application. If the latter, why don't we hear more – though you will hear some – about film studies, feminism, African-American literary criticism, cultural studies, and the like? If the former, why isn't the work more comprehensive, more deeply annotated, more historically descriptive than it is?

This book isn't a comprehensive historical study. Preeminently it's a speculative work. It attempts to locate the most potent and influential disenfranchisements of literature that theory has recently produced and respond to them. There are good guides

---

[25] See Robbins' *Secular Vocations: Intellectuals, Professionalism, Culture* (New York: Verso, 1993); Watkins' *Work Time: English Departments and the Circulation of Cultural Value* (Stanford: Stanford University Press, 1989); Fish's *Doing What Comes Naturally: Change, Rhetoric, and the Practice of Theory in Literary and Legal Studies* (Durham, N.C.: Duke University Press, 1989); Graff's *Professing Literature, An Institutional History* (Chicago: University of Chicago Press, 1987); Margo Culley and Catherine Portuges, eds., *Gendered Subjects: The Dynamics of Feminist Teaching* (Boston: Routledge and Kegan Paul, 1985); Gerald Graff and Reginald Gibbons, eds., *Criticism in the University* (Evanston, Ill.: Northwestern University Press, 1985); hooks' *Feminist Theory from Margin to Center* (Boston: South End Press, 1984); and Peter Uwe Hohendahl, *The Institution of Criticism* (Ithaca: Cornell University Press, 1982).

[26] *English Literature in Our Time and the University* (London: Chatto and Windus, 1969).

to the writers I deal with, and anyone in search of more explanatory treatments should turn to them.[27]

This began as a volume on a group of influential theorists: Paul de Man, Jacques Derrida, Harold Bloom, and Michel Foucault. But over time the emphases changed. I came to include more writers of different sorts: Roland Barthes, Stephen Greenblatt, Camille Paglia, Marjorie Levinson, Marlon Ross. But perhaps as much as the work of particular individuals, the finished book addresses concepts. One might think of this volume as organized around a set of key words and phrases that have been instrumental in the recent philosophical disenfranchisement of literature. To cultural crisis and the unconscious, the book will, as it unfolds, add blindness and insight, presence, text, ideology, power, and influence. These terms signal the shift in criticism that took place near the end of the 1960s, but they also inform, sometimes indirectly, a great deal of what is going on now under the rubrics of cultural criticism, minority studies, feminist critique, and the like.

A contemporary film critic with a feminist bent may not acknowledge extensive influence from any of the writers whose work I treat at length. But she is likely to use a Freudian theory of repression that's been touched by the blindness and insight model; likely to be skeptical about the way film mesmerizes its audiences with images, with presence; likely to want to slow the film down, to "read" it as if it were a text, by showing how it is woven ("textus") together from various other cultural discourses; likely to see it steeped in patriarchal ideology; likely to locate its misogynistic tendencies in a tradition of film misogyny, and of patriarchal culture overall, that will include Alfred Hitchcock, who is to modern film misogyny something like what Harold Bloom's Milton is to Romantic poetry. This list in fact describes many of the doctrines engaged in Laura Mulvey's vastly influential piece, "Visual Pleasure and Narrative Cinema," and to anyone versed in recent criticism, it will suggest other works.[28] I believe,

---

[27] The best of these that I have read remains Frank Lentricchia's *After the New Criticism* (Chicago: University of Chicago Press, 1980). The book offers cogent accounts of many of the writers the current work deals with, as well as brilliant analyses.

[28] Reprinted in *Feminisms: An Anthology of Literary Theory and Criticism*, ed. Robyn R. Warhol and Diane Price Herndl (New Brunswick: Rutgers University Press, 1991), pp. 432–42.

in other words, that the assumptions generated, synthesized, and refined in the early move toward theory continue to inform recent developments that seek to make categories like race, class, gender, and sexuality central. Current work is often "theorized" rather than theoretical, which is to say that it no longer argues for, but assumes the truth of, high theory.

The point of this book, it is worth stressing once again, is not to show that critical theory has nothing to teach us about art; it's not to scatter the predators from their exquisitely defenceless prey. Rather I want to show how literary art can answer the charges theory brings to it, succumbing to some yes, but also passing outside the reach of others to gesture toward futures, both linguistic and experiential, that are of human value.

The book uses "poetry" as something of a synecdoche, a part for the whole. The word should be understood as referring to any cultural creation that fruitfully exceeds destructive norms and passes beyond theory's reductive explanatory powers. The main exemplars of renovating work here will be the Romantic poets, on whom I teach most of my courses and for whom I sustain considerable admiration. There is no reason, though, why any other kind of poetry, of music – be it popular or classical – of film, of whatever cultural form you like, couldn't be measured dialectically, in a similar manner, for its power to exceed norms and productively outdistance theoretical critiques. (I will, though, want to draw some distinctions between most popular art and art that achieves a greater density, art that is harder, in other words, to interpret successfully.) If poetry itself is particularly well suited to confront disenfranchising philosophy on its own grounds, it may be in part because, after centuries of strife, poetry already contains, in ways both earnest and ludic, a great deal of philosophical notation.

So there is nothing intrinsically anti-theoretical, or anti-critical, about this book. Let theory do its worst and apply to poetry every profound doubt it can muster. Critics, when they are working in their trade, will deliver philosophical strictures to poets past and present. But they will also listen to theories, their own and others', and defend poetry where theory is superfluous, unilluminatingly reductive, or inadequate to describe the difficult, humanly enlarging pleasure that the work at hand offers.[29] At times, too, critics will perform the more difficult task of showing how accepting theory's standards, however admirable, comes at too high a price. Critics are, or ought to be, literature's public defenders: low-priced, common, serving their own time and the future, utterly necessary to sustaining culture's vitality. They discover discoveries; they bring the unacknowledged legislators' best thoughts up for popular referendum; they defend poetry; they say "Yes, but."

[29] In the introduction to *Wild Orchids and Trotsky: Messages from American Universities* (New York: Penguin, 1993), a collection of short intellectual autobiographies by contemporary academic writers working in the humanities, I offered the view that criticism is, among other things, what takes place between philosophy and poetry. But I refrained from making overt judgments about where academic criticism currently stood on the scale and why. As the book's editor, I tried to be as detached as possible. At least one reviewer took me as an unequivocal defender of Politically Correct criticism. My objective, in fact, was to show the variety of valuable work emerging from the academy (though I deeply disagree with much of the work I admire). In the present book I offer, quite directly, the views that as an editor it seemed worthwhile only to suggest.

CHAPTER I

Rhetorics of blindness: Coleridge to de Man

> And the question is still what it was then, how to view
> scholarship from the vantage of the artist and art from the
> vantage of life.   Nietzsche

Perhaps the most surprising turn in William Wordsworth's
"Intimations" ode comes when the poet calls the child, the object
of his broodings throughout the poem, the "best Philosopher":

> Thou, whose exterior semblance doth belie
>   Thy Soul's immensity;
> Thou best Philosopher, who yet dost keep
> Thy heritage, thou Eye among the blind,
> That, deaf and silent, read'st the eternal deep,
> Haunted for ever by the eternal mind, –   (109-14)[1]

Wordsworth's friend, collaborator, and sometimes competitor,
Samuel Taylor Coleridge, disliked this passage intensely, citing
it in his *Biographia Literaria* as a salient instance of "mental
bombast": "a disproportion of thought to the circumstance and
occasion."[2] What Coleridge denounces as bombast, I take to be
one of Wordsworth's best moments as a poet, a moment that,
read in its larger implications, can bring one to profitable reflections on the contemporary limitations of academic literary criticism, as well as its future promise.

---

[1] Throughout, I cite the ode as it appears in vol. I (pp. 523–9) of *William Wordsworth:
The Poems*, ed. John O. Hayden, 2 vols. (New Haven: Yale University Press, 1981).
Line numbers are given in the text.

[2] Ed. James Engell and Walter Jackson Bate, in *The Collected Works of Samuel Taylor
Coleridge* (Princeton: Princeton University Press, 1983), VII:2.136.

To put it simply, my contention in this chapter will be that criticism has followed the spirit Coleridge evinces in the judgment when it should have been attending just as much, if not more, to Wordsworth's achievement. There are material as well as intellectual issues involved in criticism's implicitly following Coleridge's verdict on the philosopher/child, and those too will need exploration.

In this chapter I shall, taking off from Wordsworth and Coleridge, offer a genealogy of Paul de Man's central critical categories, blindness and insight. The chapter will argue that de Man, despite repudiating Coleridge in "The Rhetoric of Temporality," actually operates in his spirit, though not without augmenting the Coleridgean project in a crucial way.

But why devote the opening chapter in a book on contemporary criticism to de Man, a figure who seems by now to have been doubly discredited? The discovery that de Man had, when a young man, written for collaborationist journals in his native Belgium has seriously damaged his personal reputation, and caused many to wonder if there might not be some continuity between de Man's tainted past and the deconstructive critical work that came afterwards. Then too de Man has apparently been discredited intellectually: those endorsing a return to history for literary studies are often prone to see him as a cold formalist whose work would forestall, perhaps interminably, any significant engagement with what criticism ought to attend to, politics and the material world.

But trying to construe the relations between de Man's collaborationist writings and his later deconstructive work would not bring one much closer to understanding why he commanded the influence on Anglo-American literary criticism that he did. My objective here is to show what de Man's work offered, what use it had for those in British and American universities who took it up. What did the blindness and insight figure give to critics that they needed? And, I want to add, still often seem to need? For if I am right – and it will take much of the rest of the book to fill out the argument – Paul de Man continues to be a (if not *the*) most influential figure on the current critical scene. For many critics who feel they have passed beyond de Man still operate in his spirit. In this chapter I will show why they might be prone to do so.

The topic before us is obviously a large one, but I want to enter into it modestly by asking a simple question: why would Coleridge, a critic who generally devoted himself to giving as little offense as possible, be willing to become so fierce about Wordsworth's child? What would calling the child the best philosopher have meant to Coleridge?

Coleridge placed no little stock in philosophy. On the first page of the *Biographia*, he says that one of the book's central purposes is "the application of the rules, deduced from philosophical principles, to poetry and criticism." Such an ambition would have come as no surprise to a cultivated German reader of 1817, a reader accustomed to literary criticism influenced by Kant's transcendental philosophy. Coleridge had steeped himself in German thought, and it was from his readings in Kant, Schelling, and A. W. Schlegel (all of whom he plagiarizes in the *Biographia*) that Coleridge gathered the resources to propound a philosophy of literature.

Doctor Johnson, Coleridge's great predecessor, and Hazlitt, his chief rival among Romantic literary critics, generally invoke a common-sense British empiricism when they bother to think about epistemology at all. With Coleridge things change. As René Wellek observes, "Coleridge differs from almost all preceding English writers by his claim to an epistemology and metaphysics from which he derives his aesthetics and finally his literary theory and critical principles."[3] Though what Wellek says about Coleridge's systematic disposition is undoubtedly true, it's also worth adding that besides being a lover of organic cohesion, of harmony in all things poetic and social, Coleridge was attracted to fertile disorder. His thinking – especially as it's recorded in his notebooks – frequently pays heed to the multiplicity of human perspectives, to the complexity and divergence (sometimes the near chaos) of sensory perceptions, and to the humanly uncontrollable energies of words. This sort of thinking

[3] *A History of Modern Criticism*, 1750-1950, 8 vols. (New Haven: Yale University Press, 1955–86), II:158.

may have been augmented by Coleridge's opium use, which was habitual from when he was about twenty-five, but whatever its origins it was still a consequential part of his intellectual disposition. The systematic tendency in Coleridge's work, to which Wellek and the New Critics paid heed, is surely central, but I should admit here that the version of Coleridge I will be describing, the one that has had the most influence on academic criticism, doesn't comprise the whole story.

Coleridge, the speculative organic thinker, believed, one might say, that philosophy and poetry could solve each other's problems. For philosophy, he thought, the central difficulty was that of dualism. Kant's view that we cannot know the object in itself, the noumenon, but only its representation, the phenomenon, may have been an adequate rebuttal to Humean skepticism, but it left the subject in a state of alienation, of division from the created world, that Coleridge found unbearable. (Stanley Cavell puts this sort of response to Kant's "solution" in nicely compressed form: "Thanks for nothing.") That division might be healed, Coleridge argued, through the exercise of the poetic imagination, and more specifically through the imagination's symbol-making power. The poet, Coleridge believed, had the capacity to represent the "translucence of the Eternal through and in the Temporal," fusing not only eternity and duration, but subject and object, general and particular, the many and the one.

The vast majority of philosophers would consider Coleridge's ideal of the symbol as too fanciful a response to the question of skepticism. Someone who is worried about whether or not the world actually exists – and Cavell has argued that taking the challenge of skepticism seriously is a prerequisite for being a consequential philosopher – is unlikely to be impressed by claims that something called the poetic imagination can not only guarantee the world's reality, but restore its unfallen form.

Yet if Coleridge's poetic approach to philosophy has carried little weight, his philosophical version of literary criticism has. In the *Biographia* Coleridge lays the foundation for an Anglo-American philosophical criticism by providing a systematic method for describing and evaluating poetry. Here one finds the theory of the secondary imagination with its capacity "to idealize and to unify"; the affirmation of the cohesive symbol over and against the disjunctive mode of allegory; the polemic in favor of reconciling poetic opposites ("extremes meet" was Coleridge's favorite apothegm); accounts of the disinterested pleasure to be had in contemplating resolved, organic forms.

In every case, Coleridge favors unity, favors the art work not as process or performance, but as an object that places itself outside time. There is no sense in Coleridge, as there is in such writers as Hazlitt and Richard Poirier, that the critic needs to extemporize striking metaphors to dramatize an encounter with a work of art.[4] Nor would Coleridge be likely to join Doctor Johnson in affirming that the "essence of poetry is invention." Coleridge understands his terms to be stable and of value for any verbal art work worthy of the name. Coleridge, in other words, was looking for a vocabulary that stood to art in something of the way that, as Kant saw it, the categories stood to perceptual experience. The terms transcend time and particular circumstances. "What, then, is the essence of his philosophy of art – of imaginative production?" asks Walter Pater in what continues to rank as one of the best essays on Coleridge. "Generally, it may be described as an attempt to reclaim the world of art as a world of fixed laws, to show that the creative activity of genius and the simplest act of thought are but higher and lower products of the laws of a universal logic."[5]

How successful has Coleridge's project been? The New Criticism, with its emphasis on organic unity, is difficult to conceive without it. But so too, as I will go on to argue, is that mode that succeeds New Criticism where one no longer speaks of subject and object, or phenomenon and noumenon, but of signifier and signified, and one affirms disunion as programmatically as one's predecessors affirmed harmony. As David Bromwich says, "Of our modern, exclusive, and professional criticism, with its love of method and yearning for system, the true father is

[4] In this connection see especially Poirier's remarkable *The Performing Self: Compositions and Decompositions in the Languages of Contemporary Life* (New York: Oxford University Press, 1971).   [5] *Appreciations* (London: Macmillan, 1897), p. 74.

Coleridge."[6] When criticism becomes a province of metaphysical philosophy, a collective enterprise takes shape. Yes, in the *Biographia* Coleridge argues that Shakespeare is the epitome of poetic genius and offers a set of descriptive and evaluative categories within which he stands supreme. But what about Chaucer? Milton? Spenser? How shall we measure their achievement and construct their meaning within this newly ordained sphere? Or do they compel us to change the terms, invent a new system? Now there are grounds for debate, lively arguments among critics. Hazlitt and Poirier suggest that we ought to judge criticism in the way that we would poetry: as soon as it no longer inspires a counter performance of our own, we should put it down. Coleridge's work encourages one to ask if the reading is true, or calls truth into question in some significant way.

Coleridge's philosophical criticism – in which the child, devoid of seasoned powers of judgment, is anything but the best philosopher – lays the groundwork for a profession. Coleridge in fact spoke of creating a class of learned men who might function as a secular clerisy. But it will take more than Coleridge to make literary criticism into a commanding university discipline and an effective device for the disenfranchisement of art. Against Coleridge's professional groundwork and, too, against those later professionalizing developments upon Coleridge which I take to dominate much of current academic literary criticism, the "Intimations" ode unfolds.

Coleridge's method assimilates poetry to systematic thought, sublimates art to a higher power, achieving a relationship in which, to turn now to Wordsworth, one might even say that philosophy "Broods like the Day, a Master o'er a Slave,/A Presence which is not to be put by" (120–1). The famous lines from the ode describe the child's intimations of his immortality in a puzzling way. Nor is the sentiment isolated. Later in the ode, Wordsworth will equate intimations of prior, holier life with "High instincts before which our mortal Nature/Did tremble like a guilty Thing surprised" (147–8). Ostensibly, Wordsworth

---

[6] *Hazlitt: The Mind of a Critic* (New York: Oxford University Press, 1983), p. 13.

is writing a poem in praise of the child's proximity to his immortal origins:

> The Youth, who daily farther from the east
> Must travel, still is Nature's Priest,
> And by the vision splendid
> Is on his way attended . . .

(72-5)

Then why is immortality manifest to the child in the cruel form of a master glaring down on a slave?

Scholars have traditionally been quick to locate the origins of Wordsworth's myth about the soul's preexistence in the *Phaedrus* and the *Phaedo*. Yet for his own part Wordsworth always denied Platonic influence. At first the denial seems like a shallow expression of influence anxiety, but throughout his life he had a preternatural drive to say what he thought, to tell the truth. Wordsworth recognized that this quality made him socially unbearable at times ("a very pretty piece of paganism," he growled after Keats had recited him the "Hymn to Pan" from *Endymion*), but he also thought it preserved his poetic integrity.

What would it mean to take Wordsworth seriously on this matter? How is the myth of the soul's prior existence as Wordsworth develops it not Plato's?

It pays to remember that Wordsworth's vision of "that imperial palace" from which the child comes arises through a poetic dialogue with Coleridge. In his own great ode, "Dejection," Coleridge challenged the premises of the four stanzas that initiate "Intimations." Wordsworth had written those stanzas, in which he mourns the passing of a glory that was once part of the earth, in 1802. They close with a pair of questions: "Whither is fled the visionary gleam?/Where is it now, the glory and the dream?" (56-7). Wordsworth put the poem in the drawer, the questions unanswered and presumably unanswerable, at least until he read "Dejection."

Coleridge's ode presumes to demystify Wordsworth's fragment: it affirms rather stridently that nature never fails in that it can never be more than a collection of moribund things, "objects qua objects," which as he swiftly phrases it in the

Biographia "are fixed and dead." Rather it is incumbent on the mind to transform the fallen world: "O Lady! we receive but what we give,/And in our life alone does Nature live" (47–8).[7] "O Lady" was, in one of the poem's earlier drafts, "O Wordsworth"; then, in the first published version, which appeared in the *Morning Post* on Wordsworth's wedding day, "O Edmund." Perhaps it's not a coincidence that Coleridge, whose poetic talent was, it's been said, sacrificed to his enthusiasm for Wordsworth's higher genius and stronger character, substituted the name of the Shakespearean usurper who claimed Nature as his patron goddess.

Coleridge's challenge to Wordsworth lies in insisting that, as Neil Arditi puts it, Wordsworth's relation to nature is better figured as a monologue than a dialogue. Coleridge is attempting to undo the faith that Wordsworth for many years sustained in having a special, reciprocal relationship with nature: when Wordsworth's poetry fails, even temporarily, the failure is all his. Wordsworth might have answered by affirming that a dialogue really did exist and showing once again how that dialogue could produce memorable poetic language, proof of the marriage between his mind and the "goodly universe." Or he might have broken through into radical subjectivism – as he seems to do in the great Simplon Pass scene of *The Prelude* – thus admitting that Coleridge was right: "we receive but what we give."

What Wordsworth actually chooses to do is much more impressive, at least as I see it. With an inventive stroke he attempts to make Coleridge's premises and those of the reigning philosophy of the day if not obsolete, then at least peripheral. Wordsworth refuses to take up Coleridge's challenge and keep on talking about subjects and objects. He simply walks away from *that* discussion. He refuses to work out a poetic solution to the problem of dualism, the problem that Kantian philosophy has supposedly bequeathed to poetry.

Instead of letting metaphysics circumscribe poetry, he challenges its foundations:

[7] *The Complete Poetical Works of Samuel Taylor Coleridge*, ed. Ernest Hartley Coleridge, 2 vols. (Oxford: Oxford University Press, 1912), I:362–8. Line numbers are given in the text.

> Our birth is but a sleep and a forgetting:
> The Soul that rises with us, our life's Star,
>   Hath had elsewhere its setting,
>   And cometh from afar:
>   Not in entire forgetfulness,
>   And not in utter nakedness,
> But trailing clouds of glory do we come
>   From God who is our home . . . (58–65)

The first stroke against systematic philosophy is not to be confined by its methods; one must affirm invention at the expense of argument. Wordsworth offers fresh tropes when he is supposed to traffic in sufficient reason.

Yet surely they are anything but fresh, for they are Plato's; they are metaphysical philosophy's. The degree to which they *may* still be philosophy's images is, I think, what Wordsworth is recording when he depicts immortality as an authoritative, perhaps even a sadistic, presence, one that "Broods like the Day, a Master o'er a Slave." The child, which is Wordsworth's most common image for poetic power, is threatened by the celestial spirit; it makes him guilty. And yet it's the spirit of the child, the spirit of poetry, that is being rediscovered in the myth of the philosopher who banished poetry from his ideal state.

Wordsworth's gambit is to try to reinfuse Plato's images with a sensuous and vital force. He wants to reclaim some of philosophy for poetry, to show that systematic thought is nothing but poetry that has gotten frozen and also – remember the image of the imperial palace – institutionalized. This reinfusion is bound in the long run to fail, in part because society is far more on the side of rules and concepts than of invention. Culture encourages the child to be blindly with his own blessedness at strife; or, if you like, encourages poetry – and, too, poets like Coleridge – to turn to metaphysics. Coleridge was always saying that Wordsworth would become the world's first truly philosophical poet, but what Wordsworth is up to here is something quite different. He is, as I see it anyway, responding to a cultural moment infatuated with Kantian premises, and doing so by trying to renew a myth, which he would have thought was originally born with the poets, so vigorously that for a while we can't think of Plato.

That "for a while" is all that one can expect to possess: the concept, Coleridge, the imperial palace, will always return, but on that temporary space of freedom depends the kind of life that exceeds the condition Coleridge memorably evokes when, looking out in dejection on the stars and moon, he murmurs, "I see them all so excellently fair,/I see, not feel, how beautiful they are" (37–8).

So when Wordsworth calls the child the best philosopher, what he is saying, I take it, is that the child, whenever he lives, simply does not need the mournful consolations that metaphysical philosophy gives; for philosophy, in this understanding, is the decayed memory of images that once were poetry.

But of course, one may say, that is not philosophy at all. Look, for instance, at the forms in which philosophy comes to us: dialogues, lecture notes, fragments, examinations, essays, aphorisms, meditations, discourses, hymns, critiques, letters, summae, encyclopedias, commentaries, investigations, tractatuses, prolegomena, pensées, confessions, and, of course, poems (to purloin a list from Danto). To enumerate these forms is to evoke our sense of philosophy not as a footnote to Plato, as the consolidation of talismanic terms, the crystallization of paradigmatic narratives, or the search for disciples, but rather as the mind's quest to enlarge its scope, to provide more, and more valuable ways of talking about crucially important subjects. In "Intimations" we see philosophy at its most poetic, as myth, and also at its most prohibitive and disenfranchising, appearing to poetry as a strict father appears to a guilty child, appearing in the guise of what Freud would call a punishing super-ego, an *Über-Ich*.

To philosophy, poetry can look like childishness, for philosophy demands that we mature. Recall how, in the tenth book of *The Republic*, Plato insults poetry by suggesting that it stimulates childish emotions and depends upon childish credulity. Philosophers, in Plato's account, are as far away from children and women as you can get. Is there in Plato, in Aristotle, in Descartes, Kant, Hegel, any positive image of childhood?[8] (Is it entirely a

---

[8] But note Richard Rorty's tender reflections on childhood and humiliation in *Contingency, Irony, and Solidarity*, pp. 89–90. Unlike de Man and Derrida, who purvey knowing theories about the impossibility of stable knowledge, Rorty conveys his

coincidence that such a large proportion of the major philosophers were childless?) Just by affirming the image of the child, Rousseau and Wordsworth strike a blow against the philosophical insistence on seeking maturity. When Wordsworth, toward the end of "Intimations," speaks of the "years that bring the philosophic mind," he is using "philosophic" in the sense Coleridge approved, to denote a state of mind that can face human limits with mature resignation. But if Wordsworth is willing finally to become a philosopher in the most conservative sense, others, because of him, will not rest there. His "visionary gleam" becomes Shelley's "intellectual beauty" and then his "wild west wind," as it becomes Emerson's "gleam of light which flashes across [the] mind from within." Philosophy, it's been said, involves learning how to die, an idea from which, I imagine, arises Harold Bloom's observation to the effect that poets begin by rebelling more strongly against the inevitability of their own deaths than do other men and women. To both of these observations, Wordsworth helps one to reply that perhaps we are all in some manner both teaching ourselves to die and rebelling – periodically, unsuccessfully, and grandly enough to make it worth recording in the exalted form of an ode – against the tutelage.

My point here is not to read "Intimations" as an allegory in which poetry and philosophy hold down specific sites. Rather I mean to suggest that one of the ways poetry proceeds is by putting concepts that have become the property of philosophy into a dramatic and musical play, putting them into symbolic action. Wordsworth feels he can do this, I think, because, at times, imagination is more humanly necessary than wisdom, poetry than philosophy. The vitality of the Romantic connection with the child is so great that it empowers a raid into the provinces of knowledge. Thus to the question "What is philosophy?" Wordsworth helps us to find one good answer: philosophy is one of the forces that challenges, intimidates, and inspires the very best

anti-foundationalism in an ironic, but also appealingly open style, a style that suggests an experienced *and* a receptive temperament. He owes something to James and Dewey and Nietzsche, but also something to the Romantic discovery of childhood. Rorty greets the disappearance of Truth in a spirit that is markedly different from the spirits of the great truth-finders, thinkers like Aristotle, Kant, and Hegel, and that, presumably, is as it should be.

poets of a given time. And literature? Perhaps, from one angle anyway, it's what philosophers strive to create an encompassing theory for, what they hunger to transform into knowledge. If the philosopher's injunction to the poet is to grow up, then the poet, in his highest moods of confidence, replies that one ought to devote oneself to living in such a way that death will present a contrast.

If Sigmund Freud had read "Intimations" in an especially irritable state of mind, the state in which he composed the essay "Creative Writers and Daydreaming" where he claimed that literature uses form to occupy the critical faculties while the unconscious revels in wish fulfillment, he might have assimilated the great Ode to his reflections in *The Future of an Illusion*. Freud, in his most reductive mode, would be inclined to read through all of Wordsworth's subtle ruminations on past existence, and to understand them as a form of religious nostalgia. Religion, Freud said in one of his best-known and bluntest epigrams, is the longing for the father. Wordsworth, the case might continue, wants the freedom of living in a post-Christian world, but will not give up the deity: in fact he even speaks at one point, of "God, who is our home." But his objective overall is to use evasions such as metaphor and metonymy, or, as they are known to analysts, condensation and displacement (remember Trilling's reflections on this matter), to achieve the desired emancipation along with the desired security.

In a slightly more tractable frame of mind, Freud might see, in what appears to be a detail, some subtler implications in the poem. The child "lies," the ode says, "with light upon him from his father's eyes" (90). That light, presumably, is the light of the super-ego, being conveyed to the child. All of the imaginative structures of authority the child concocts, like the imperial palace, will be nothing more than precipitates of the initial transfer of power that takes place in the Oedipal encounter. It would be of interest here that the light of paternal power falls on the child just after he's been "fretted by sallies of his mother's kisses" (89).

Freudian readings such as this one are a thing of the past, and for obvious good reasons. Many patients free associating on the couch might be capable of displacing their fixations on authority from one image to the next: what was once the father becomes the state, becomes the dome of the capital building, and other such things. But those fixations, those longings for the father, will not result in the "Intimations" ode.

And yet, did criticism really give up Freud so easily? I think not, and understanding how he has been transformed and put to use can bring us closer to understanding the way a good deal of current academic criticism works. Paul de Man, or a reader indebted to him, would be likely to find ratios of blindness and insight active in Wordsworth's image of the soul's prior life. Blindness and insight, de Man's central conceit, is a figure for dramatic irony, the kind of irony that arises when speakers say more than they know, and in situations where the surplus of meaning is taken in by some third party. This is the case for all of the critics that de Man considers in his first published volume: they are unable to apprehend the insights that are inconsistent with their idealizing critical models, but that those models allow them, paradoxically, to produce. De Man argues, for instance, that Georg Lukács pushes his organic model for understanding the novel far enough to reveal temporality's power to disrupt the claims that novels make for epic-style cohesion. Yet this dissonance reveals itself not to Lukács, whose own view is that novelistic temporality contributes to the text's organic form, but rather to de Man. To him, Lukács' book gives "the elements to decipher the real plot hidden behind the pseudo-plot, but the author himself remains deluded."[9]

In *Blindness and Insight*'s central essay, on Derrida's reading of Rousseau, "The Rhetoric of Blindness," de Man takes time to summarize the pattern that arises from his analyses of the various critics:

It is necessary, in each case, to read beyond some of the more categorical assertions and balance them against other much more tentative utterances that seem to come close, at times, to being contradictory to these assertions. The contradictions, however, never cancel each other out, nor do they enter into the synthesizing dynamics of a dialectic. No

---

[9] *Blindness and Insight: Essays in the Rhetoric of Contemporary Criticism* (Minneapolis: University of Minnesota Press, 1983), p. 104. Henceforth cited in the text.

contradiction or dialectical movement could develop because a fundamental difference in the level of explicitness prevented both statements
from meeting on a common level of discourse; the one always lay hidden
within the other as the sun lies hidden within a shadow, or truth within
error. (pp. 102–3)

This, presumably, is something like what happens when Oedipus
lays his curse upon the murderer of Laius. At that point the
audience, familiar as it is with the Oedipus legend, is in a position
to detect the self-usurping sense in the protagonist's brave words.
As D. C. Muecke, the author of a fine study of irony, puts it,
"[T]here is a special pleasure in seeing someone serenely unaware
of being in a predicament, especially when this predicament is
the contrary of the situation he assumes himself to be in. It
would be difficult to account for this pleasure in purely humani-
tarian terms."[10] Muecke, with an urbane irony of his own,
indicates that dramatic irony involves a reversal in established
relations of authority. The audience can suddenly claim superiority to the speaker. So for de Man, the author is someone who
says more than she knows, and whose authority is accordingly
usurped by the reader, who will become prey to a similar dynamic
in turn.

Freud's interest in drama, and tragic drama in particular, is
well known. Sophocles' *Oedipus Rex*, along with Shakespeare's
Hamlet, helped Freud to formulate the Oedipal complex, but
Sophocles' play also gave Freud an image of how psychotherapy
proceeds. "The action of the play consists in nothing other than
the process of revealing, with cunning delays and ever-mounting
excitement – a process that can be likened to the work of
psychoanalysis – that Oedipus himself is the murderer of Laius,
but further that he is the son of the murdered man and of
Jocasta."[11] Freud is probably thinking here of the way that
Tiresias draws out Oedipus, compelling him, through a sequence
of questions, to come face to face with his actual state. Tiresias is
the one character on stage who knows how to interpret the
dramatic irony that infuses much of what Oedipus has to say.

[10] *Irony* (London: Methuen, 1970), p. 63.
[11] *The Standard Edition of the Complete Psychological Works of Sigmund Freud*, trans. James
Strachey et al., 24 vols. (London: Hogarth Press, 1953), IV:261–2. (Hereafter "*S.E.*")

The prophet seems to understand that the threats Oedipus makes against him are evidence that he is suffering intimations of his own guilt. Soon the rage he is directing at Tiresias will be aimed at himself.

Similarly, the psychoanalyst must also be attuned to dramatic irony. She must understand that patients say more than they know, and help them to uncover the hidden dimension of their words. She divines the words within their words. In an early phase of Freudian therapy, the objective of such uncovering was what Freud called catharsis. Suddenly the patient would recall the repressed scene in its full intensity, and discharge the energy that had kept that scene locked in the unconscious, inaccessible to the daytime mind. The moment in which the repressed returns, Freud indicates, is comparable to what Aristotle described in terms of the discharge of fear and pity. In therapy, such discharge left the patient, as it presumably left the spectator after *Oedipus Rex*, in a state of exhausted tranquility.

Freud eventually gave up the cathartic method, which seemed to produce only temporary release from symptoms. He replaced it with analysis based on transference, analysis in which the physician takes up the role of one or another significant figure in the patient's past (sometimes a composite of such figures, sometimes a few in sequence). By replaying patients' deeply internalized ideas about their relations with key figures in their psychic histories, transference analysis functions as a kind of theater. The patient and the analyst take on roles, but they also observe the unfolding of the play. The revelations that occur are intentionally less cataclysmic, less dramatic, than those in the kind of therapy aimed at catharsis. In analysis through the transference, the patient's ego is present on the scene and can take possession of the repressed events, or hitherto hidden information, as knowledge. Ego can comprehend something more of the id, the it; insight can displace a strategically disabling blindness.

This formulation gestures toward a connection between de Man and Freud, a connection I think I can render plausible by returning to "Intimations." Wordsworth's "vision splendid," the light that the child sees and feels emanating from his other-worldly origins, would qualify, to a deconstructive reader of de Man's sort, as a disturbingly mystified phenomenon. It would look like an exercise in symbol making, or metaphor, or blindness, or theory, depending upon the period in de Man's career from which the reading arose. That is to say Wordsworth's celestial light promises to give full access to knowledge, presence, unity, a being outside of time, and all of the states that de Man dismissed as illusory, human efforts to put on godlike powers.

The "vision" might be undermined, or deconstructed, from within. Consider, for instance, the metaphor that Wordsworth uses to record the child's gradual estrangement from his exalted vision: "Shades of the prison-house begin to close/Upon the growing Boy" (67–8). The "prison-house" might be understood as a reference to the inevitability of mediation. The play of shades, which presumably becomes constitutive of all experience, could be identified as a play of textual traces actively deconstructing illusions of full presence. One might speak here of a prison house of language, from which it is futile to try to escape. (The conventional association of shades with death could suggest, to the deconstructor, that an unwillingness to live with language, a wish for an unmediated vision, was bound up with unwillingness to face death.) From this perspective, what matters most in the poem is the reference to an intervening structure that compels reading and interpretation, and undoes, or at least challenges, the illusion that equates knowing and seeing.

I cannot say whether de Man would find the poem sufficiently self-conscious to be credited with undermining its own "naive" vision and forecasting the terms of its future misreading, as certain of Rousseau's texts are said to do in "The Rhetoric of Blindness." If de Man did find the poem sufficiently self-questioning, Wordsworth would be congratulated as a subtle ironist capable of affirming blindness and shadow as forms of self-subverting insight. But then it is likely that a critic or two would be summoned forward – as Derrida is in "The Rhetoric of Blindness," and Jean Starobinski is more than once in de Man – to represent the kind of mystified reading that is in need of correction.

But how far have we come from Freud? Are we not still talking about ratios of repression? Consider this passage:

All patients seem curiously doomed to say something quite different from what they meant to say. . . It seems . . . that . . . insight can only be gained because patients are in the grip of a peculiar repression; their language gropes toward a certain degree of insight only because they remain oblivious to the perception of this insight. The insight exists only for the therapist in the privileged position of being able to observe the repression as a phenomenon in its own right.

The passage, which could fit quite easily into one of Freud's papers on therapeutic technique, derives from de Man.[12] Along with a few syntactical changes, I have made some substitutions in diction: "repression" for "blindness," "patient" for "critic" (though in some cases de Man would have said poet; in this case he could easily have said Wordsworth), and "therapist" for "reader" in the privileged position. The term "insight" is apposite to both deconstructive and psychoanalytical claims, with the qualification that de Manian insight is likely to involve repressed affirmations of temporality, contingency, and ultimately of death, while the Freudian analyst listens for echoes of the Oedipal drama.

De Man's criticism – and here I come to one of this chapter's central points – fuses Freud with Coleridge. Now I understand that even if one accepts the linkage between de Man and Freud (a figure whom de Man rarely mentions), the association with Coleridge will sound, at least initially, rather odd. For it would seem that what de Man achieved as a critic is inseparable from the turn against Coleridge that he executes in "The Rhetoric of Temporality." Where Coleridge denigrates allegory as a "mere picture language," de Man, in what's been called the most photo-copied critical essay written, celebrates its capacity to deliver readers from comforting illusion and to unveil – the

---

[12] The relevant passage in de Man reads:

All these critics seem curiously doomed to say something quite different from what they meant to say . . . It seems, however, that this insight could only be gained because the critics were in the grip of this peculiar blindness: their language could grope toward a certain degree of insight only because their method remained oblivious to the perception of this insight. The insight exists only for a reader in the privileged position of being able to observe the blindness as a phenomenon in its own right. (pp. 105–6)

terminology betrays residues of his debt to existentialism – "an authentically temporal destiny" (p. 206).

De Man's critique is aimed against Coleridge's aesthetic of the symbol. In *The Statesman's Manual* Coleridge offers the well-known and influential description: "[A] symbol is characterized by a translucence of the Special in the Individual or of the General in the Especial or of the Universal in the General. Above all by the translucence of the Eternal through and in the Temporal."[13] Allegorical writing, as de Man describes it, is self-consciously literary, which is to say artificial. Rather than referring to a natural unity outside of the text, allegory signifies by making reference to other writing: it gestures toward an expanding universe of words. The ongoing process of construing inter-textual meanings, of moving from passage to passage, book to book, somehow functions, for de Man, to represent the rhythms of being within time. (I'm not sure why this image of interminable interpretation isn't understood as being suggestive of interminable life, and thus itself a wish fulfillment.) Yet, as de Man sees it, those temporal rhythms are frequently subdued by the allure of the symbol, by illusions of full understanding that find all the world in a grain of sand or, as in the "Intimations" ode, in a prior world from whence we supposedly come. Thus the movement of even the most attentive reading is from allegorical and temporal authenticity to seduction (de Man's diction is overtly puritanical) by this or that symbolic bower of bliss (p. 206).

The symbol/allegory dualism, like the blindness/insight and theory/undecidability dyads that follow upon it, is supposed to encompass what matters most about literary experience, and about interpretation overall. De Man greatly expands the meaning of "allegory" and the application of both allegory and symbol. Thus he is able to talk about allegory as characteristic not only of Jean de Meung, but also of Defoe, Wordsworth, and Rousseau. In fact, de Man argues that the rediscovery of allegory is chiefly what distinguishes the Romantic achievement.

Doesn't this separate de Man from Coleridge and his aesthetic

---

[13] *Lay Sermons*, ed. R. J. White (Princeton: Princeton University Press, 1972), p. 30.

of the symbol? Nominally yes, but not, in my opinion, much more than that. De Man actually concurs with Coleridge on a number of matters. Like Coleridge he makes rhetorical terms central to his proceedings; his prevailing critical mode is technical. Like Coleridge, he focuses on epistemological issues, on the truth or falsity of certain modes of reading: allegory is authentic, the symbol delusory. Like Coleridge, de Man is a formalist. The content of the symbol matters less to Coleridge than the fact that it makes contact with the eternal. Just so, de Man is not attuned to the subject of the allegory, but rather to its formal, inter-textual dynamic. The movement de Man chronicles from allegory to symbol and back to allegory seems to me to replay Coleridge's sense that experience, even at its best, must consist in symbolic contact with the numinous realm inevitably followed by reimmersion in the world of objects – which "qua objects are fixed and dead." If, as Coleridge says in "Dejection," we receive but what we give, it follows that our powers of creative response will inevitably ebb and flow, even during the best times.

To put matters in summary form: de Man has recourse to Coleridge's rhetorical binaries, symbol and allegory, but values them in an opposite manner. He prefers allegorical disjunction to symbolic unity. By using Freud (though without quite saying as much), it is possible to reinforce that value distinction by insisting that one side, the allegorical, has been systematically repressed, not only by Coleridge, but by critics like Wasserman, Wimsatt, and Abrams, who have reproduced Coleridge's position in the twentieth century. *With* Coleridge, one can commence the systematic study of literature. With Coleridge and Freud, one can have a philosophical study of literature in which the power relation between poet and critic is comparable to the relation between patient and analyst. By recourse to Coleridge's terminology, the Freudian dimension becomes a touch harder to detect. By using Freud's trope of the unconscious, what is rather conventional in Coleridge takes on the aura of a hidden and subversive knowledge.

But can't one justly think of de Man as a defender of poetry against philosophical disenfranchisement? Might one not say, for instance, that de Man's achievement lies in getting to poetry before Derrida did? Derrida, this case would continue, deemed virtually all texts susceptible to deconstruction. De Man comes on then, in "The Rhetoric of Blindness" and elsewhere, to point to some works that encode the patterns of incomprehension to which their presumptuous readers will inevitably succumb. Such writings are self-deconstructing. Those texts that record, allegorically, how they will be misunderstood, and also proffer images for their own correct deconstruction, their own "rigorous unreliability," are, de Man teaches, worthy of being called literature. Doesn't this qualify as a subtle defence of poetry?

No. First of all the canon of so-called literature that de Man and his disciples worked up was minuscule: one encounters respectful de Manian readings of Rousseau, Wordsworth, Rilke, Rousseau, Hölderlin, more Rousseau, more Wordsworth, and very few others. By this standard, there is very little literature indeed. Presumably most of what one conceived as literature before is blinded discourse. Then too, when the standard for being literary is deploying a formal structure, blindness and insight, it seems clear that conceptual categories, continuities, have taken precedence over whatever might be singular in this or that literary work. Theory, in other words, can do the job better. It's not clear to me that poetry profits from de Man's formalism much more than from Aristotle's.

Where Coleridge, Freud, and also de Man significantly concur is in their unwillingness to celebrate the child. After Freud's reflections on the child's Oedipal passions take cultural hold, the affirmations familiar to us from Rousseau, Wordsworth, Emerson, and Whitman become all but untenable within literary high culture. Childhood becomes the source of the neuroses. Freud's defence of sublimation, like Coleridge's of philosophy, depends on denigrating the kind of spontaneity the Romantic child embodies. When James Dickey begins his great lyric, "The Other" (a poem to which I shall return in the next chapter), with the lines "Holding onto myself by the hand,/I change places into the spirit/I had as a rack-ribbed child,/And walk slowly out through my mind," he brings us back to the Whitman of "Out of the Cradle," – "A man, yet by these tears a little boy again" – and declares himself an uninhibited, and potentially archaic,

Romantic vitalist.[14] Is there, on the other hand, any voice in contemporary writing as severe, knowing, unsurprised, as compulsive in its maturity, as de Man's?

The child as ideal is something that, in the wake of Freud, one must leave high culture to find. Stephen King, the vastly popular horror writer, almost always chooses for his heroes boys who have not yet crossed over into puberty. They are the sorts of boys who, as Emerson puts it, are sure of a dinner and would be loath to say or do anything to conciliate the authorities. King's heroes aren't yet corrupted, aren't fully broken to social forms, and as one might expect they exhibit an Emersonian self-trust. If they see it – no matter what *it* is – then it's there. Not only are King's heroes children, but the effect he chiefly induces, primal fear in the midst of a bland, smiling, and unselfconsciously corrupt society, is designed to bring the reader back to childhood, "moving about in worlds not realized" (146), as Wordsworth has it.

Being scared without actually being physically threatened (an experience Edmund Burke associated with the sublime) is, in our current culture, one of the few routes back to the childhood self, and we would be rather arrogant, I think, to trust so entirely in psychoanalysis and the philosophical tradition – both of which augment their power by turning against childhood and the kind of poetry associated with it – that we are unable to credit the human need a writer like King fills. The recourse to childhood has been for some time a mode of resistance to oppressive social forms. To call upon the child in this way is to indict society for not providing enough possible futures that reflect the energy and promise perceptible in children. It is also to suggest that we might try greeting the disappearance of secure foundations and transcendent Truth not with de Man's knowing skepticism, but with a receptive, buoyant curiosity, a childlike curiosity. "The Intimations Ode" – in fact virtually all of Wordsworth's best poetry – proves, at least to me, that the recourse to childhood *remains* a valuable gesture.

The state of knowing that has a superior relation to childhood (to poetry, to trope) is the one that Wordsworth, you'll recall,

---

[14] Dickey, *Poems, 1957–1967* (Middleton, Conn.: Wesleyan University Press, 1967), p. 34 and Walt Whitman, *Complete Poetry and Collected Prose*, ed. Justin Kaplan (New York: Library of America, 1982), p. 388.

refers to as "the philosophic mind": it looks *through* death and presumably through all human fictions. The philosophic mind finds ultimate meanings (or ultimate patterns by which meanings are undone). It affirms the sort of Coleridgean categories that exist on high (a form of transcendentalism, perhaps), or the suppressed forces that Freud favored (descendentalism, if you like). Then too the philosophic mind can combine those two approaches in de Man's fashion. What is lost in addressing poetry by way of Coleridge, Freud, and de Man is the ability to see how poems get out ahead of us, creating fresh prospects, new hope. Theory interests itself in the past, in what is already known; poetry would create the future. In "Intimations," Wordsworth puts his words into play between poetry and systematic philosophy actively enough to make us doubt both categories, and to believe that everything is always and inevitably literature, a world of trope, which is a world of freedom, temporarily at least. Could Freud conceive of someone who succeeds in submitting his internal agency of authority, his super-ego, to imaginative metamorphosis, and so gives it, for all practical purposes, another shape? No more than Wordsworth could conceive of living his whole life as one stable human structure.

Surely there is a use for conceptual criticism, for the intervention of general ideas that summarize a particular author, period, or genre. I think, in fact, that literature that can be effectively summarized by such categories is no longer worthy of the name. Knowing as much about this or that work can be of value. And yet what Wordsworth shows is that metaphysical principles can be put back into play, reduced to fiction, by the actions of ambitious poets. A key measure of a poet's prowess lies in her ability to possess, transform, and surpass the reigning conceptual modes, writing in such a way that no existing theory can account for the work. But this dialogue between poetry and systematic philosophy is rendered invisible by stabilizing analyses that presume to put a stop to the mutually animating exchange.

It is my view that approaches like de Man's, approaches that work variations on Freud's theory of repression, have become commonplace in academic literary criticism, and by the end of this book, I shall have pointed to a number of elaborations on the blindness and insight motif. It will not be my contention that everyone writing theoretical criticism – the kind of criticism that can produce disciples – has been influenced by de Man per se. Instead I think that de Man, rather shrewdly, reduced and codified a dynamic that can result in institutional and perhaps even broad cultural authority for academic criticism, though at a cost.

Consider the situation of criticism in the university. The university system, as Louis Menand has pointed out, was built with a positivistic model of research in mind. "According to this model, knowledge develops by the accumulation of research findings, brick piled onto brick, until the arch of knowledge about a field stands clearly defined against the background of mere undisciplined information. All the requirements and rewards of academic work – doctoral dissertations based on 'original research,' tenure review, publication in specialized and refereed journals, and so forth – were established to encourage the production of more bricks."[15] And the system seems to work quite well, at least for the hard sciences.

But what about literary criticism? The major critics in the Anglo-American tradition who wrote prior to criticism's comprehensive institutionalization, writers like Johnson and Hazlitt and Virginia Woolf, would have been hard pressed to see their work as contributing to some looming structure of knowledge. Criticism succeeded in the university not because it modified its conception of knowledge to include Johnson's *Rambler* essays, or the pieces Woolf brought out in the *Common Reader* collections, but because criticism changed to meet academic requirements. Criticism followed Coleridge's lead and became more like an organized field of knowledge. By adapting the theory of the unconscious, criticism took another step forward in that it offered the potential for subversive interpretation and esoteric insight, insight inaccessible to outsiders in that only a licensed, that is a university, critic could tell you authoritatively whether the subtext you had found was actually there or not.

How does a senior practitioner know that the latent sense a junior aspirant has pointed to ought to be credited? As Frank Kermode indicates in an essay titled "Institutional Control of

---

[15] Review of *Tenured Radicals* by Roger Kimball, *New Republic*, July 9 & 16, 1990, p. 38.

Interpretation," that is an unanswerable question: those in power simply know, and that's all there is to it.[16] Here the comparison to psychoanalysis becomes illuminating. If the junior practitioner of therapy brings forward an interpretation of the patient's symptoms and the supervising elders feel that it is wrong, another source of appeal exists, the patient. If the patient is being helped by the "insight," then the elders must, presumably, stand aside. But in literary studies, there is no comparable system of checks and balances.

If your reading is dismissed by the elder critics (and no matter how senior you might be, there are always elders), then presumably you can go out and set up a school of your own, something like what Jung did when he and Freud became incompatible. The important point, though, is that you can only set up a school if you have a vision of the latent sense, a vision of which disciples can make use. De Man succeeded in transferring the Freudian model of repression from the sphere of analytic therapy to that of rhetorical analysis, thus making Freud compatible with the linguistic turn that has characterized much of contemporary thought.

Throughout his career, de Man renamed the symbol/allegory dyad, speaking of blindness and insight, metaphor and metonymy, truth and ignorance, theory and undecidability, always indicating that the latter term was subject to programmatic repression. In so doing he perpetuated the myth of a specially sanctioned realm – comparable to the unconscious in psychoanalysis – to which one might gain secure access only in a department of literature. For there one could find authorities, professors who might trace themselves back, as Freudian analysts like to do, to the founder, and whose judgments about the repressed sense of the text one might take as binding.

At the close of his essay, Kermode confesses that to him whatever mild oppressions universities commit in controlling interpretation are worth putting up with because they allow us to "preserve the latent sense." The situation, he says, "might even be cause for mild rejoicing." But why this latent sense is of value, Kermode never actually says. Kermode, most all of whose writings

---

[16] *The Art of Telling: Essays on Fiction* (Cambridge: Harvard University Press, 1983), pp. 168–84.

exude a temperate irony that, I take it, signifies genuine intellectual modesty, might submit that the pressure of a latent sense keeps alive a feeling of salutary doubt, of due compunction about one's interpretive authority.

But not everyone has Kermode's highly civilized conception of the latent sense. It seems to me that one of the chief values of the latent sense, when it is established using the psychoanalytical model, is institutional. It preserves the English department and helps it to grow within the softly Darwinian environment of the university. ("It's a sheep eat sheep world," my colleague Gordon Braden says of the academy.) As many students of professionalism have noted, every group that wants to establish itself as a profession must have access to some hidden knowledge from which the public is excluded.[17] In the merger of systematic philosophy and psychoanalysis, criticism, I think, finds one sort of such knowledge. By turning from the play of figurative language to affirm truth (or the programmatic impossibility of discovering truth), you gain a certain kind of institutionally negotiable power. You acquire a way of knowing that's not altogether embarrassing when compared to what goes on in the physics department.

And also a kind of knowledge that can produce disciples. In fact, no critic in recent memory has equalled de Man's power to create devoted students. At de Man's memorial service, Barbara Johnson, perhaps his best-known and most gifted follower, said that "The last thing he probably would have wanted to be was a moral and pedagogical – rather than merely intellectual – example for generations of students and colleagues, yet it was precisely his way of *not* seeking those roles that made him so irreplaceably an exception, and such an inspiration. He never sought followers; people followed him in droves. He was ironic toward discipleship; the country is dotted with his disciples."[18] Others who delivered tributes at de Man's memorial service go further than Johnson in professing their fascination with him and their allegiance to his memory and teaching.

What was it about de Man that made him so good at creating

[17] See Magali Sarfatti Larson's *The Rise of Professionalism: A Sociological Analysis* (Berkeley: University of California Press, 1977).
[18] "In Memoriam," *Yale French Studies*, 69 (1985), p. 10.

devoted students? Despite Johnson's tribute, he did in fact profess some overt interest in founding a school. If in "The Rhetoric of Blindness" de Man writes condescendingly about discipleship, he takes a different view in his second book, *Allegories of Reading*. There, having submitted an example of deconstructive reading, he observes that, "The whole of literature would respond in similar fashion, although the techniques and the patterns would have to vary considerably, of course, from author to author. But there is absolutely no reason why analyses of the kind here suggested for Proust would not be applicable, with proper modifications of technique, to Milton, or to Dante, or to Hölderlin." Then a memorable line: "This will in fact be the task of literary criticism in the coming years."[19]

A long-time student of dramatic irony might be expected to restrain himself from making regal pronouncements like this. And surely anyone who feels that a "return to history" came on not long after *Allegories* was published and overthrew deconstructive hegemony will be likely to relish de Man's bit of hubris. Yet, as I've said, I am not sure that de Man had it entirely wrong; I'm not sure his influence isn't alive still, in however displaced a form, creating disciples.[20]

Like psychoanalysis, de Man's deconstruction initiates a self-perpetuating order. It is well known that one psychoanalyst must analyze another: there is the training analysis that inaugurates the career, but Freud also felt that even practiced psychoanalysts should return periodically to treatment. Just so, one de Manian reader must disclose the ratios of blindness and insight produced by the other. As a student, one is read, one's blindnesses disclosed, one's coincident insight taken up and made the motive for fresh readings which will in turn yield occlusions and opportunities.

This relay of readings lends itself well to an institutional setting. It reinforces hierarchically established roles. Under de Man's dispensation, one is always reading as a teacher, seeking points

---

[19] *Allegories of Reading: Figural Language in Rousseau, Nietzsche, Rilke, and Proust* (New Haven: Yale University Press, 1979), pp. 16–17.

[20] John Allman reflects shrewdly on de Man's influence in "Paul de Man, Deconstruction, and Discipleship," *Philosophy and Literature*, 14:2 (October 1990), pp. 324–39.

of mystification in the text, then becoming the object of scrutiny in one's turn, being read as a student. Every deconstructive reading that works is a teacher's reading of a student. Derrida is, at least in "The Rhetoric of Blindness," a pupil of de Man. The identities of student and teacher shift perpetually (with one exception, that I'll describe shortly), but you always play one or the other of the university's two major roles, making those roles appear more natural than they otherwise would. So subversive deconstruction reaffirms the institutional structure and the profession that it ought, presumably, to question.

Yet can't one usurp power by reading the senior reader, by deconstructing the master? In the early days of psychoanalysis, Freud suffered considerably from something comparable: his best disciples and heirs were always rebelling. The most famous insurrection was that of Carl Jung, who said that his suspicions about Freud began during an incident on the boat trip they made to America, where Freud was to lecture at Clark University. The two took to analyzing each other's dreams to pass the time. One day Freud reported a dream, Jung began the analysis, but then, to go further, needed to ask Freud some personal questions. Freud refused to answer. When asked why, Freud said it was because he did not want to risk losing his authority.[21]

Freud had invested a great deal in the hope that the extraordinarily gifted Jung would succeed him as the head of the psychoanalytic movement. But the problem that Freud encountered was that the more creative his followers were – and Jung was probably the most creative of all of them – the more they were disposed to rebel against him. That is, they emulated his drive to speculate, and frequently what they speculated on, using and enlarging the Freudian method, was Freud himself.

At one point in his work, de Man observes that the question of his own readerly blindness is one that he is, by definition, incompetent to pose. Surely one of the attractions of his kind of deconstruction is that it allows one to read the senior reader, deconstruct the deconstructor. But the process will always repeat the original structure of blindness and insight. Thus de Man

---

[21] Peter Gay provides a brief account of the episode in *Freud: A Life for Our Time* (New York: W. W. Norton, 1988), p. 225.

arrived at a way to sanction, and to circumscribe, the tendency of the disciple to rebel. The terms that Jung would have used to analyze Freud's dream would be quite particular to Freud – and quite painful because of how personal they were. (The dream at issue seems to have involved Freud's relations with his wife.) The terms that de Manian analysis deals in are coolly impersonal enough, and so often repeated, that using them will always be a tribute to the founder.

In "The Frame of Reference: Poe, Lacan, Derrida," Barbara Johnson acts as de Man's stand-in in a critical power struggle with Derrida and Lacan.[22] She claims, contra Derrida, that there is in fact a primal scene, but that, contra Lacan, we cannot represent it authoritatively. Rather, argues Johnson, the primal scene consists in the trauma of facing an undecidable interpretation, the trauma of having to acknowledge oneself as blinded in a way that doesn't solidify into a presumptuous theory of blindness. In "Deconstruction, Feminism, and Pedagogy," Johnson argues that de Man's insights about the ways that linguistic structures determine personal identity and actions effectively destabilize received ideas about what it means to be a human being, possessing an effective will.[23] But at the same time, de Man, perhaps blindly, transfers the terms customarily associated with agency to language. In doing so he performs an act of personification that betrays nostalgia for the kind of humanity he's busy calling into question. Johnson seems to be de Man's agent in the first piece, his critic in the second, but her recourse to the blindness and insight motif in both cases renders each essay an act of homage, albeit of a highly intelligent order. After the first de Manian reading, there is, in a certain sense, no other.

Why then was de Man so effective at generating disciples? First, because he offered an apparently subversive mode of interpretation, one that was difficult to acquire and that provided arcane knowledge. And too, he offered it to a generation of graduate students who, given the experience of the '60s, were highly skeptical about any claims to authoritative truth. Yet

[22] *Psychoanalysis and the Question of the Text*, ed. Geoffrey Hartman (Baltimore: Johns Hopkins University Press, 1978), pp. 149–71.
[23] *A World of Difference* (Baltimore: Johns Hopkins University Press, 1987), pp. 42–6.

this interpretive method acted to shore up university structures, making them more appealing to those who nursed allegiances to institutional authority. Then, though the blindness and insight motif seems rebellious, it provides no very satisfying way to rebel against the master. The method forms a self-perpetuating order which is pleasing to inhabit and hard to break from. One might recall in this connection how, in *The Republic*'s tenth book, Plato derided Homer for not producing disciples, and affirmed, albeit indirectly, the true philosopher's power to create "a host of disciples to love and revere him" (p. 330). In the disenfranchisement of art, the ability to garner disciples is crucial, for there is too much literature out there for one critic to do the job alone.

Yet perhaps I am being unfair. Just because a style of interpretation meshes smoothly with institutional protocols, just because it effectively produces disciples, just because it can't record what one poem, the "Intimations" ode, achieves (at least according to me), does that mean the interpretive style ought to be discarded?

Surely one does not want to stop using the concept of dramatic irony to illuminate literature and life. Dramatic irony, in its classical manifestations, acquaints us with our tendency to overestimate ourselves, to claim more by way of knowledge or power than it's given human beings to possess. The classical dramatists made characters the object of dramatic irony when they assumed they could control future events, subdue nature, live in perpetual happiness. Contact with the tragic sensibility may induce us to temper our own ambitions and utterances; de Man's attraction to dramatic irony (which never led him to adopt a corresponding irony of tone) should in no way undermine the concept's value. It is, rather, the merger of dramatic irony with the theory of repression and the unconscious that I wish to resist.

But am I saying here that the unconscious does not exist? Doesn't everyone who refuses to believe in God believe in the unconscious? To that question I can only answer, alas yes, almost everyone. The unconscious is an explanatory term, the matrix for narratives accounting for phenomena that are otherwise inexplicable. But because the unconscious is the realm of the repressed, we cannot, by definition, know it. Its existence can only be inferred: its actions can be guessed at, diagnosed, but never demonstrated. We can only judge the unconscious as a category for understanding by studying the effects of those interpretations that rely upon it.

Whatever the effects of the theory of repression within clinical psychoanalysis, it seems clear that when a literary critic makes use of that theory the result is an immediate shift in power from author to critic, writer to reader. There is no rebuttal to the charge of repression (no chance for "Wait a minute, I wasn't repressing that!"), and no text or writer has ever, as far as I know, voluntarily transferred interpretive power to a critic the way a patient transfers it to a physician. I wonder then if it is possible to describe a literary critical invocation of repression as evidence of anything but a personal, professional, and institutional will to power over the writing at hand.

But am I not myself using the blindness and insight motif to read de Man? Isn't this chapter an attempt to expose de Man's blindness to the actual ramifications of his method, and to the true reasons for its success? I think not, and for a few reasons. First of all, the blindness and insight model, like the theory of repression, is designed to disclose the origins of the object at hand. De Man believes that the source of Lukács's book, *The Theory of the Novel*, lay in his suppressing a critical truth, the truth of temporality. I do not care in the least where de Man's books came from, what enabled him to write them. (In fact, a major argument threading through this book is that one ought to be wary of all theories that pretend to disclose the origins of cultural works, rather than their use and value.) This chapter concerns itself with what de Man's writings do, what influence they have in the world.

Nor do I think that de Man, or a disciple of his, would be constitutionally unable to comprehend the argument I'm making here and respond intelligently to it; they wouldn't be "blind" to the views this chapter unfolds. I do think that the results of de Man's work are stabilizing and even stultifying where he took them to be disruptive, but I put this view forward as a disagreement with him, not as a disclosure about the hidden, or repressed, nature of his project. If you use the term blindness loosely enough, then any disagreement with de Man can be written of as an exercise in his method, a piece of unwitting homage.

My chief doubt about the deployment of Freud's concept of repression – Platonism in reverse – by de Man and others is socially pragmatic. Theories of interpretation should catch on because they offer opportunities not only to understand texts, but to understand people. How shall we talk about ourselves? How shall we describe others? These are the kinds of questions that bring many students into literary studies. Such students are often rightly skeptical about the scientific pretensions that disciplines like psychology and sociology sustain. They seek ways of talking more attuned to individual idiosyncrasy, more respectful of mystery. And criticism can, or ought to, work in collaboration with literature to enlarge such expressive resources.

Making the theory of repression central to your interpretive procedures induces you to stop questing for more and more varied ways of representing experience and to find repose on an absolute truth. When Kenneth Burke called the unconscious Freud's god-term, he meant, among other things, that invoking it indicated a desire for arguments and interpretations to come to an end and for faith to take over. Burke's (and my) conception of a literary culture is one in which the arguments don't come to an end, in part because no one can play the intellectual traffic cop, lifting a hand to stop things where they are.

It's also, I think, a bad idea to contribute in any way to the view that once one is versed in the theory of repression, or of blindness and insight, one can, by definition, know others more authoritatively than they can know themselves. For the assumptions that inform the theory of repression contribute, I think, to creating a culture of mutual surveillance. Having to submit to other people's construction of your unconscious motives, having to take that kind of intrusion seriously, can be a harsh impediment to self-trust, a virtue rarely in excessive supply to begin with. But of course, one might reply, you *don't* really have to take such things seriously. When people offer a free and unbidden analysis of your psyche's secret workings you can tell them, with whatever ceremony you deem appropriate, to go to hell.

Matters aren't always so simple, though. Too often the person deploying psychoanalytic resources also holds power over the analyzed one. The interpreter in question can be the boss, the physician, the social worker, the teacher, someone on whom one is compelled to depend, someone who can make life less palatable than it already is, or maybe ease the pressures a degree or two. In order to survive in the environment such interpreters control, you are often well advised to entertain, and sometimes to accept, their assessment of your deep identity and of course your attendant problems, then work along the prescribed lines to become healthy, productive, and good. I think that I am not overstating the case when I say that a lot of what passes for education, rehabilitation, psychological care, and social work in the West now entails encouraging the so-called client to accept the therapeutic construction of him- or herself to which the presiding expert holds the key. That key is, almost inevitably, the theory of repression.

My criterion here is pragmatic: I don't ask whether the theory of the unconscious is true (even from an empirical perspective one cannot, as I suggested above, get a satisfying answer to that question), but whether it is good in the way of belief. I think it's not: yet the power it offers, especially to literary critics looking to strengthen their discipline's standing and their own authority, is most attractive. Maybe the task of literary criticism in the coming years will entail resisting such power.

But a fear arises. If academic critics gave up on the notion of repression, seeing it as a damaging thing to believe in and use, then would they have anything to do? What would they write? Who would read them? Can criticism survive without the unconscious?

For an answer we can continue looking at Wordsworth. Coleridge's response to the first four sections of "Intimations" precipitated a key insight for his friend: Wordsworth saw that continuing to talk about subjects and objects was not going to be conducive to human vitality or to the writing of great poems. He understood that the question was tired, and that something new needed to be invented. Thus he took up the stance of the critic between systematic analysis and poetry.

Criticism, understood along these lines, demands that poetry measure itself against certain concepts and narratives, against certain "principles of reality." Thus criticism, working in Robert Frost's mode, tests the reach of metaphors, finding the points where they give way, and are no longer of value. In "Education by Poetry," Frost writes that unless you've had a "proper poetical education," you're "not safe anywhere . . . You don't know the metaphor in its strength and its weakness. You don't know how far you may expect to ride it and when it may break down with you."[24] What Wordsworth sees in his guise as critic is that his old mapping (Nature and I) won't hold up when Coleridge presses it: maybe it is a monologue he's been sustaining. Lately though, rather than showing how tropes fail to illuminate a given situation and then, perhaps, gesturing toward new possibilities, critics have been taking the short cut that recourse to the theory of repression, of blindness and insight, offers.

With that move, a good deal of criticism has lost another major virtue, the power to show how poetry has overcome, or troped beyond, the prevailing theories of the day. Wordsworth does exactly that, rejecting Coleridge's Kantian problematic, but from the perspective of Coleridge and Freud, the achievement is difficult if not impossible to detect. Under their tutelage one looks for an object, not a performance, for what is locked in the past, not for what remains new, remains out ahead of current norms. With the turn to Coleridge and Freud and, too, to de Man, criticism loses its capacity to defend poetry from unimaginative philosophical critics who insist on the preeminence of ideas, principles, and stories that literature has already assimilated, or has no need to assimilate.

Then, too, the effective literary critic – standing between the poets and the systematic thinkers – challenges philosophy when it devolves into a meager conceptual apparatus, challenges it with the fluidity of poetry, which is inseparable from the temporal fluidity of experience. Among other things, good literary criticism gets philosophers worried about what to do with fictional discourse when they're concocting stiff definitions about what counts as a

[24] *Selected Prose of Robert Frost*, ed. Hyder Cox and Edward Connery Lathem (New York: Collier Books, 1968), p. 39.

true sentence. What happens, the critic asks, when the cat sitting
on the mat becomes a feline figure embroidered in the carpet?
Given the existence of self-consciously fictive statements which,
by way of generic affiliations, bear an unending variety of relations
to mimesis, can we actually use a simple binary distinction, true
and false, sense and nonsense, to describe every statement?
Literary critics, in one of their dimensions – and they have plenty
of others – are the people who stir up trouble between poets and
philosophers, the kind of trouble that keeps them in productive
dialogue and competition. It's also true that by staging dialectical
encounter between tropes and systems critics can provide those
momentary stays against confusion that serve as images for how
to organize, however fleetingly, human life.

All noble enough, but not quite the end of the story. When
Wordsworth called the source of prior life "the imperial palace,"
he was still enough in sympathy with the French Revolution to
be, to say the least, ambivalent about imperiums and palaces.
Getting so stolid and respectable an image into play was no
small task and, as I've suggested, the play doesn't last for very
long: it's only a few lines before the child has run through the
stages of humanity, "all the Persons, down to palsied Age" (105).
The imperial palace is the sort of image that attaches itself to
philosophy (as seen by literature), and I take Wordsworth to be
rather prescient in sensing the natural attraction between august
institutions and stable ideas. At the University of Virginia, where
I teach, the imperial palace has been appealingly democratized:
Jefferson's Rotunda is an agreeable alternative to the kind of
palace of wisdom that Wordsworth figures in "Intimations."
But, as Jefferson would be happy enough to concede, the Rotunda
(its dome the very image, it's been said, of an Enlightenment-style
cranium) is a far more apt architectural trope for philosophy
than for poetry.

That is, even if criticism aims to stay vital by sliding between
concept and trope in response to the way that the passage of
time kills some metaphors and quickens others – makes some
strictures more just, others less – when criticism takes up residence
in the imperial palace, or even close by the Rotunda, it's disposed
to freeze, to become a discipline. Insisting on certain standards

of plausibility is a function of criticism, granted, but in the context of the university, critics are likely to forget to slide in the other direction, toward the affirmation of those works that make the current principles seem superannuated.

These remarks about institutional placement offer me a chance to reflect on the style of this book. It's often the case, as the reader will have already noticed, that I use the analytic (or institutional) style that I want to interrogate. But in my conception of criticism there is nothing wrong with doing so: criticism moves between analytic and responsive writing, with many permutations in between. There are times when generality and assimilation are apt, particularly when one encounters writings like de Man's that claim more novelty than they possess. The larger challenge is to convey the energies one finds in works of art. One can do this by making metaphors, but that's not the only way. There are many kinds of style, as I suggest in the final chapter, that *transfer* fresh energies from art to the reader of criticism. Whether I have found styles to convey what it is like to encounter the works I value, the reader will judge: suffice it to say that it doesn't follow from this book's argument that such styles be operative all the time.

Criticism, as I'm describing it here, serves time by keeping a dialogue going. Thus understood, criticism is no more progressive than Hazlitt believed the arts to be, and it is much more disposable. But if criticism were willing to sign away its own intimations of immortality, its own urge to permanence, it might be in a better position to infuse literary and academic culture with the energy that could accrue from living simultaneously in the public and the academic world. Right now we have, at least as I see it, an enervated literary culture in part because the critics are not talking to – or defending – the poets any more: they've gone hand in glove with the other people in the school of arts and sciences. Critics haven't been historicist enough, in other words, to read the needs of the time and serve them: rather they've been marching glumly in step with the conceptualizers. This capitulation to concept over and against dialectic, this affirmation of critical progress (now that we've added political critique to deconstruction, we're really getting somewhere), is, I think, inseparable from a wish not to die, to align oneself with something that's going to last. The hostility of academic critics to literary journalists may in part be informed by unease at their brazen will to be transient, du jour, of the day.

Critics' unwillingness to turn in the direction of poets and novelists and offer them, say, deconstruction (that is, Derrida at his best, not de Man) as the day's equivalent to Plato's charge that they don't know what they're talking about has something (and maybe more than something) to do with the spinelessness, the lack of intellectual content, in a lot of today's fiction. Most writers simply don't know what to do with deconstruction, or with any of the more or less current philosophical challenges to fiction and poetry, and this is in part because theoretical critics have opted out of the dialogue with them, opted, that is, out of the kind of dialogue that's so productive for the likes of Wordsworth and Coleridge.

In the title story of Christopher Tilghman's much-praised collection, *In a Father's Place*, for example, one encounters a young woman with brown hair pulled back in a bun, a combative expression, and a copy of *Of Grammatology*, which she reads over breakfast.[25] And that's really all you need to know about her. She will go on to have the same violently, pointlessly nihilistic effect on the established family she's visiting as deconstruction, we are encouraged to imagine, would have on the sort of traditional fiction we're in the process of enjoying. The woman can't provide an interesting challenge to the family, one that makes the reader stop and reassess his or her own reading of the story, which has, for the most part, identified itself with the father and his place, in part because the author has no developed reading of deconstruction: it's just something he feels instinctive hostility toward.

To phrase it swiftly, a culture's imaginative writing can devolve toward ongoing wish fulfillment without criticism to deliver the strictures that come from, among other places, philosophy and the social sciences. For their part, the conceptual disciplines are likely to go authoritarian, intoxicated with the universal pre-

---

[25] New York: Farrar, Straus, Giroux, 1990.

sumptions of theory, when their practitioners forget that poetry (childhood, power, and play) exist. Surely there are exceptions to the case I am making here. Don DeLillo and Salman Rushdie seem to have read, or imbibed, a good deal of what's out there in the theoretical ether. Some critics continue to conduct the difficult dialogue between poetry and philosophy.

Yet most of us seem to have forgotten that from the beginnings of Western culture, poetry has been on trial, and that by acting exclusively as prosecutors, we do in sophisticated ways what practical, ambitious cultures have always tended to do, if more crudely: discredit what seems to be childish, extravagant, useless, and weird. Emerson is right when he says that criticism ought to be able to consider literature ephemeral and entertain the possibility of its disappearance, the possibility of its being sentenced to oblivion, or death. But literature, though never simply innocent, often provides the resources for answering our worst doubts about it. In literature critics can sometimes find a worldly innocence, a state we shouldn't be afraid to defend.

CHAPTER 2

Polemics against presence

The greatest thing a human soul ever does in this world is
to SEE something and tell what it SAW in a plain way.
Hundreds of people can talk for one who can think, but
thousands can think for one who can see. To see clearly is
poetry, prophecy and religion – all in one.   John Ruskin

The visual is *essentially* pornographic.   Fredric Jameson

Blindness and insight: in putting these categories at the core of
his work, Paul de Man offers psychoanalytical resources to
philosophy in its ancient quarrel with the poets. But the terms
do something more to place de Man at the center of contemporary
theoretical criticism. The blindness and insight model traffics in
the ocular rhetoric with which theorists in the past three decades
have been engaged, sometimes to the point of obsession. De
Man's ironic use of the term insight (ironic because insight, though
initially desirable, will inevitably solidify into a standard mode
of perception, a form of blindness, and must thus be regarded
with some suspicion) conveys a much more measured and dialectical position than most theorists hold.

For the majority of those writers who have had major impact
on Anglo-American literary criticism in the latter part of the
century have been uninhibitedly anti-visual. That is, they have
aimed their polemical energies at forms of thinking that, as they
understand it, uncritically use the experience of seeing as an
ideal image for understanding. A few examples will bring the
tendency to mind: consider Lacan's critique of immersion within
the visual world of the Imaginary, Rorty's of philosophical
mirror-language, Baudrillard's of media-generated illusion, "the

precession of simulacra," Foucault's of all-surveilling panoptic society, the feminist critique of the male gaze, and Derrida's polemic against the metaphysics of presence. One could easily go on. All of these critical imperatives urge us to withdraw, or severely qualify, our investment in thinking about knowledge as ideally modeled on sight, and to reconceive intellectual acts in new terms.

Exactly why is this hostility to the visual, this polemic against presence, so pervasive in current theory? What are its sources? What relation does it have to the study and criticism of literary art? Where, if anywhere, does the anti-ocular critique fit into the quarrel between philosophy and poetry? What are the institutional and professional dimensions of the anti-visual polemic? For whom does it work? Who benefits? Who loses?

I want ultimately to focus on Jacques Derrida, the writer who seems to me to have developed the most original, subtle, and influential anti-visual polemic to be found in contemporary theory. But I will make my way to Derrida, and to the larger issues this chapter will consider, by way of an essay by Roland Barthes called "The World of Wrestling." The essay, which is one of the earliest examples I have encountered of post-structuralist criticism, will perform a number of functions, including bringing us into initial contact with the cultural politics that inform contemporary theoretical polemics against presence.

By wrestling Barthes does not mean the Olympic event with its classical intricacies, but the kind of costumed pageant in which all moves are rehearsed, the sort of thing that in its current American form is likely to star Hulk Hogan and Rowdy Roddy Piper. Until recently, the match might also have featured a cameo appearance by Cyndi Lauper singing, or lip-syncing, "Girls Just Want to Have Fun." Barthes begins his semiological analysis of the sport by comparing it to boxing:

A boxing-match is a story which is constructed before the eyes of the spectator; in wrestling, on the contrary, it is each moment which is intelligible, not the passage of time. The spectator is not interested in the rise and fall of fortunes; he expects the transient image of certain passions. Wrestling therefore demands an immediate reading of the juxtaposed meanings, so that there is no need to connect them. The logical conclusion of the contest does not interest the wrestling-fan, while on the contrary a boxing-match always implies a science of the future. In other words, wrestling is a sum of spectacles, of which no single one is a function: each moment imposes the total knowledge of a passion which rises erect and alone, without ever extending to the crowning moment of a result.[1]

Wrestling grants the spectator the satisfaction of one perfectly legible tableau after another. Every physical gesture is fully comprehended, every dramatic signifier fully invested by an unambiguous sense. Wrestling "imposes the total knowledge of a passion which arises erect and alone." Boxing, on the other hand, is the realm of narrative. The emphasis is temporal, not spatial; one must interpret the signs in relation to one another rather than simply taking satisfaction in their perfect expressiveness. Two aficionados might read a boxing match quite differently, especially in its middle rounds. The response to a well-choreographed wrestling match will be unanimous. The audience will concur and coalesce around its agreement.

The key to wrestling's appeal, Barthes thinks, is that in it "everything is presented exhaustively" (p. 25). All meanings are immediately accessible, nothing is deferred. Take the case of Thauvin, one of the standard villains. Thauvin is "a fifty-year-old with an obese and sagging body, whose type of asexual hideousness always inspires feminine nicknames." He "displays in his flesh the characters of baseness, for his part is to represent what . . . appears as organically repugnant." The spectators revel in Thauvin because he is exactly what he appears to be. One glance and you know him. The crowd, Barthes says, will "let itself be frenetically embroiled in an idea of Thauvin which will conform entirely with this physical origin; his actions will perfectly correspond to the essential viscosity of his personage" (p. 17). Once you have certain knowledge of someone or something, you can stop interpreting and indulge yourself in the pleasures of unqualified, passionate response.

[1] *Mythologies*, trans. Annette Lavers (New York: Hill and Wang, 1957), p. 16. Henceforth cited in the text.

The kind of reading that goes on at the wrestling match troubles Barthes in part because it releases a vulgar enthusiasm in the audience. Another way of putting the matter is to say that it turns the audience into a crowd. The crowd's passion reminds Barthes of religious passion and of the sort of fear and pity provoked by ritual drama. In fact, the three forms, tragedy, the high mass, and the spectacle of wrestling are all scapegoating rituals. Barthes says at one point that wrestling "enacts the exact gestures of the most ancient purifications" (p. 21). And the figure who is sacrificed is naturally "the bastard." "What the public is looking for here," Barthes writes, "is the gradual construction of a highly moral image: that of the perfect 'bastard.' One comes to wrestling in order to attend the continuing adventures of a single major leading character, permanent and multiform" (p. 23), and to watch that character pay, Barthes goes on to indicate, for his transgressions.

What worries Barthes the most – and provides what I see as the dramatic undercurrent of the essay – is the political plot that he finds buried in the mass-cultural phenomenon. The match, Barthes says, dramatizes "the great spectacle of Suffering, Defeat, and Justice" (p. 19), and in so doing, one might add, follows the rhetorical plot frequently laid out by the brown-shirted orator who declames on the denigration of the *Volk* at the hands of this demon or that, the sorrows of unwarranted degradation, and then the impending – and just – rise of the new empire. In wrestling's obsession with the drama of scapegoating, in which the "bastard" is made to pay, I think that Barthes means us to see shades of the kind of demonizing and brutality visited on the Jews and other supposed outsiders little more than (remember that Barthes is writing in the mid-50s) a decade before.

And then of course there is the hero, the sum of the people's will to power, capable of being "possessed by moral rage, magnified into a sort of metaphysical sign." That one may see the hero at the end of the bout, as he "leaves the wrestling hall, impassive, anonymous, carrying a small suitcase" (p. 25), reminds us of the crowd's power to inflate almost anyone, even a clownish house painter, into a figure of destiny. To Barthes, I think, the spirit of the fascist political rally, and of fascism proper, infests the apparently innocuous world of wrestling.

All of this is communicated indirectly: one is compelled to read "The World of Wrestling" by adopting the authorial position that Barthes develops for himself. But what exactly is the stance that the interpreter offers? The essays collected in *Mythologies* play off the boom in anthropological studies created by Lévi-Strauss and his followers. Barthes's conceit in the volume is to cast himself as an anthropologist investigating the tribal behavior, not of the Jivaro or the Nambikwara, but of the French petit bourgeois and, as is the case in the wrestling essay, the lumpen proletariat.

So the essay is in a certain sense an ironic one, relying as it does on an unstated but significant reversal. It is also something of an allegory in that it uses the phenomenon of the wrestling match to tell a larger story about the politics and ethics of signification. But in the penultimate paragraph, lest anyone has missed the implications, Barthes turns and decodes the piece:

In wrestling, nothing exists except in the absolute, there is no symbol, no allusion, everything is presented exhaustively. Leaving nothing in the shade, each action discards all parasitic meanings and ceremonially offers to the public a pure and full signification, rounded like Nature. This grandiloquence is nothing but the popular and age-old image of the perfect intelligibility of reality. What is portrayed by wrestling is therefore an ideal understanding of things; it is the euphoria of men raised for a while above the constitutive ambiguity of everyday situations and placed before the panoramic view of a univocal Nature, in which signs at last correspond to causes, without obstacle, without evasion, without contradiction. (pp. 24–5)

In light of this passage, it is surprising that any number of Barthes's critics have refrained from decoding the piece.[2] Some are oddly content to read "The World of Wrestling" as a benevolent highbrow's appreciation of popular culture.

I agree that "The World of Wrestling" is a highbrow's piece

---

[2] These include Steven Ungar, *Roland Barthes: The Professor of Desire* (Lincoln: University of Nebraska Press, 1983); Jonathan Culler, *Roland Barthes* (New York: Oxford University Press, 1983); Annette Lavers, *Roland Barthes: Structuralism and After* (Cambridge: Harvard University Press, 1982); George R. Wasserman, *Roland Barthes* (Boston: Twayne, 1981).

of work, but I'm not sure how benevolent it is. Note the way Barthes wants to imagine the members of the audience. According to him they come to the wrestling matches to escape "the constitutive ambiguity of everyday situations." They cannot live with the anxiety of not knowing the truth, cannot live amidst the proliferation of signs without origin, secure referent, and stability. They flee from this condition rather than making the best of it. Barthes's moral message, if I understand him correctly, is that this urge to flee is inseparable from a taste for the kinds of transparent meanings and puerile symbolic dramas – and sometimes dramas that are more than symbolic – that fascism offers. There's an equation being drawn here between fascism and the hunger for presence.

But does Barthes really know what's going on in the mind of his crowd? Isn't it possible that the crowd is as aware of the fictive nature of the matches as Barthes is? Just as Thauvin plays the bastard, maybe the people gathered at the arena play the part of crowd. Maybe what Barthes is seeing is in some measure a satire on, or a self-conscious playing along with, a clichéd version of group behavior. (Viewers of ABC's *Monday Night Football* know how vividly members of the stadium crowd turn themselves out – in costumes, face paint, with flamboyant banners, and the rest – the better to get themselves filmed. If you're going to be immortalized as part of the football audience, you've got to prepare your role shrewdly and play it with exuberance.) Is indulging the fiction of total knowledge an act of bad faith when one recognizes it as a fiction?

If I'm crediting the crowd with too much here, it may be by way of reaction: Barthes gives them no credit at all. "The World of Wrestling" ought, I think, to be seen as an installment in the ongoing depiction of the mob by European proponents of high culture. The essay fits in particularly well with Freud's view in *Group Psychology* of the crowd projecting the super-ego function onto the leader, much as the subjects of a hypnotist do, the better to act out, with his indulgence, their baser tendencies. Closer to Barthes is Nietzsche, who himself saw the Christian ritual of scapegoating as integral to the herd morality. One also thinks of Dickens (*A Tale of Two Cities* comes particularly to mind), of Balzac with his royalist's disdain for the masses, and later of Le Bon (who influenced Freud), and of Elias Canetti and his magisterial *Crowds and Power*.[3]

Like these writers, Barthes is interested in helping his readers recognize themselves as – or become – the sort of people who aren't susceptible to the crowd mentality. The writers offer an implicit image of strong individuality, which they encourage their readers to assume, with all the attendant burdens and satisfactions. Freud, for instance, offers us the ideal of the hyper-masculine scientist who doesn't need to escape the demands of his super-ego by joining the mass. Barthes's essay, operating in a similar way, is a piece of literary education: it teaches you to repudiate a certain sort of reading, and perhaps too a certain class, or your own class identity. The essay is divisive. Its quiet message runs, "We read this way; they read that."

"The World of Wrestling" stigmatizes the crowd for its authoritarian fantasies, but were (and are) the members of the European intelligentsia less susceptible to fascism than the masses? Remember that Heidegger, whom some see as Europe's most gifted intellectual of the period, had surprisingly little compunction about running a swastika arm band up his sleeve. Is Barthes, by putting all the heat on the proletarians, performing a sort of scapegoating in his own right, a ritual of exoneration for his own intellectual class? What is at stake, in social and political terms, in Barthes's polemic against presence, and in other such polemics that operate in its mode? To answer these questions, I shall have to widen my survey considerably.

"The World of Wrestling" was published more than ten years before Jacques Derrida's key works of 1967 and well in advance too of the essays collected in *Blindness and Insight*. Yet the piece is alive with many of the tendencies to be found in post-structuralist theory. The two reading styles that Barthes describes at the beginning of the essay, one attuned to boxing's "science of the

---

[3] Freud's *Group Psychology and the Analysis of the Ego*, S. E., XVIII:65–143; Nietzsche, *The Genealogy of Morals*; Gustave Le Bon, *The Crowd: A Study of the Popular Mind* (New York: Macmillan, 1896); Elias Canetti, *Crowds and Power* (New York: Viking, 1962). Patrick Brantlinger offers a survey of such writing in *Bread and Circuses: Theories of Mass Culture as Social Decay* (Ithaca: Cornell University Press, 1983).

future," the other to an unambiguous "spectacle," predict with an apparent charming ease the distinction that de Man will go on to draw between allegory and symbol, and that Derrida will describe in terms of "writing" and "the metaphysics of presence." To de Man, you'll recall, the aesthetic celebration of the symbol comprises an attempt to bypass the mediations of language and of time, and to succumb to illusions of perfect presence. Allegory wrests one away from the bad faith the symbol cultivates by compelling the reader to interpret the text at hand in terms of other writings (and those in terms of still others), thus inaugurating a movement of mind that represents the movement of temporality. For Derrida, more concerned with philosophical than literary writing, it is the transcendent concepts of metaphysical philosophy that need to be reconceived as signifiers within a web of other signifiers, as mere words with multiple meanings and verbal associations. Thus the transcendental concepts – Derrida sometimes calls them philosophemes – when read from multiple perspectives lose their clear purity, surrender their purported being outside of time and chance. Thauvin, who to the crowd at the wrestling match supposedly "displays in his flesh the characters of baseness," whose identity is purely, immediately, and unarguably present, is the pop culture equivalent of de Man's symbol and Derrida's philosopheme.

"The World of Wrestling" predicts any number of developments in post-structuralist theory. It lays out, quite clearly, the polemic against presence that will become pervasive; it elaborates this polemic not only thematically, but also by insisting at every opportunity that visual phenomena be rendered in rhetorical or literary terms; the essay is a semiological translation of things seen. Thus it carries out what one might call a sublimation, a refinement of crude phenomena into something higher. It effects a critique and a transformation on a pop cultural event. As I said, the essay helps the audience to recognize itself as, or evolve into, an elite.

Yet there is a significant way in which "The World of Wrestling" does not predict the direction of post-structuralist thought: it does not thoroughly practice the habits of reading that it seems to affirm. Derrida, in other words, would find the essay all too easy to deconstruct. The allegory and the irony become by the end of the piece, when Barthes climbs onto the box and gives his closing oration, nearly as fixed, intelligible, and comprehensive as the kind of thinking that he attributes to the crowd. When Barthes speaks of "the constitutive ambiguity of everyday situations," he has become formulaic and literal in his commitment to the indeterminate. His simple statement recalls the facile satisfactions of de Man's symbol and Derrida's philosopheme. A latter-day deconstructor would presumably be as critical as Barthes of the transparent signs and the "panoramic view of a univocal Nature" that wrestling supposedly provides. And the antidote would be a mode of reading the event that stressed temporality, irony, and displacement, that aimed to undo all illusions about stability, including one's own, the kind of reading we find most highly developed in Jacques Derrida.

Derrida's critique of what he takes to be the currently presiding mode of outworn authority takes the form of a polemic against presence. Identifying the metaphysics of presence and calculating its costs are his key critical objectives; the displacement of metaphysics in favor of something else (but what precisely?) is his central goal. This much is evident even in his earliest works.

Derrida came onto the American scene with an analysis of structuralism. The essay "Structure, Sign, and Play in the Discourse of the Human Sciences," which he read at Johns Hopkins in 1966, argued that structuralism, an unnerving foreign import that many members of the audience had, I'd guess, yet to assimilate, was not the breakthrough its most aggressive proponents claimed.[4] By satisfying themselves that they had demonstrated how the human subject is inhabited and determined by numberless systems, structured like languages, committed structuralists came to believe they had demystified the received, humanistic version of man. The doctrine that one is fixed by language overall and shaped by a variety of systems that work to delimit possibilities for perception and thought – the system of romantic love, of male friendship, of advertising, of cuisine – demoted the will

[4] Collected in *Writing and Difference*, pp. 278–93.

and the cogito and provided a version of human limitation that, to some, seemed to fit the experience of living in a mass society.

Cultural codes penetrated experience at every level and provided the constricting horizon for human possibility. Men and women were understood as functions, not originators, as spoken not speaking; their knowledge was, at best, confined to various mediating forms, whose final relations to things in themselves were outside their powers of determination. To Kant's view that the noumena were beyond secure human knowledge and came to us transformed in inscrutable ways by the senses and the categories of understanding was added another alienating qualification. Phenomena themselves were now to be understood as occluded by language, and by their relational roles in systems structured like languages.

To some this might seem harshly secular enough. The version of the self that arises from the structuralist enterprise looks to be at significant variance with the humanism of Matthew Arnold or Lionel Trilling, and of the figure an entire generation of French intellectuals had to pass into maturity by repudiating, Jean-Paul Sartre. But Derrida found in structuralism not ultimate lucidity, a world beyond superstition, but rather a displaced nostalgia, a nostalgia for the center. Structuralism had supposedly passed beyond humanism (which, it was said, made a god or potential god of the human subject) in that it denied the power of the cogito fully to know itself and to transform itself by that knowing. (Just so humanism, it was said, had claimed to surpass deism by finding meaning in the autonomous self and that alone.) But both of these so-called developments, Derrida argued, continue to preserve the old commitment to the center, the father, the law, and the truth. They were not so authentically secular as they took themselves to be in that the wish for a god, or godlike powers, haunted their conceptual designs, as well as their grammar and tropes.

Structuralism's nostalgia for the center was manifest in its attachment to what Derrida called "the structurality of structure." For the many languages that determined the subject retained symmetrical, coherent, centered form. The structuralists too innocently conceived that one could do what Barthes assumed himself to be doing in "The World of Wrestling," place oneself at one or another commanding midpoint and achieve maximum insight without distortion, pure presence. As Derrida understood it, structuralism was another in a sequence of metaphysical systems promising disinterested (and thus benign) apprehension of all that mattered in experience, while being in fact exclusionary, oppressive, totalizing and thus – potentially – totalitarian.

As in Kant, Hegel, Husserl, and Heidegger, in Barthes and his structuralist colleagues, presence is the ultimate objective. Structuralism was thus continuous with the major trajectory of Western thought whose arc begins with Plato. Not a break with tradition, structuralism actually condensed and intensified the central tenets of reigning intellectual practice, making them available for critical analysis and accordingly for subversion, displacement, deconstruction. In its devotion to form at the expense of force, structuralism provided, albeit unwittingly, a cold X-ray of Western thought. And by its insistence on language as the central site for analysis, it offered a cue for the activity that would – perhaps – bring about the undoing of itself and the tradition that it summarized.

What is at stake in Derrida's critique of the metaphysics of presence? First of all, power. Metaphysics – and to Derrida metaphysical philosophy concentrates the form of virtually all Western thought, including the most common and day to day – is a technique for achieving mastery. Yoked to a scientific world view, saturated by the impulse that reaches a point of concentration in Descartes to divide the world into subjects and objects, metaphysics enjoins what Derrida with Heidegger in mind calls "the domination of beings." Thus: "it is the domination of beings that *différance* everywhere comes to solicit, in the sense that *sollicitare*, in old Latin, means to shake as a whole, to make tremble in entirety. Therefore, it is the determination of Being as presence or as beingness that is interrogated by the thought of *différance*."[5]

But there is another, more expansive way to conceive of Derrida's work. Derrida is in a certain sense a descendant of the Enlightenment; he wants to help void the world of vulgar super-

---

[5] *Margins of Philosophy*, trans. Alan Bass (Chicago: University of Chicago Press, 1982), p. 21.

stition. For Derrida, God (the ultimate presence) is only ostensibly deceased: He has been displaced into a number of cultural forms, chief among them, perhaps, reason. The situation comprises a paradox in that it was reason that began to separate us from superstition to begin with: Derrida, much like the members of the Frankfurt School, contends that Western reason has become a deity in its own right and must be submitted to debunking critique.

But it's not enough for Derrida to do away with God and his culturally licensed replicas. Like Nietzsche, whom he generally admires, Derrida seems to be questing for a culture that, though void of sanctified beliefs, doesn't devolve into nihilism. Nietzsche famously portrayed such a nihilistic culture with his vision of the last man in *Thus Spoke Zarathustra*. "The earth has become small," says Zarathustra, "and on it hops the last man, who makes everything small."[6] The last man has his little pleasures for the day and for the night: he's petty, a creature of the herd, cautious, calculating, and full of secret rancor. "We have invented happiness," the last man says, then he blinks. The last man has done away with God in anything but a courageous way. He has simply shrunk his horizon to the point where God's being or nonbeing is beside the point. He's killed God not by realizing that, as Blake observed, all deities reside in the human breast, but by demoting himself into an insect incapable of conceiving anything higher than the life of the colony or the hive.

Nietzsche was devoted to imagining ways of life that acknowledged the death of God, but that didn't surrender to the kind of nihilism the last man exemplifies. So too for Derrida, it's not just a matter of evolving beyond religious superstition, but of coming up with a form of being that, having cleansed the cosmos of its majestic ghosts, isn't prey to despair. For what it may be worth, I find the quests that both Nietzsche and Derrida enter on to be of central value. I share their Enlightenment suspicions about transcendental belief, but also their concern that in giving up religion one risks losing vitality and creative purpose. Thus in the pages to come I will be paying considerable attention to

---

[6] Trans. Walter Kaufmann (New York: Penguin, 1954), p. 17.

Derrida's critique of presence, as well as to his proffered alternatives. Like Nietzsche's image of the Eternal Return, which challenges us to arrive at a point where we could will that our lives
be repeated over again and again eternally, Derrida's image of
différance challenges us to engage in a new way of interpretation
that is also a new way of life.

Another name for *différance*, common in Derrida's earlier writing, is play. In the 1966 paper he describes a "Nietzschean
affirmation, that is the joyous affirmation of the play of the world
and of the innocence of becoming, the affirmation of a world of
signs without fault, without truth, and without origin which is
offered to an active interpretation."[7] Reading in a way that
gestures toward that affirmation, that disperses "truth" by ex-
ploiting the figurative power words have to generate an expanding
universe of signification, is Derrida's by now well-known technique
for undoing Western epistemological hubris.

One might note here the large actual distinction – and the
perceived continuities – between Derrida and de Man. Academic
criticism has become accustomed to lumping them together under
the rubric of deconstruction, and of course there are obvious
likenesses: the emphasis on close reading, the concern with epistemology, the background in Heidegger and Freud, the skeptical
disposition. But de Man is preeminently a dialectical thinker: he
charts all discourse with polar terms: blindness and insight,
metaphor and metonymy, theory and undecidability. Derrida,
though he is attuned to the power metaphysics has to recuperate
and normalize antithetical gestures like his, also is willing to
affirm at least the possibility of a full unbinding from transcendental truth. His images of play and of writing put him in contact
with Romantic visions of emancipation. Derrida has remarked
on his interest in English Romanticism, and one imagines him
encountering ideal forms like Shelley's Prometheus or Blake's
Milton with far more sympathetic interest than de Man could
muster. (For de Man, *writing* would always lapse into a theory
of writing ripe for critique; Prometheus and Blake's Milton will
inevitably solidify into idols.) *Différance* puts Derrida in some

[7] *Writing and Difference*, p. 292.

relation, though as I will show, a rather vexed one, with visionary poetics.

Does Derrida rely, like de Man, on a theory of repression? I find this a difficult question to answer with confidence. Granted Derrida will talk about the repression of writing by speech in the West. And surely he gains some of the license for his interpretive practice from Freud's theory of dream interpretation. Derrida, in his readings of Plato, Descartes and Kant, might be understood as compelling the text of Western philosophy to engage in free association. In psychoanalysis the term free association is something of a joke: let the ego play at ease and it will begin compulsively circling its own magnetic north, the complex of traumas and repressions that make it what it is. There's nothing free about it. Just so, Derrida seems to think, will the texts of Western metaphysics surrender their secret holdings when one simply listens and takes them at their words. And this sounds a good deal like the analysis of a philosophical unconscious. Philosophy, apparently, has done to language what the subject frequently does to unpalatable drives. Derrida, like Freud, would seem to be out to lift repression.

And yet it is also true that Derrida is always compelled to release the entrapped meanings from philosophy texts in a way that *demonstrates* how precisely the writer, or the tradition that forces his hand, has worked to bind language, delimit meaning, and thus constrict perceptions of difference. Derrida in effect tries to show that there are more relevant distinctions at hand than the writer takes into account. One can argue with a Derridean reading, claim that it is too ingenious. One may say that it travels too far beyond the bounds of regulating cultural contexts in the meanings it finds. Against a way of reading like de Man's that comprehensively relies on the theory of repression there is no civilized rebuttal. Derrida's best readings are performances: one is surprised by the range of associations that he can bring into play. Of de Man it has been said accurately that no matter where he starts, he ends in the same place. And it is, I believe, this virtuoso aspect of Derrida, manifest especially in his power to stretch the bounds of interpretation, that makes his kind of deconstruction dependent on individual prowess, not susceptible to routinization, and thus not as institutionally negotiable as de Man's.

Yet the key distinction between Derrida and de Man seems to me to lie in Derrida's confidence (though to be sure it is not consistent) that the West might pass beyond the age of metaphysics. His insights about language in philosophy need not be reabsorbed by containing structures. By deconstructing the authority certain key philosophical texts have over their readers – an authority that they supposedly achieve by appearing to master the unmasterable free play of language – Derrida offers an image for how one might respond to any authority that claims to have dominated time and chance. The ideal result of a comprehensive labor of deconstruction would be the full liberation of those energies now absorbed by meretricious figures of truth. From Derrida's perspective, one might say, every commitment to presence or a transcendental signified grants the illusion of stability, but depletes human energies. We might think of *différance* as, among other things, a name for those powers that Derrida's deconstruction strives to release. *Différance*, one might say, is the Derridean equivalent of the child in Wordsworth's "Intimations" ode, a figure for hope and vitality.

Derrida attempts to inaugurate, or exemplify, the release from outworn forms in a sequence of remarkable essays aimed at the fathers of Western philosophy. In my view he is at his best when he writes about an author who is driving hard for authority by trying to exert maximum control over the interpretation of his texts. He is very fine on Husserl, Kant, Hegel, some aspects of Rousseau, Lévi-Strauss and Lacan; on Plato and Freud he seems to me splendid. The more determined the writer is to create a transparent text, and to confine the reader exclusively to literal meanings, the more invigorating it is – and the more plausible – when Derrida goes to work flushing out connotations. When a writer doesn't seem to care much for that kind of authority, when the objective seems to be a proliferation of meanings, Derrida's treatments tend to lack strict enough focus to matter much: no consequential cultural work is getting done.

In one of his finest essays, "Plato's Pharmacy," Derrida's technique is simply to refuse to disallow any of the meanings

that accrue to Plato's key terms: "pharmakon," Plato's trope
for writing, means remedy and poison; it is associated with
"pharmakeus," the word for wizard, and "pharmakos," scape-
goat.[8] In a remarkable moment, Derrida is able to show how
Socrates' systematic philosophy, which sublimates the accidental
into the essential and banishes phenomena that do not fit the
encompassing structure, finds its logical culmination in scapegoating generally, and Socrates' own scapegoating by the citizens
of Athens in particular. Systematic compression and exclusion
are antithetical to the expansive powers of words. Plato's desire
to restrict meaning to a univocal sense seems almost to compel a
reaction from language: tied in conceptual knots, it chafes,
expands, bursts, devolving in the final moments of the essay to
something like a primal linguistic flux. Verbal energy presumably
undoes the cold dream of Western mastery, returning us to the
untruth of time and chance. Presence dissolves into play.

From one angle, Derrida seems to be trying to do to philosophy
what Samuel Beckett did to theater, what Jackson Pollock did
to painting, what Art Ensemble of Chicago does to jazz, and
John Ashbery to poetry. Derrida, from this perspective, pushes
the form toward an apparent disorder. Yet the disorder reveals
the conventions and the constitutive elements that other practitioners have been taking for granted.

Pollock's action painting reminds one that painting always
takes place in two, not three dimensional, space. The flatness of
a Pollock deconstructs the conventions of perspective which,
beginning in the fifteenth century, have held considerable sway
over Western art. As Robert Hughes observes, perspective "sim-
plifies the relationship between eye, brain, and object. It is an
ideal view, imagined as being seen by a one-eyed motionless
person who is clearly detached from what he sees. It makes a
god of the spectator, who becomes the person on whom the
whole world converges, the Unmoved Onlooker."[9] Pollock's work,
more I think than that of any of the modernists before him,
manages to assault conventions in perspective, and to say, in
effect, that all the intoxicating sense of lifelike depth was achieved

[8] In *Dissemination*, trans. Barbara Johnson, (Chicago: University of Chicago Press, 1981),
pp. 61–171.
[9] *The Shock of the New* (New York: Alfred A. Knopf, 1991), p. 17.

through an artificial deployment of material, of paint. Conceive, more or less, of the metaphysics of presence as the philosophical version of perspective; think of Derrida as trying to call attention to words as Pollock tried to call attention to paint.

But – and the second phase of Pollock's effect matters as much, I think, as the first – once you've moved into a critical relation to convention, observe the sense of vitality, of action, that you can convey. You can stir perceivers, vitalize rather than lull. (Can we say something comparable, I'll be asking, of Derrida?) Pollock's assault on convention functioned, for many, to open up new possibilities. It brought a cultural activity back to confront its primary, and forgotten, assumptions and offered the possibility of beginning as if anew.

Pollock's work resonates better in a museum, in the company of lots of other paintings, than it does hanging alone in someone's living room. (So Derrida reads best in a course with Plato, Descartes, Kant, and Hegel.) The Pollock acts in relation to other art: it's as though someone had detonated a Dutch Master a few rooms down, sending its elements back into fruitful chaos. To be brought into contact with their conventions and materials is often a fine thing for artists; it loosens them up, shows how much room there is to extemporize, because what had become for them, through habit, necessary elements of their endeavor are now up for grabs. The sense of license that Pollock supplied has inspired some marvelous American painting.

Just so Beckett, however tiresome one might find his more languorous performance pieces, helped enfranchise a younger generation of playwrights that includes Pinter and Stoppard. By breaking up naturalistic conventions for dialogue – demonstrating, that is, the artifice in naturalism – Beckett opened the way for an uncanny dramatic speech. He allowed for characters who, in ever-shifting ratios, could be simultaneously humdrum and other-worldly. Such characters (from whom David Mamet has lately been wringing the last life) satisfied both our hunger for bracing, often unsavory fact and the urge to guess at larger meanings.

So Derrida suggests that the primary elements for literature and philosophy are the same, and that the two kinds of writing differ, chiefly, in the conventions they have imposed on linguistic matter. Is it possible, then, to imagine a philosophically trained intellect more sympathetic to the literary imagination than Derrida? For one might say that Derrida, with his focus on figurative language, discloses the literary dimension of philosophical writing. And if philosophy is a tissue of words, manifold in their associations, then how can philosophy conceivably function as a stable template to discipline and delimit literary range, to disenfranchise poetry? Doesn't Derrida do, quite programmatically, something like what I took Wordsworth to be doing in the last chapter when I said that he was restoring the mythical dimension to Plato's "philosophical" story about anamnesis and a prior life? Doesn't Derrida show that literature and philosophy share the same primary source, language, and thus put an end to the ancient quarrel?

Given what we know about that quarrel, it surely pays to beware of philosophers bearing gifts. The true relevance of Derrida's work for literary study is one that it will take some time to unfold. The inquiry will take us from a mythical topos, to the philosophical tradition that Derrida claims to deconstruct, into the work of Camille Paglia, and back again to Barthes and popular culture. Finally, though, we shall be in a position to see how Derrida's polemic against presence – epitomized in his observation that there is nothing outside the text, nothing that does not require reading – carries the struggle between poetry and philosophy to a level of extraordinary and unprecedented refinement.

One of the earliest names that Derrida gives to the experience of self-presence, the sense of consolidated self-identity that must be dispersed by deconstruction, is auto-affection.[10] It is in pondering this term that we will begin to see what role Derrida actually plays in the contention between the philosophers and the poets. The illusion of a full and coherent being occurs most intensely, Derrida says, at the instant of "hearing oneself speak." When you speak, the words become an integral part of your ongoing

---

[10] For useful discussion of auto-affection in Derrida see Rodolphe Gasché's *The Tain of the Mirror: Derrida and the Philosophy of Reflection* (Cambridge: Harvard University Press, 1986), pp. 18, 194–5, 231–6.

bodily processes. The signifier is naturalized, its status as mediation occluded; its problematic relations to other signifiers past and to come is forgotten, as words become as intimate and immediate as the breath that forms them.

In Derrida's view, this moment of hearing oneself speak has been understood, quite erroneously, as the primal scene of language, the moment when language reveals itself as what it is, a natural essential entity, fully continuous with physical being, identical in fact with life itself. The belief that language can establish presence, that the signifier can convey the signified without remainder, is inseparable from this so-called primal experience. Derrida will go so far as to say that it has been *a*, if not *the*, defining moment for the self from Plato to the present. Hearing oneself speak is, Derrida believes, a founding moment for metaphysics. As he observes in *Speech and Phenomena*, auto-affection is "not something that happens to a transcendental subject; it produces it. Auto-affection is not a modality of experience that characterizes a being that would already be itself (*autos*). It produces sameness as self-relation within self-difference... "[11] And what cures the subject of auto-affection, presumably, is encounter, or re-encounter, with that primal self-difference. Writing, which differs and defers endlessly, breaks up the illusion of self-presence and self-perfection engendered by the primal scene of hearing oneself speak. *Différance* functions, for Derrida, as a form of linguistic therapy to be administered to a linguistically motivated error in self-apprehension.

As Derrida sees it, the principle of auto-affection is internally at odds. If a self is to know itself and constitute itself through the act of knowing, it must take up an interpretive distance on itself. It is compelled to split. That splitting, and the subsequent knowing, entail an act of interpretation, an interpretation of the self by itself. And such an interpretation can itself be interpreted. One may then take up yet a fourth perspective, and so on. Thus the technique by which the ego of metaphysics seeks to establish its identity reveals to the critical observer the terms for its undoing. Auto-affection functions to exclude the third perspective, the

[11] Trans. D. B. Allison (Evanston, Ill.: Northwestern University Press, 1973), p. 82.

perspective that makes it possible. As Derrida writes in "Economimesis": "The negative is its business and its work. What it excludes, what this very work excludes, is what does not allow itself to be digested, or represented, or stated – does not allow itself to be transformed into auto-affection by exemplorality. It is an irreducible heterogeneity which cannot be eaten either sensibly or ideally."[12]

Auto-affection, it should be clear, is a kind of self-love. It is an infatuation not with one's physical form per se, but with the words that emanate from one's body. Beautiful, complete, coherent words, rather than a perfect bodily image, confer the erroneous sense of self-identity. And this erroneous self-conception must be revised through the intervention of a different kind of words, words that dramatize fragmentation, not facile coherence. To use this plot to describe the genesis of self-identity is, as I have been implying, to have commerce with the Narcissus myth. (In *Of Grammatology*, Derrida in fact refers to the myth quite directly to describe his practice.[13]) In the hands of such writers as Milton, Freud, and Lacan, the myth becomes a story about the genesis of a certain kind of self, a self mesmerized by images and in need of instruction. Beginning at least with Milton, the Narcissus myth is frequently a narrative that iconoclasts revise and disseminate to demonstrate the power of words over images. And that too is how the myth functions for Derrida, but with a crucial – and quite brilliant – refinement.

In Milton, the voice that comes on to draw Eve from fascination with her image in the reflecting pool is a celestial voice; it arrives from on high. It commends attachment to displaced self-images: to Adam ("hee/Whose image thou art") and to Eve's future children ("Multitudes like thyself").[14] The voice asserts the power of word over image; logos over desire. To a pious reader, the voice is what saves Eve from the fate of Narcissus, who is so transfixed by the lovely image in the pool that he pines away

---

[12] Trans. R. Klein, *Diacritics*, 11: 2 (Summer 1981), p. 21.
[13] Trans. Gayatri Chakravorty Spivak (Baltimore: Johns Hopkins University Press, 1974), pp. 36–7.
[14] *John Milton: Complete Poems and Major Prose*, ed. Merritt Y. Hughes (Indianapolis: Bobbs-Merrill, 1957), IV:471–2, 474.

and dies. "There," says Eve, "I had fixt/ Mine eyes till now, and pin'd with vain desire,/Had not a voice . . . warn'd me."[15]

In Freud, the warning voice is that of the super-ego, the precipitate of the father's, crucially verbal, castration threat. The authoritative voice, Freud says in his great 1914 paper, "On Narcissism," breaks up the child's illusions about his own self-perfection.[16] Freud, an admiring reader of Milton, saw the necessity for the super-ego's intervention, but believed that often that inner authoritative agency had to be revised. The super-ego tended, particularly in a culture largely without persuasive images of reasonable authority to educate it, to stay as it was in childhood. It often remained too fierce, too punitive, issuing strictures apt for the child, but too limiting for the mature adult.[17] And too, as Freud argues in *Civilization and Its Discontents*, the super-ego had the tendency of accruing to itself all the energy that would have been discharged in the acts that it, often needlessly, prohibits.[18]

Freud's solution? Implicitly, and here I interpret him, it is to revise the sadistic voice, either through therapy or through contact with the humanely authoritative voice of his writings. One's inner voice of authority, Freud thought, might become more humane, more ironic, worldly, cultivated, more, in short, like his own voice. And this solution, despite the shades of authoritarianism one might find in it, does not seem to me entirely bad. For in Freud's sensibility one encounters traces of much of the best thought that informs the Western tradition. He could, as I see it, quite legitimately claim to be the living renewal of major elements he found in Goethe, Milton, and Shakespeare. One could do worse.

In Freud's purported disciple Lacan, we find a revision of the Narcissus topos in the essay on the mirror stage.[19] Lacan believes that the ego is precipitated by a misapprehension: despite the fragmented inner experience of the child who consciously takes in his mirror image for the first time, the coherent specular self

---

[15] *Milton: Complete Poems*, IV:465–7.   [16] *S. E.*, XIV:67–102.

[17] I compare Freud's and Milton's versions of the Narcissus myth in *Towards Reading Freud* (Princeton: Princeton University Press, 1990), pp. 55–86.

[18] *S.E.*, XXI:57–145.

[19] "The Mirror Stage as Formative of the Function of the I," *Écrits*, trans. Alan Sheridan (New York: W. W. Norton, 1977), pp. 1–7.

becomes the presiding, and delusory, image for who he is. It is whole, beautiful, and complete, where he is, in actuality, a piecemeal, discordant being. He often spends the rest of his life attempting the impossible: attempting to become identical with that total, self-sufficient image. Only by initiation into the Symbolic, the realm of representation made necessary by the absence of the thing represented, can one recover contact with that early, authentic state of absence and alienation that preceded the mystified mirror phase. And if the Oedipal passage, the first initiation into the Symbolic, fails, then one must have recourse to the analyst's Word, Lacan's Word, to guide reinitiation.

Each of these elaborations on the Narcissus myth could sustain much more extended commentary, but overall one might note how inevitably an authoritative voice intervenes on a state of self-infatuated error, an error that is visually generated. Each retelling of the story is an exercise in iconoclasm, a kind of polemic against presence. The image is the antagonist; the word purifies.

And here is where Derrida comes in. For what he does is not to deconstruct or disable the Narcissus story, but to refine it. In Freud, the authoritative logos, the voice of the super-ego, comes on to dispel narcissistic self-enclosure, but then that voice needs to be revised in its turn. In Derrida, the contention is between a view of language in which words are understood as offering presence, and one in which presence is fully placed into verbal circulation. Auto-affection must give way to *différance*. What Derrida offers, as I see it, is an iconoclasm yet more refined than Milton's, Freud's, or Lacan's. If Freud, in line with the Judaic tradition, puts the image per se under harsh critical scrutiny, then Derrida questions those words that convey images. He intervenes with language upon language, raising the intensity of abstraction to an altogether new degree. Freud's residual respect for the image – manifest in his view that the ego is always bodily; that is, always at least in some measure narcissistic – is here challenged. In Derrida's revision of the Narcissus topos the polemic goes a step further. Now we have a distinction between verbal icons, and shattering, iconoclastic words, Derrida's deconstructive words.

When writers offer a new version of Narcissus, they are bound to supply an alternative to the self-infatuated state they've de-picted. They have to offer some fresh relation between desire and prohibition: thus Milton's celestial voice, Freud's therapeutic words, Lacan's initiation into the Symbolic all offer new relations to authority. What, we are now in a position to ask, precisely is Derrida's alternative to auto-affection? What is at stake in prof-fering *différance* as the alternative to the epistemological narcissism that supposedly informs the metaphysics of presence?

Freud, I believe, would have been divided about Derrida's alternative. He would have been both respectful and wary of *différance*. In *Moses and Monotheism*, Freud writes with admiration about the Jewish feat of trying to keep faith with an invisible God. He calls the capacity an advance in intellectuality, and to it he ascribes many of the Hebraic virtues. In prohibiting graven images, "a sensory perception was given second place to what may be called an abstract idea – a triumph of intellectuality over sensuality or, strictly speaking, an instinctual renunciation, with all its necessary psychological consequences."[20] Freud sug-gests that renouncing images is crucial for the development of civilization. It prepares the mind for scientific reflection, for ethical and philosophical speculation, for all those areas of inquiry where one must proceed abstractly, working with symbols that are removed from things in themselves.

But where Freud's humanity comes into play is in sensing just how much this renunciation of sight is likely to hurt. For the pleasures of seeing are great, and the pleasures of a life based on the sensuous joy in vision are not lightly put by. An aesthete, says Camille Paglia (about whom I'll have more to say later), is not necessarily someone obsessed with fashion, decor, and art; an aesthete is someone who lives by the eye.[21] To develop one's powers of abstraction is often to lose contact with the gorgeous world of appearance, and for that, I believe along with Freud, one generally suffers.

Freud overall admires the willingness to renounce visual pleas-ure and assurance. In describing Judaism in terms of its com-

[20] *S. E.*, XXIII:113.
[21] *Sexual Personae: Art and Decadence from Nefertiti to Emily Dickinson* (New Haven: Yale University Press, 1990), p. 60. Henceforth cited in the text.

mitment to the invisible at the expense of the seen, Freud is establishing continuities with his own non-faith of psychoanalysis, which asks men and women to place the invisible realities of the inner life before external factors. The scholar Yosef Yerushalmi is right, it seems to me, to understand *Moses and Monotheism* as the book in which Freud establishes the genetic link between Judaism and psychoanalysis.[22] George Steiner, for his part, is willing to attribute a fair measure of anti-Semitism to Gentile rancor against the Jews for taking the satisfactions of idolatry away from them, an observation that, whatever its ultimate truth (Hannah Arendt's political understanding of anti-Semitism seems to me closer to being accurate), Freud would probably find congenial.[23]

By pursuing the power of abstraction, by affirming word over image, science over narcissism, humanity evolves. Yet Freud, who believed that one must not ask humanity to renounce too many basic satisfactions, is humane enough to see that abstraction imposes suffering. In positing narcissism as a primary developmental stage, Freud, who always attributes a certain prestige to origins, asks us to sustain some regard for visual allure. When Freud says that the ego is a bodily ego he means, among other things, that our sense of self-identity is inseparable from our abiding internal vision or fantasy image of our physical form. Freudian therapy is attuned to the idea that in the beginning is the image. To proceed in therapy, or in life, as though this narcissism were of no consequence would be too burdensome for almost anyone. Though he is tempted by an iconoclasm as severe as that of John Milton, one of his favorite writers, Freud nevertheless sustained respect, if not affection, for the culture of the eye.

Derrida doesn't. For him even words that convey images are an affront. Every form that can be shattered must be. On the matter of therapy Freud observed that better is too often the enemy of good, and in Derrida's fierce iconoclasm he would, I

---

[22] *Freud's Moses: Judaism Terminable and Interminable* (New Haven: Yale University Press, 1991).

[23] Steiner develops this idea in "Through That Glass Darkly," *Salmagundi*, 93 (Winter 1992), pp. 32–50. Arendt offers thoughts on anti-Semitism in *Origins of Totalitarianism* (Cleveland and New York: Meridian Books, 1958) and *Eichmann in Jerusalem: A Report on the Banality of Evil* (New York: Penguin, 1963).

suspect, find an excessive assault on a basic satisfaction, for which people would have to pay in hard coin. And yet, Derrida would argue, the rigors of his work – for given the cold severity that his writing exudes it is to say the least disingenuous to call it play – are worth it. The deconstructive ritual of purification can lead us out of fanaticism, away from misplaced faith. *Différance* can compel us to surrender the wish to dominate, and induce us to recognize and appreciate differences. By conceiving the world in terms of word and image, or true word and image-word, then affirming language's non-truth, one can, Derrida suggests, remake oneself in salutary ways.

And Derrida, as I observed at the opening of this chapter, is anything but alone in his polemic against presence. The desire to overcome fixation on images informs much of the best writing we have come to call theory. In fact, to speak very broadly, we can place a fair amount of theory within the territory mapped out by the Narcissus myth. In Rorty, Foucault, and Baudrillard, and, as I have mentioned, Lacan, to name a few current theorists of consequence, one finds considerable skepticism about metaphysics and also about vision. They are all, I would suggest, like Derrida, polemicists against presence, figuring it variously as the mirror-language of philosophy, the Imaginary, panoptic society, and the precession of simulacra. Like Freud and Derrida (and the Mosaic code that influenced them) they mistrust the attractions of the visual and affirm the value of word against image.

In Lacan's version of Narcissus, the myth takes a rather authoritarian form in which the analyst's Word purportedly reinitiates the subject into the Symbolic. Rorty's version is appealingly open. In *Philosophy and the Mirror of Nature* noncoercive conversation is the verbal form that breaks up philosophical mirrorgazing and helps people remake themselves.[24] Jean Baudrillard's prophetic voice cries out against disabling immersion in the hyper-real world of electronically generated images.[25] Foucault's voice – sardonic, superior, sometimes attaining to prophetic wrath –

[24] Princeton: Princeton University Press, 1979.
[25] *Simulations*, trans. Paul Foss, Paul Patton, and Philip Beitchman (New York: Semiotext[e], 1983).

pits itself against a culture of surveillance epitomized by Bentham's all-seeing panopticon.[26] These modes of thinking are different in many ways but they share a tendency to split experience into two opposing registers, verbal and visual, and to put forward scenarios in which a more enlightened word intervenes on a scene of visually generated error. In this tendency, a good deal of contemporary criticism has followed them. From the feminist film critic decrying "objectification," to the Foucauldian literary critic who finds in theatrical spectatorship a rehearsal for social surveillance, to leftist intellectuals who follow Barthes with their polemics against the ideological designs of popular culture, the image is understood to be the root of a good deal of contemporary cultural evil.

In an essay on the prevalence of anti-ocular critique in contemporary French thought, the intellectual historian Martin Jay has effectively summarized the tendency at hand, one that has become as active in America and England as in France. "The link between privileging vision and the traditional humanist subject, capable of rational enlightenment, has been opened to widespread attack. The illusions of imagistic representation and the allegedly disinterested scientific gaze have been subjected to hostile scrutiny. The mystifications of the social imagery and the spectacle of late capitalist culture have been the target of fierce criticism. And the psychological dependence of the ideological 'I' on the totalizing gaze of the 'eye' has been ruthlessly exposed."[27]

To turn against image culture means turning against metaphysics, displacing the old subject–object mapping supposedly characteristic of metaphysical thinking with another system of metaphors in which language is central. As Fredric Jameson observes, "The notion of textuality, whatever fundamental objections may be made to it, has at least the advantage as a strategy, of cutting across both epistemology and the subject/object an-

---

[26] *Discipline and Punish: The Birth of the Prison*, trans. Alan Sheridan (New York: Pantheon, 1977). Henceforth cited in the text.

[27] "The Empire of the Gaze: Foucault and the Denigration of Vision in Twentieth-century French Thought," in *Foucault: A Critical Reader*, ed. David Couzens Hoy (New York: Basil Blackwell, 1986), p. 178.

tithesis in such a way as to neutralize both, and of focusing the attention of the analyst on her own position as a *reader* and on her own mental operations as *interpretation*."[28] Derrida, as I see it, occupies the forefront of this movement toward textuality because his polemic is not only against images per se, but against even those linguistic forms that translate readily into visual imagery.

And yet I am skeptical about a key claim that informs the polemic against presence in general and Derrida's advanced form of that polemic in particular: that is, the claim to have passed beyond metaphysics, and to be working out another way for representing experience. To explain my view, I need to turn for a moment to a worldly thinker of major distinction, Hannah Arendt. In the first volume of *The Life of the Mind*, Arendt provides a survey of the ways that philosophers have represented the act of thinking. The book, seen from one angle, is a history of the tropes that thinkers from Plato to Bergson have applied to their own most central activity. Some major tendencies, according to Arendt, traverse this, the metaphysical tradition. One of these is a distinct lack of interest in the simple delights of everyday perception. "Nothing perhaps is more surprising in this world of ours," she writes in a memorable sentence, "than the almost infinite diversity of its appearances, the sheer entertainment value of its views, sounds, and smells, something that is hardly ever mentioned by the thinkers and philosophers."[29] The sheer entertainment value of life: no mode of thought intent on teaching us how to die, or how to live with just equanimity, is likely to be caught up in such distraction. In fact, it is from that world of the senses that philosophers, when they think, take leave. We must, Plato said in an image particularly significant for this chapter, close the eyes of the body in order to open the eyes of the mind. For we live, in a yet more famous Platonic image, amidst shadows cast on the walls of a cave. To be enlightened means to leave that cave, which is the sensible world, and enter into the sunlight of intelligible being. As Arendt observes, "to find out what truly *is*, the philosopher must *leave* the world of appearances among

---

[28] *The Ideologies of Theory: Essays 1971–1986, Volume 1: Situations of Theory* (Minneapolis: University of Minnesota Press, 1988), p. 18.   [29] *Life of the Mind*, p. 20.

which he is naturally and originally at home – as Parmenides did when he was carried upward, beyond the gates of night and day, to the divine way that lay 'far from the beaten path of men,' and as Plato did, too, in the Cave parable."[30] Appearances – Kant's insistence on this seems to me of central import for metaphysical philosophy – must have their grounds in something that is not mere appearance.

Arendt attends, roughly speaking, to the same line of thinkers that draws Derrida's deconstructive energies, and in fact this line seems devoted to affirming some region beyond the merely sensible: there is Plato's distinction between the ideas and worldly forms, Kant's between phenomena and noumena, Hegel's between the appearance of historical disorder and the actual workings of the world spirit, Heidegger's tension between the covering over and the revelation of Being, and, one might add, the distinction that Freud, who was not terribly friendly to philosophy, makes between the repressed and the manifest content: one could go on. What becomes clear is that most of the thinkers Derrida has criticized have been, *like him*, polemicists against presence.

Yet there is a difference. In the metaphysical turn against worldly presence, another kind of presence has, as Derrida sees it, usually come to the fore: forget the shadows on the wall of the cave, put your mind on the eternal forms. But those forms themselves become as mesmerizing, as false, as the appearances they displace, suggests Derrida. What Derrida is doing, at least as I understand it, is bringing the philosophical tradition's suspicion about the image another step forward, refining it.

He is not – and this is the point that matters – doing what he claims, trying to put an end to metaphysics; rather he is improving on it: making it more severe, abstract, unworldly than it has previously been. For metaphysics does not privilege presence per se, as Derrida insists; rather it turns against exterior presence to affirm inward or supernal presence. The imaginary worlds of metaphysical true being were simply not free enough of appearance for Derrida's taste, and he went on to purge them. Thus when he speaks of the metaphysics of presence in traditional philosophy, one must take the word "presence" in a highly ironic, even a sarcastic sense: it is as though someone were saying that the local socialists, who want to share the material wealth equally, are addicted to the politics of greed because they don't bother to figure out a way to share cultural and intellectual riches, too. They're not willing to take it to the next level. Any mode of thinking that accepts the cloven fiction of image and word, and makes that fiction constitutive of its workings, is operating, as I see it anyway, in continuous relation to the Western metaphysical tradition. And that tradition may have established itself – Nietzsche, Havelock, Danto, *and* Derrida suggest as much – as the true antidote to what is most harmfully deceptive in art, and in particular in philosophy's closest competitor, literary art.

Beginning with the view that Derrida is working to extend the tradition he claims to repudiate, it would be possible to found an entire critique of metaphysical philosophy, quite as comprehensive as his, calling attention not to its addiction to presence, but to its view that presence must be overcome. Arendt chronicles the first stage in this polemic against appearance; one might then locate a second stage in which writers such as Derrida, Lacan, Barthes, Baudrillard, and all of us – literary critics included – who have almost unanimously stopped talking favorably about images and spoken nearly exclusively of words, language, tropes, and text would play some part. For if our reading of de Man demonstrates the ways that literary criticism has frequently surrendered to a philosophical form of psychoanalysis, our inquiry into Derrida thus far should demonstrate how much reliance on the trope of the text comprises a surrender to another philosophical stricture, the commandment against presence.

This is not to say that a mode of critique ought to be written off merely because it offends this or that prerogative traditionally attached to literature, in this case the prerogative of creating visual images with words. If a philosophy comes along to realize Hegel's prediction to the effect that everything consequential in literature will, in time, be absorbed by concepts – or even by *the* concept – then so be it. Criticism, as Emerson indicated, must be cheerfully willing to conceive the total disappearance of literature.

The standard I want to offer here is pragmatic and indebted to the Emerson of "Compensation," who knew that every gain is likely to entail some loss. An uncompromising drive on behalf of secular values, the drive to make the self merely mortal in the provinces of its own mind, animates Derrida's work and renders it, to me at least, both promising and moving. But it's still a matter of tallying accounts. My view of Derrida as being within the metaphysical tradition, not its fearsome terminator, is of value here not because it debunks Derrida out and out (it doesn't), but rather because it allows us to see his work within the context of the ancient quarrel, and thus more readily to apprehend its price. So in the remaining pages of this chapter, I will be reading Derrida not as the figure who makes the philosophy/poetry opposition obsolete, but as someone who brings it, invaluably, into contemporary focus. To do so I need to take one more detour, this time into the work of a critic who stands almost alone in her defence of what Derrida would teach literary and cultural criticism to repudiate without trial, the gorgeous pagan image.

In 1990 Camille Paglia, a professor at the Philadelphia College of Art, brought out a book that managed to traduce almost every current academic assumption. ("There's something to offend everybody in here," Paglia's editor told me.) Not least among *Sexual Personae*'s targets was the idea that Derrida did so much to inject into the critical mainstream, the idea that almost every culture experience could be illuminatingly conceived in terms of reading and textuality. Paglia's book asserts that the academic fixation on language (one can now speak of reading a painting, a film, a TV commercial, not just a book) is a manifestation of culture's attempt to domesticate art's erotic and violent energies. For this and for a dozen or so other reasons, *Sexual Personae* has been accorded rough treatment in the academy, when it hasn't been ignored out and out. Yet *Sexual Personae* has its virtues, not the least of which is to take the part of the visual – the part of Narcissus, one might say – against the insufficiently examined convictions about presence and textuality that reign in current intellectual life.

What would it mean to create an erotics of art? That is what Susan Sontag, one of Paglia's major influences, called for at the close of her well-known 1964 essay, "Against Interpretation."[31] Most of that piece was given over to a polemic against the so-called depth analysis current in academic criticism. That is, to speak broadly, it was a protest against the domination of art by philosophical and psychoanalytic categories. But Sontag, whose own critical sensibility has generally been remote, gave little indication then or later what such an erotics would be like. Paglia's book, published twenty-five years later, *is* an erotic history of Western literature and visual art: written in an aggressive, nervous, seductive style, it's the kind of criticism that Sontag prophesied but didn't produce.

Paglia's first provocation is to locate the origins of Western art and culture not in Greece, as scholars predominantly have, much less among the Old Testament Jews. What matters most in Western art is, to Paglia, neither Hebraic nor Hellenic, to recall the Arnoldian terms that map out the dialectical boundaries for a good deal of subsequent humanism. The progenitor, rather, is imperial Egypt, that most "eye-intense" of cultures. "The Egyptians invented *elegance*," Paglia writes. "Elegance is reduction, simplification, condensation. It is spare, stark, sleek. Elegance is cultivated abstraction." Egyptian high culture has been underestimated, Paglia says, "because of the moralistic obsession with language that has dominated modern academic thought. Words are not the only measure of mental development. To believe that they are is a very western or Judeo-Christian illusion. It stems from our invisible God, who talks creation into existence ... The most ancient conflict in western culture, between Jew and Egyptian, continues today: Hebrew word-worship versus pagan imagism, the great unseen versus the glorified thing" (p. 61).

That our view of Egypt as a culture of the eye might be determined in part by the fact that we still cannot confidently read its hieroglyphics could temper Paglia's view somewhat. But she is not prone to clog her arguments with too many

---

[31] Reprinted in *A Susan Sontag Reader* (New York: Farrar, Straus, Giroux, 1982), pp. 95–104.

distinctions. The dualism she sets up between word and image is crude, but not unrelated to the way Western thinkers, even the most sophisticated metaphysical philosophers, have frequently operated. Paglia's distinction lies in being an articulate proponent for the side of the argument that's generally left undefended: the throngs dancing around the golden calf, or crowding into the holy brothels of Corinth, don't publish much criticism.

Pagan imagism, Paglia thinks, continues to animate art in the West, despite the efforts of humanism in its varying forms to quell or sublimate it by transforming passion into respectable knowledge. For her, Egyptian iconophilia attains its modern apogee in the glamorous, sexually charged world of the movies. To Paglia, all art that matters aspires to the condition of cinema. In the contention between Hebrew word worship and Egyptian glorification of the thing, Paglia's allegiances are, without qualification, with the visual.

The flavor of Paglia's project comes through when one compares her reflections on Donatello's *David* with those of H. W. Janson, one of the deans of contemporary art history and the author of an influential textbook for beginning college students. "The Middle Ages would surely have condemned it as an idol," Janson observes. "Nudity, clearly, is his natural state, although he resembles a classical statue only in his beautifully poised *contrapposto*. Donatello has chosen to model an adolescent boy, not a full-grown youth like the athletes of Greece, so that the skeletal structure here is less fully enveloped in swelling muscles; nor does he articulate the boy's torso according to the classical pattern."[32]

What does it mean to say that nudity is a figure's natural state? A puzzling remark, but my guess is that Janson means to imply that if it's natural, then surely it's not to be taken as an erotic provocation, a turn on. This is one in a series of gestures that attempt to cue the student's response: don't, above all, be sexually aroused by this work. The account in fact begins with a reference to prohibition: the Middle Ages would have condemned the piece as an idol. Note also the number of negative constructions

---

[32] *History of Art: A Survey of the Major Visual Arts from the Dawn of History to the Present Day* (Englewood Cliffs, N.J.: Prentice-Hall, 1977), p. 387.

("not a full-grown youth," "nor does he articulate,") and qualifications ("resembles a classical statue only," "less fully enveloped"). Such gestures tend to bring the intellect to the fore and demote other responses. But Janson's most important distancing devices are the multiple contexts he calls forward. He assiduously places the sculpture with reference to the Middle Ages, ancient Greece, Classical art. His account works to blur the piece's immediate sexual aura, its presence. Janson doesn't see *David* as an object of intrinsic fascination; rather, he "reads" it as something of a signifier in the text of art history. The work is contextualized. The cultural objective, presumably, is to teach the student how to overcome, or at the very least to qualify, a certain kind of immediate pleasure in the interest of the more refined (but presumably less intense) pleasure associated with art historical knowledge.

Thus the questions that Paglia, throughout *Sexual Personae*, compels one to ask: Might it not be one of the key social functions of historical criticism to discipline aesthetic pleasures? Do art history and literary criticism strain to make us address in an exclusively rational way works that might also incite passion?

Where would Derrida stand on this matter? He, I suspect, would want to take Janson a step further. Derrida would be inclined to think that Janson's contextualizing categories, the sorts of categories put to work by numberless other humanistic intellectuals, would themselves devolve into idols. They would become objects of fascination, breeding the kind of epistemological hubris deconstruction purportedly works to dissolve.[33] Deconstructing these categories would mean releasing the viewer from bondage to them by allowing each one – the Middle Ages, Greece, Classical art, and what have you – to modify, shift, and finally displace the others until one reached the point where there was neither a visual nor a conceptual ground from which to apprehend the work. "Each element appearing on the scene of presence," as Derrida puts it in a key passage, "is related to something other than itself, thereby keeping within itself the mark of the

---

[33] Derrida's most sustained reflections on the visual arts, reflections that those familiar with his earlier work would have had little trouble anticipating, occur in *The Truth in Painting*, trans. Geoff Bennington and Ian McLeod (Chicago: University of Chicago Press, 1987).

past element, and already letting itself be vitiated by the mark of its relation to the future element."[34]

Derrida would be likely to object here and assert that one objective of deconstruction is to undermine philosophical oppositions like visual/verbal. He would perhaps try to demonstrate that both Paglia's and Janson's approaches were installments in the history of the kind of philosophical criticism that's devoted to sustaining illusions of presence. Whether it's verbal or visual presence that's at issue probably wouldn't matter very much. In fact the reason I have chosen presence as a mode of access to Derrida's work is that his relation to that state seems to be unremittingly negative, rather than dialectical. Vision and the image won't be preserved or transformed by Derridean deconstruction; they must be displaced pure and simple. In short, I think that Derrida would do to Janson something very much like what Janson does to Donatello, turn against the visual properties in the interest of a more refined cognitive abstraction.

Now here is Paglia on *David*: "David's contrapposto is languorously Hellenistic. The hand on hip and cocked knee create an air of sexual solicitation. From the side, one is struck by the peachy buttocks, bony shoulderblades, and petulantly protruding boy-belly. The combination of child's physique with female body language is perverse and pederastic . . . The *David*'s shimmery, slithery bronze is a frozen wet dream" (pp. 147–8). To Janson, *David* seems to be the product of the lengthy tradition of Western sculpture, a figure that takes its place in a conceptual development; the sculpture is all but devoured by its antecedents. Though Paglia's approach isn't immaculately ahistorical and experiential – she refers to the Hellenistic tradition, uses the technical term contrapposto, and later has many illuminating things to say about the relations between the sculpture and other, later works – her chief objective is to render *David* as a figure of erotic fascination. He's a sexual persona, the beautiful boy. To Janson, I suspect, Paglia has committed a major naive error: at certain points in her account she suspends talk about the work of art, which is a gesture within a historical tradition of gestures, and

<hr />

[34] *Margins of Philosophy*, p. 13.

begins to sound like the *David* is more person than statue. To deconstruct Paglia, someone like Derrida, who would be as appalled as Janson at her idolatry, might run her brief description together with a number of versions of the Pygmalion myth, in which the central figure brings a statue to life. The myth presumably betrays the common metaphysical desire to get beyond representations and possess the thing in itself.

Paglia believes that her sexual personae compel fascination from virtually all perceivers, no matter what their professed sexual orientation. The personae (which include the beautiful boy, the femme fatale, the male heroine, the androgyne of manners, etc.: all, it is worth pointing out, variations on the theme of the androgyne) are, to Paglia, art's proper material, the primary colors with which Western artists are supposed to work. Every artist must recast them to create fresh human desires. The personae are culture's variations on nature's incessant biological themes. Thus the glory of art lies in its power to extemporize fictive identities that swerve away from biology's literal insistence on what we are. For Paglia is a biological essentialist: men are men, women women. Anatomy is, as Freud thought he knew, destiny.

In Paglia, nature plays the role of Harold Bloom's precursor, from which living poets must differentiate themselves. Yet Paglia thinks that there is some pure and true version of Nature out there for everyone to apprehend. And that true version is the Marquis de Sade's sado-masochistic hell in which the desire to copulate inevitably braids with the desire to torture and kill.[35] To matter, art must take account of the fact that nature truly is red in tooth and claw, etc., etc. But de Sade's sado-masochistic fundamentalism is merely a reading of nature, an interpretation. Paglia ought to see that the artists she admires are responding not to nature but to representations of nature they find all around them, including of course those in the work of other artists. Because conventional gender roles seem to have an early provenance,

---

[35] For a clear and relatively compressed rendition of de Sade's thinking on nature the best source is probably his *Philosophy in the Bedroom*, which appears in *Justine, Philosophy in the Bedroom, and Other Writings*, comp. and trans. Richard Seaver and Austryn Wainhouse (New York: Grove Press, 1965), pp. 177–367.

Paglia is determined to think they are literally true. One of Paglia's idols, Oscar Wilde, could have shown her that nature always comes to resemble the works of the day's better artists. ("Where, if not from the Impressionists," writes Wilde – stealing a bit from Whistler, and setting himself up, I'd guess, to be stolen from by T. S. Eliot – "do we get those wonderful brown fogs that come creeping down our streets, blurring the gas lamps and changing the houses into monstrous shadows?"[36]) Her work's vitality, though, its capacity to provoke riveted attention, is due in part to using nature as a god-term, and in that way establishing a point of stability that a deconstructive reading would quickly – and quite usefully – explode.

Of course for such an operation Paglia would have only scorn: she refers to Derrida's writing as masturbation without pleasure. Paglia is that rarity, an extremely gifted and expansive critic with no appetite for philosophical reflection. She reacts to contemporary theorists like Derrida in much the way that Byron, another superficial genius (in the best sense), reacted to Coleridge, against whose *Biographia* he pointed *Don Juan*. "Explaining metaphysics to the nation," Byron mutters, "I wish he would explain his Explanation."

I said that to Paglia all art that matters aspires to the condition of cinema, but perhaps a better way to put it is to say that Paglia's project consists in encountering major canonical art work as though it were a certain sort of popular art. For popular art, it seems to me, often attempts to persuade us of its complete novelty: you've never seen anything like this before. Such popular art aspires to skim the surface of the times and to deliver for our pleasure what makes our moment distinct from any other (which can be quite a valuable aim). It aspires to make us feel that, to modify Milton's Satan a touch, "We know no time when we have been as now." So even when Paglia talks about the ancestors and descendants of an art work, something she can do with considerable authority, it's generally peripheral to her major drive, which is to reproduce the experience of being overwhelmed by a great work in its pure, visual immediacy, its being in the present.

[36] *Literary Criticism of Oscar Wilde*, ed. Stanley Weintraub (Lincoln: University of Nebraska Press, 1968), p. 187.

Madonna, to cite one of Paglia's particular favorites, has worked overtime to provide up-to-the-minute renderings of the way sex, power, and material lust blend. Next year it will all have to be reimagined as fresh extravagances are brought out into the light of common day for acceptance and approval. Such productions are possible to put into context, of course, and plenty of academics have done Madonna the favor by exposing her roots in Weimar night clubs, among Zola's nineteenth-century French courtesans, and wherever else. Perhaps one measure of popular art is how well it gets at what's singular about a given moment and how difficult it is to contextualize convincingly. One current development that I think Paglia is tapping into is the unfolding, if still anxious, receptivity to bisexuality and androgyny: finding such tendencies throughout Western art places her book in energizing contact with current, if contested, perceptions about sexuality.

We might compare Paglia's populism to the refining urge we located in Barthes' piece on popular culture. Paglia wants to affirm the visual dimension; Barthes to translate visual experience into verbal. In "The World of Wrestling" the crowd becomes a rather debased group of readers, a bad interpretive community, and the match becomes a text. This drive to render an intensely visual experience in verbal terms – to transform narcissistic gazing not only into words, which criticism obviously cannot avoid, but to use a rhetorical vocabulary, language to the second degree, one might say – this drive is something one often encounters in the cultural criticism that has followed Barthes.[37] Even those writers who find something to praise in popular culture (usually they call it subversion), tend to use textual or coldly formal terms to render the work. In so doing, they can rhetorically undermine the sensuously charged creations they want to savor and endorse.[38]

The tradition from which critics almost inevitably draw, the

[37] In his excellent *William Empson: Prophet Against Sacrifice* (New York: Routledge, 1991), Paul H. Fry offers shrewd remarks on the dangers of taking language as paradigmatic of all sign-systems: see pp. 90–1.

[38] For a fine account of the difficulties twentieth-century American intellectuals have had in coming to terms with popular art forms, see Andrew Ross, *No Respect: Intellectuals & Popular Culture* (New York: Routledge, 1989). His discussion of Marshall McLuhan, pp. 114–34, bears in particular on the concerns of this chapter.

metaphysical tradition, in which I include Derrida, with its polemic against presence, is based in part on the philosophers' urge to separate themselves from the many, from the crowd. (Recall how in *The Republic* Plato stigmatized the poets by associating them with democracy, philosophers being aristocratic by temperament.) Derrida concerns himself with philosophy, but as a pedagogical technique his kind of reading, taking the polemic against presence a step further, draws the student another pace away from the energies and pleasures of day-to-day life, the "infinite diversity of . . . appearances" that Arendt calls attention to. If one can say that Thauvin is a pop-culture philosopheme, one can also say that for Derrida the Enlightenment Kant is too popular a philosopher, not severe, not harsh enough in the demands he places on his readers. As the wrestling match is to Barthes, the *Critique of Pure Reason* is to Derrida.

Paglia is the least elitist of critics, and that too, at least when she encounters something other than a certain sort of popular art, can produce difficulties. But it remains to say a little more about her achievement. The quality Paglia tries to locate is akin to what Benjamin, a critic with more palpable religious longings, called the aura. Paglia simply refers to it as charisma, the glow that emanates from a narcissistic personality, or, presumably, from a work of art that exudes a beauty, poise, and self-possession that seem more than human. If a good deal of criticism in the West, at least since Arnold, has, to speak very broadly, aspired to play the role of the authoritative presence that intervenes on one or another form of naive infatuation, then Paglia is, as far as I know, the first critic to side with Narcissus out and out.

Whatever the shortcomings of Paglia's book it still serves as a salutary warning. It announces that contemporary criticism, in its drive to produce ever more sophisticated elaborations on the authoritative cultural voice, has often lost touch with the vital dimensions of art. *Sexual Personae* works as what Saul Bellow, in an invaluable phrase, calls a "contrast gainer." For Western education, Western humanities, following the Arnoldian dictum and trying to use art to produce good citizens, have often ignored the visual and the erotic in favor of somber meditations on the

Word. Among these meditations none demands or promises more than Jacques Derrida's.

What putting Paglia beside Derrida should suggest is that the cloven fiction of image and word that's dramatized in the Narcissus story, and that has guided so much of Western reflection, is inadequate to the complexity of both art and life.[39] This much I think a number of the English Romantics knew when they tried to rewrite the Narcissus story.[40] I am thinking here not only of such direct retellings of the myth as Wordsworth's Winander Boy sequence and Shelley's *Alastor* but of the poets' attempts to present certain sorts of self-images in their work. These self-images exude a charismatic glow, a "narcissistic" glamor. But they sustain this allure while engaging fate, limitation, and authority.

When Coleridge, for instance, depicts himself as the inspired bard in "Kubla Khan," the figure is without a doubt of considerable erotic interest:

> His flashing eyes, his floating hair!
> Weave a circle round him thrice,
> And close your eyes with holy dread,
> For he on honey-dew hath fed,
> And drunk the milk of Paradise.[41]

Of this image Paglia remarks, "The poet is a beautiful youth in the Hellenistic style, an ephebic kouros of female emotionalism. His flashing eyes and floating hair combine masculine power with feminine beauty" (p. 329). "He has an eerie sexual iridescence. Masculine and feminine dilate around him like a solar corona" (p. 330). Coleridge's poet is, Paglia's suggestions seem quite right, a prototype for the male rock star, Elvis Presley or, from a later generation, Axl Rose or Kurt Cobain, a figure who's both macho and tender: dangerous, but vulnerable, and to no one so much as himself.

---

[39] The fiction is deeply enough ingrained so that W. J. T. Mitchell can speak quite persuasively about iconoclasm among leading art critics and historians, those who, one might assume, would be inclined to preserve some affection for graven images. See *Iconology: Image, Text, Ideology* (Chicago: University of Chicago Press, 1986).

[40] In *The Heresy of Self-Love: A Study of Subversive Individualism* (New York: Basic Books, 1968), Paul Zweig fruitfully questions the hostile suspicion that variations on the Narcissus myth have generated in the West.   [41] *Poems*, I:298.

But that's not the end of the story. First of all, Coleridge's poem confronts us with some degree of difficulty; it's not an easy pleasure. From a very few hints – hair, eyes, "honey-dew," "milk of Paradise" – one has to construct a whole figure, a complete scene. There are other issues of interpretation as well. Why weave the circle thrice, not two times or four? Is it the Christian three, evocative of the trinity, and thus a counter-spell against pagan charisma? Or does the number have an ancient or esoteric provenance? And why close our eyes? To shut out the poet's influence? Or to reproduce his possible Homeric blindness? What are we to make of the incantatory rhythms that animate the passage? Does the chant-like quality ask us to join a community of resistance to the poet's powers, or do the lines mesmerize us with their rhythms, drawing us into a Dionysian troupe? Such questions involve matters of interpretation; they depend for their answers on how we construe suggestive words and ambiguous verbal rhythms. And this activity of interpretation complicates the clear portrait, the glowing persona, that Paglia would like us to see in the poem. *Sexual Personae* doesn't quote a great deal of poetry, and when it does, often isn't responsive to the multiple meanings that major verbal art generates.

With Presley and Axl Rose, the pleasures are, at least in my view, intellectually much easier than with Coleridge's poet; the personae they present and their musical designs require virtually no interpretation. (Though that doesn't mean that their insubordinate energies don't matter.) Perfect immediacy is the aim of a lot of pop culture, whereas art that offers more difficult pleasures demands that we respond with a mix of passion and intellection. At summoning forth the former, Paglia is brilliant.

Part of the difficulty in responding to the poet in "Kubla Khan" involves bringing the right ancestral images to bear. Coleridge's poet is a rejuvenation of other figures in literature and myth: of Apollo the creator god, Dionysus, Orpheus, Christ (thus part of the poem's scandal, eroticizing a sacred image), Collins' "rich-haired Youth of Morn," and possibly of the young Milton, the Lady of Christ's College. To me, a great poet ought not to be seen as contending against his precursors so much as drawing them into the present, making them live within his own time. He finds what in their work speaks best to culture's current needs and tries to renew it. There is, granted, a certain measure of aggression here, for the predecessor's image must be changed. An unironic depiction of Apollo won't do, either in Coleridge's time or our own. "Phoebus is dead, ephebe," says Stevens in *Notes toward a Supreme Fiction*. But the same poet puts forth the figure of the youth as virile poet, a refinement on Apollo meant to sustain a more skeptical gaze.

This activity of literary renewal (about which the final chapter on Harold Bloom will have more to say) is probably best seen not in terms of an internecine war among poets, but as an act of faith in poetry, a saving reaction to the ways in which the passage of time, shifts in belief, changes in ways of talking and thinking threaten to render great poems of the past obsolete. Poets who matter allow us to see why the writers they have loved continue to be worth our attention; they bring into the present elements in their predecessors' work that still count. So Coleridge's bard gets us to recall his ancestors, *even as* he exerts a powerful fascination. One thing that distinguishes Coleridge's image from many pop culture icons is the poet's wish to evoke past art, to make it live in the present.

Further on in time Coleridge's poet makes contact with, and is revitalized by, James Dickey's Other who, anything but a Lacanian Other, represents a form of Apollonian authority and pleasure that Dickey seeks to embody, if only for moments at a time, by fiercely dedicating himself to poetry. In "The Other" the poet finds an ideal-I that will inspire him throughout his writing life:

> . . . I talked all the time through my teeth
> To another, unlike me, beside me:
> To a brother or king-sized shadow
> Who looked at me, burned, and believed me:
> Who believed I would rise like Apollo
>
> With armor-cast shoulders upon me:
> Whose voice, whistling back through my teeth,
> Counted strokes with the hiss of a serpent.[42]

[42] *Poems 1957–1967*, p. 34.

The initial presentation of the Apollonian Other may, to a more severe reader than I, be too gaudy, bordering on what Coleridge (thinking of Plato, actually) called "gorgeous nonsense." But part of what redeems the image is the poet's willingness to describe the price for sustaining his glowing, self-made ideal-I. The compensatory cost for a nearly Homeric ideal turns out to be a drive to keep unfolding and refining his art. This drive persists even when Dickey's strength for it fades: the "looming brother but more/Brightly above me is blazing." The ideal-Other will not allow the poet to relent and savor the autumnal phase of his life, or as Dickey puts it, "turn wholly mortal in my mind."[43]

And here I think we find something else that distinguishes demanding art from many popular cultural forms. All too often popular art will not tally costs; it ignores the Emersonian laws of compensation. Coleridge's great passage on the bard comes at the end of "Kubla Khan," a poem that, in Coleridge's account, is terminated when a Man from Porlock comes to the door and destroys the reverie. Coleridge, in effect, has gone too far in imagining himself as an inspired figure; he's incited his orthodox censor, and he pays for it by having his potentially great long poem cut off. The warning stands: if you want to see yourself in such gorgeous sexual terms, and to write the poems that the rich-haired youth would write, you had best be ready to withstand inquisition by a harsh, quotidian spirit whose name carries intimations of poverty and enclosure. So at the foot of Donatello's *David* there is Goliath's severed bleeding head. It's an image, perhaps, for the helpless spectator who is struck dumb, who loses his reason, his self-control, his head, over the boy's coldly poised beauty.

Popular art often tries to insist that the glamor comes free, without compensatory cost. But if such glamor is initially exhilarating, it is often, in the long term, demoralizing, as we learn that the charismatic ones do not need us at all, and will not recognize us as among the elect. So popular films often take one, temporarily, into a glowing world, inducing beautiful reveries. But when the curtains close, we're left on the far side, palely loitering. Is this sense of exile part of the reason that people so

---

[43] *Poems 1957–1967*, p. 36.

often leave the movies in a state of grumbling discontent? A neurotic, says Lacan, is someone who thinks that others exist who are always happy and whose lives are ever beautiful: pop art à la Madonna, and difficult art as it can be transformed by Paglia's brilliant descriptions, could make us believe in that land of eternal allure. Difficult images like Dickey's and Coleridge's don't give in to wish fulfillment, though they may come perilously close. And they also resist reduction or facile abstraction; they resist becoming forms of knowledge purchased through the loss of erotic and emotional power.

Have I made things too easy for myself by choosing glamorous male images? Had I chosen complex erotic female images, wouldn't I have had to encounter the critique of the male gaze? Maybe so. There are, it's true, exploitative and vulgarly degrading images of women in cultural circulation. Critics should point them out where they occur and attempt to persuade their readers to concur in the assessment. Yet overall I should much rather that we democratize the pleasures of looking and of sensuous life – the world of appearance that Whitman loved so much and rendered with his peculiar wild delicacy – than succumb to a pervasive iconoclasm. Is the drive to sexual objectification (probably as available now to women as to men, at least in our rich corner of the world) integral to the mimetic or representational drive that lives in almost every artist? If so, to what degree does the feminist critique of the so-called male gaze entail yet another attempt to disenfranchise art?

Just as Derrida would end epistemological hubris by deconstructing virtually everything written, so it seems that some critics, fired by a nearly puritan iconoclasm, want to put an end to all forms of pleasurable seeing. In the essay on representations of women in film that I mentioned earlier, Laura Mulvey observes, "It is said that analysing pleasure, or beauty, destroys it. That is the intention of this article."[44] Mulvey finds the world of film almost as pervasively culpable as Derrida finds the world of philosophy: I would prefer to draw distinctions among different cultural works.

But uninhibited celebration of charisma is, as I have been

[44] *Feminisms*, p. 434.

arguing, also insufficient. However valuable Paglia may be in bringing Coleridge's bard to life, what she says is inadequate without reference to the tradition he rejuvenates, to the poem's difficulty, and to its responsiveness to the laws of compensation. The achievement of glamor in a context that also evokes some version of the reality principle is what distinguishes Donatello, Coleridge, and Dickey, and frequently, I would suggest (though there is hardly space here to demonstrate as much), that writing we call literature. Literature often displays personae that are as fascinating as anything Hollywood can give us, but that also compel interpretation and tally costs.

Poems like Coleridge's begin, perhaps, in the conviction that society has become far too restrictive and artificial, that nature (which each writer conceives in something of an individual way, Keats's being a far different thing than, say, Wordsworth's or Dickinson's) is being overwhelmed by civilization. And yet a renovating poet, like Coleridge or Shelley, Stevens, Dickey, Amy Clampitt, or James Merrill, cannot succeed merely by offering glamorous images and leaving it at that. It is the achievement of beauty within the context of authority and limit that matters, that prevents the spirit from being merely fascinated then let down on the one hand, or drawn to a sterile abstraction on the other. The poets aspire to become, however temporarily, liberating gods, as Emerson called them, when they offer images of a world in which desire and limit need not be at *perpetual* strife, and where discipline may be a spur to creation, not merely its inhibitor. The quality I am describing here is akin to what Richard Poirier calls "density," a quality he finds in works of art that offer strong initial pleasures but that also reveal themselves as complexly textured, and that fruitfully resist our routine powers of understanding.[45]

The pornographic image and the fascist icon have no texture, no density – they aim fully to absorb. Poetry of the sort I am describing may well traffic near the borders of pornography and propaganda. (Is there a refined eroticism in Wordsworth's depiction of childhood in "Intimations" and elsewhere?) In fact –

---

[45] *The Renewal of Literature: Emersonian Reflections* (New Haven: Yale University Press, 1987), pp. 130–4.

and here is part of Paglia's value – we need to be reminded in the midst of a humanistic culture that this is so. But one must also have the perspective of H. W. Janson, if not Jacques Derrida, to sustain the cultural detachment that guards one from total immersion and lets one perceive how fate and limit are recorded in major works of art. To put it in compressed form, what I mean to evoke here is something that Freud's terminology can express, but that Freud himself resisted conceiving: Coleridge's poet and Dickey's Other are figures for an "eroticized super-ego." The allure of such images is far less assimilable to Kant and his notion of disinterested pleasure than it is to Stendhal, who speaks of beauty as a promise of happiness.

But am I saying anything more here than what Horace says when he claims that poetry aspires both to delight and to instruct, or what Angus Fletcher does when he observes that art gives us difficult pleasures? (Thus Yeats: that which delights is the most difficult among things not impossible.) I mean only to suggest that when pleasure and instruction come together the two tendencies can transform one another in ways that are as significant to human life as they are hard to describe in general terms. The *specific* achievement of a work of art may lie, at least partially, in the way it manages to blend pleasure and instruction so that neither is perceptible in its pure form. I have tried to say something of the shape that blending takes among the Romantics, whose revision of the Narcissus topos brings them most immediately into the provinces of my discussion. Criticism, as I understand it, should be capable of describing the intermingling of eros and cultural reference in any given work and, too, be ready to comment on the possible social consequences.

Derrida's deconstruction, with its ascetic rigor, is as sure a philosophical proof as I know of against the fanaticism that can come from being mesmerized by images and by offers of fully present truth. And yet the weakness of Derrida's position lies in what one must surrender in order to pass with him beyond illusion. For Derrida, at his most rigorous, compels one to turn against pleasure, against the allure of seeing, against worldly things and the things of the earth. To me, such renunciation is too costly.

For Derrida there is indeed very little literature: that is, there is very little writing by poets and novelists with an aversion as severe as his to visual and verbal presence. Most of what we call literature is fair game for deconstruction. Derrida decides nearly every encounter with the image in advance: whatever can be deconstructed must be. He offers an uncompromising ascetic discipline that, I believe, could contribute quite palpably to purging the world of fanaticism (if it did not become a fanaticism in its own right). Abiding in the background of Derrida's best work is a vision of the nation that became intoxicated by images, the swastika, the leader, the parading torches, and went to work to ruin the world and to obliterate the culture that has done the most – I believe Freud's implications to be right in this – to civilize mankind.

Perhaps the glamorous self-images that I found in Coleridge and Dickey, and that traverse literature in general and Romantic writing in particular, can be intoxicants. But that judgment ought to come from a critic who measures and remeasures the *specific* work's ratios of pleasure and density within the context of the cultural moment as he or she embodies it, and not of the disenfranchising philosopher who decides the game in advance. To live by the image alone is to invite fanaticism, but the ethos of *différance*, noble as it in many ways is, threatens to purge life of vital force. Between these two alternatives lies an ongoing critical activity. Surely that activity may fail and lead us, at times, to error, reduction, or excess. But it's that kind of risk that makes criticism worth doing. There's something disturbingly mistake-proof about the way Derrida and Paglia think.

Imagine a class of intellectuals who were not devoted to the ascetic vision or a reactive over-estimation of popular culture, who gave up the dualism that informs the Narcissus myth in which words fight it out eternally and on high with glamorous images (or seductive image-words). Such critics would, without sacrificing their intelligence and learning, engage on equal terms with the surrounding culture. They would be less interested in making themselves and their students into a self-contained elite through harsh philosophical discipline than in having an ongoing effect on the thinking of their fellow citizens. Such intellectuals would see television and electronic culture not as fearsome

opponents or, following McLuhan and Paglia, as the all-con-
quering wave of the future, but as opportunities for exercising
responsive critique, and too for disseminating their ideas. The
ascetic priests, says Nietzsche, become extraordinary, and – he's
forced to admit – extraordinarily interesting creatures, by their
willingness to repudiate the world and all merely human pleasures:
for, no matter what the circumstance, they desire to be different;
they desire to be elsewhere. Yet the price of being different and
elsewhere has been, for contemporary Anglo-American intellectuals, that of having all too little cultural influence. The risk of
wishing to be elsewhere and different lies in the possibility that
the wish will come entirely true.

CHAPTER 3

Real history

Someone chronicling the past twenty-five years of Anglo-American intellectual life might describe it as the time when textuality triumphed, when the forces of deconstruction, led by Jacques Derrida, successfully stormed the Bastille of logocentrism, demonstrating that all writing, whatever its pretensions, was prolific with tropes, unstable, decentered. The writer could go on to show how the professors of English colonized the other university departments. She would point out how often anthropologists, historians, philosophers, psychologists, economists, law professors, and even scientists were compelled to give up their belief in transparent language and confront their work's rhetorical dimension.

Richard Rorty found figurative biases in the purportedly neutral language of analytical philosophy; Stanley Fish excavated legal rhetoric; Hayden White located the major historians' master tropes; Clifford Geertz focused on how anthropologists represent themselves as authors; Donald McCloskey analyzed the rhetoric of his fellow economists.[1] Progressively more scientists gave Thomas Kuhn – whose paradigm functions as a sort of *langue* in which the *parole* that is the individual datum acquires its sense – an extended hearing.[2] Everyone in the university, it sometimes seemed, had to learn to read all over again as the pupils of the

---

[1] Rorty, *Philosophy and the Mirror of Nature* and *Objectivity, Relativism, and Truth* (Cambridge: Cambridge University Press, 1991); Fish, *Doing What Comes Naturally*; White, *Metahistory* (Baltimore: Johns Hopkins University Press, 1973); Geertz, *Works and Lives: The Anthropologist as Author* (Stanford: Stanford University Press, 1988); McCloskey, *If You're So Smart: The Narrative of Economic Expertise* (Chicago: University of Chicago Press, 1990).

[2] *The Structure of Scientific Revolutions* (Chicago: University of Chicago Press, 1962).

literature professors: there was nothing, and no one, outside of the text.

But the story our fictive chronicler told would be at best a partial one. The struggle between philosophy and poetry was ancient in Plato's time, and it would be presumptuous, as I have been arguing throughout this book, to think that we have terminated it in ours. In the past twenty-five years, the language of literary criticism has moved progressively further away from the languages of poetry and fiction, accepting more and more terms from the analytical disciplines. Though we literary critics may have enforced an ethics of reading on our colleagues in other departments, they have also had a potent effect on us. As it frequently happens in the political world, a sort of reverse colonization has been taking place. To call a literary critical study authentically interdisciplinary at present is to pay it the highest compliment. What that compliment usually means is that the work in question has succeeded in translating the language of literature repeatedly into the terms of more generalizing and accordingly more stable areas of knowledge.

Eminent among these areas has been historiography, not history writing per se, but philosophical reflection upon the ways that history might be written. While the other departments have been, in varying measures, going textual, a good deal of literary criticism has turned from the critique of truth sponsored by Derridean deconstruction (though not from its polemic against the visual) and adopted historical categories, particularly Marxist/Hegelian categories, for the analysis of literary works. No longer primarily concerned with philosophical approaches to the question of understanding, many critics have gone to the philosophy of history. Thus the term "ideology," crucial to any Marxist account of culture, has become of central import. Consider some consequential titles: *Criticism and Ideology, The Romantic Ideology, The Ideologies of Theory, The Ideology of the Aesthetic, Ideology: An Introduction*: one could cite more.[3]

---

[3] Terry Eagleton, *Criticism and Ideology: A Study in Marxist Literary Theory* (London: Verso, 1976); Jerome J. McGann, *The Romantic Ideology: A Critical Investigation* (Chicago: University Of Chicago Press, 1983); Jameson, *The Ideologies of Theory*; Eagleton, *The Ideology of the Aesthetic* (Cambridge, Mass.: Basil Blackwell, 1990); Eagleton, *Ideology:*

Writing philosophy, as Havelock suggests, virtually always entails conferring auras on particular words. The major philosophers choose new and surprising terms; their followers add a little to the lustre and disappear. A more literary prejudice is well expressed in Robert Frost's observation that after you've repeated a truth a couple of times, it becomes less true. Say it with any frequency, and it won't be true at all. (On this subject Oscar Wilde is charmingly extreme: When people agree with me I always feel that I must be wrong.) One way to conceive of criticism, as I have been arguing in these pages, is as writing that plays itself out between certain philosophic and poetic tendencies. I think that in this, the moment of the interdisciplinary, and despite the efforts of Derrida, Rorty, and others to undermine fixed conceptions of truth, the practice of submitting literary writing to categories, particularly of a moral and political sort, may be at an all-time high. Among these categories, "ideology" is commonplace, a puzzling matter given recent political and intellectual developments. One is, in fact, surprised to find the term still in circulation at all. Yet it persists, thrives, and, given its import in cultural studies, seems to have a shining future ahead of it.

The term ideology goes back at least to the French thinker Antoine Destutt de Tracy, whose main work began to appear around the period of the French Revolution, but it is Marx and Engels who give the concept its contemporary sense. A well-known passage from the *Contribution to the Critique of Political Economy* is, with some qualification, representative of Marx's views on the matter. "The mode of production," Marx observes there, "conditions the social, political and intellectual life process in general. It is not the consciousness of men that determines their being but, on the contrary, their social being that determines their consciousness."[4] And if someone's social identity entails ownership of the means of production, then his consciousness is likely to be

An Introduction (London: Verso, 1991). All of these works arise in a significant relation to Louis Althusser's 1969 essay "Ideology and Ideological State Apparatuses," collected in *Lenin and Philosophy and Other Essays*, trans. Ben Brewster (New York: Monthly Review Press, 1971), pp. 127–86.

[4] (Chicago: C. H. Kerr, 1911), pp. 11–12.

skewed – as well as socially preeminent. As Marx puts it in *The German Ideology*: "The class which has the means of material production at its disposal, has control at the same time over the means of mental production, so that thereby, generally speaking, the ideas of those who lack the means of mental production are subject to it. The ruling ideas are nothing more than the ideal expression of the dominant material relationships, the dominant material relationships grasped as ideas; hence of the relationships which make the one class the ruling one, therefore, the ideas of its dominance."[5]

Yet Marx and Engels are not always so blunt. At times they suggest that various superstructural formations that ought, strictly speaking, to be enclosed by ideology possess a relative autonomy. Balzac, Royalist that he was, still lays bare the material dynamics of Parisian life, anatomizing history as class struggle: he shows you more than he knows. Engels is generally more flexible than Marx, claiming in a well-known letter to Joseph Bloch that the determining element in history may *ultimately* be material production and reproduction, but that elements of the superstructure influence historical struggles and even at times determine their outward form.

Yet even with these qualifications on record, the classical Marxist conception of ideology relies upon a split between base and superstructure: ideology is finally a cover story. The deep truth is within the material dynamic that Marx, with the aid of scientific methods, uncovered.

Roland Barthes has said that modern myth – but he might also have said ideology – is the transformation of history into nature.[6] "What the world supplies to myth," Barthes observes, "is an historical reality, defined, even if this goes back quite a while, by the way in which men have produced or used it; and what myth gives in return is a *natural* image of this reality... The world enters language as a dialectical relation between activities, between human actions; it comes out of myth as a harmonious display of essences."[7] Note that in Barthes's semiological

---

[5] Karl Marx and Frederick Engels, *The German Ideology*, ed. C. J. Arthur (New York: International Publishers, 1976), p. 64.   [6] *Mythologies*, p. 129.
[7] *Mythologies*, p. 142.

translation of Marx there is an opposition between the relational way in which the world purportedly enters language and the display of essences that characterizes myth. The opposition reproduces the metonymy/metaphor split on which structuralist and post-structuralist thinking both rely. Yet at the same time Barthes keeps alive the notion of the base, "what the world supplies," and a mystified structure that disguises it, the artificially natural image. This effort to translate, without maiming, the classical notion of ideology persists into the present; only the techniques of assimilation have changed.

Though there are many ways to define ideology (Raymond Geuss's *The Idea of a Critical Theory* lists most of them) Barthes's lines about transforming history into nature are close to the center of Marx's thinking.[8] Marx did not want anyone to forget, at least until socialism had triumphed, that no social condition was stable, and that we were the products, much more than the producers, of historical change. Barthes's, in other words, is a good brief characterization of ideology provided you know – as Marx thought he did – what history and nature are. To Marx, history was materially motivated class struggle, a condition of flux; nature is unregenerate and unchanging. Part of bourgeois hubris consisted in believing that capitalism was the natural, and therefore eternally just, fulfillment of the instinct for material accumulation endemic to human beings at all times. The free market was, to the bourgeois mind, human nature translated perfectly into social form. Given Marx's confident view of the world, the concept of ideology follows directly. Those whose place in the human food chain, in which the great capitalists, as Marx memorably said, devour the lesser, inhibits them from seeing the truth are likely to be creatures of ideology: they live the life of false consciousness.

Two events intervened on left-wing intellectuals to make Marx's view of ideology harder to hold onto. The first one was the gradual decline and fall of communism throughout most of the world. The internal collapse of the Soviet Union and the break up of its foreign empire cast virtually everything associated with

[8] *The Idea of a Critical Theory: Habermas and the Frankfurt School* (Cambridge: Cambridge University Press, 1981).

Marx and his thought into discredit, at least for many. Russia's fate has been taken as witness to the fact that Karl Marx was comprehensively wrong.

The second event, less consequential by far, was the onset and dissemination of post-structuralist thinking. Can one take, say, Lacan seriously when he associates the drive to possess the truth with the quest for that supremely determining nonentity, the phallus, and still talk about ideology? For to use ideology as an analytical category, one must have a verifiable doctrine to oppose to bourgeois error. "Like it or not," Foucault has said, ideology "always stands in virtual opposition to something else which is supposed to count as truth."[9] How much of Marx would remain intact after a Derridean reading had brought his latent religious affiliations – the teleology, the apocalyptic vision, the prophetic identification, and the rest – to the forefront?

In my view one of the signal failings of Derrida and his disciples has been their unwillingness to read Marx in the way they have so eagerly read Hegel and Kant. The question of whether, or to what degree, Marx's commitment to a univocal standard of truth, his truth, inspired his various disciples, from Lenin to Guzmán, to commit their barbarities remains one worth investigating. For Derrida could surely have found in Marx, who is Hegel's most consequential heir, and thus in some sense the major heir of metaphysics, rather than in Heidegger, the culminating move in an intellectual tradition devoted to suppressing different interpretations, and perhaps too to suppressing different people, by whatever means necessary. It is still worth asking whether Stalin, and indeed Pol Pot, were acting in Marx's spirit when they decided to fabricate intermediary stages of economic development, with all that entailed, in order to create the new society.

Even during the height of Derridean textualism, various thinkers actively tried to keep Marx's vision alive. For some time the objective of a lot of left-wing theorizing was to preserve the notion of ideology in a form that Marx would have been able at least dimly to recognize, while being responsive to those

---

[9] *The Foucault Reader*, ed. Paul Rabinow (New York: Pantheon, 1984), p. 60.

influential theorists who undermined claims to fixed truth. Post-structuralist thinking seemed to scare theoretical Marxists away from any but the most recondite notions of ideology. In the work of Althusser, Macherey, and the Terry Eagleton of *Ideology and Literature*, one finds attempts, often strained, often intellectually brilliant, to keep talking about ideology but to do so in ways that won't entirely traduce post-structuralist skepticism.[10]

The result is that these thinkers refine the concept of ideology to a point where it loses significant impact. Here, for example, is Eagleton elaborating Macherey and Althusser: "If the literary work can be seen as an ideological production to the second power, it is possible to see how that double-production may, as it were, partly cancel itself out, invert itself back into an analogue of knowledge."[11] The gist of this sentence is that when an ideology is submitted to the workings of literary form, then that ideology becomes more readily available to consciousness. Yet a phrase like "analogue of knowledge" seems to me a piece of sophistry: it gestures toward Derrida's style of interminable analysis with the word analogue, suggesting that the result of a successful ideological interpretation will be a mere analogue and itself interpretable. At the same time, the word "knowledge" indicates that there is a ground beneath all the reading, a ground that, given a Marxist understanding of the ultimately determining material base, we have access to. Though one may make a show of reading one's reading and so on, the truth is nonetheless available, perhaps always in hand.

At least for many, the force of Marx's thinking lies in its materialism. Simply open your eyes and look at the way most people are compelled to lead their lives, Marx insists. Put your theories and intellectual constructions in abeyance, and look at how many suffer, how grievously, and why. When one takes to manipulating rarefied abstractions, talking about "ideological production to the second power," then the immediacy, the tough-minded materialism, and the direct ethical vision are in danger of passing out of mind.

So why do so many critics writing in England and America in

---

[10] See Pierre Macherey, *A Theory of Literary Production* (London: Routledge and Kegan Paul, 1978).   [11] *Criticism and Ideology*, p. 85.

the latter part of this century bring the concept of ideology, and the philosophy from which it derives, into play? Why use it, given that Marx's version of ideology is for the most part too crude, and that post-structuralist versions, which beat the concept to an airy thinness, seem too remote? How, given these drawbacks, can a critic effectively put the concept of ideology to work? And why would anyone want to? To answer these questions, and a few others as well, I will turn to the writing of two accomplished younger critics, Marjorie Levinson, author of *Wordsworth's Great Period Poems*, and Marlon Ross, whose first book is titled *The Contours of Masculine Desire*.[12] Levinson and Ross embody some of the main tendencies in contemporary leftist historical criticism: their work will illustrate the power and the price of this energizing mode.

Levinson's first chapter on "Tintern Abbey" has, according to Paul Cantor, become a classic in the field of Romantic literary criticism.[13] Since Cantor's fine essay came out, her piece has been considered at some length by a pair of estimable writers, Thomas McFarland and Morris Dickstein.[14] Levinson's essay deserves the attention it has gotten. It is a richly researched piece that displays command of the whole field of Wordsworth scholarship, an awareness of major developments in contemporary literary theory, and a capacity for resourceful close reading. Ross's too is remarkable work; taking up a great range of writers from the Romantic period, it begins with a critique of gender politics in the Romantic poets and goes on to affirm a line of female writers who were their contemporaries and are, Ross thinks, worth studying now.

Yet neither of these critics qualifies as a major force in the way that de Man and Derrida, Foucault and Bloom undoubtedly do. Why then include them? Because they are representative, in

---

12 *Wordsworth's Great Period Poems* (Cambridge: Cambridge University Press, 1986); *The Contours of Masculine Desire: Romanticism and the Rise of Women's Poetry* (New York: Oxford University Press, 1989). Both books will be cited in the text.

13 "Stoning the Romance: the Ideological Critique of Nineteenth-Century Literature," *South Atlantic Quarterly*, 88:3 (1989) pp. 705–20.

14 McFarland, *William Wordsworth: Intensity and Achievement* (New York: Oxford University Press, 1992); Dickstein, *The Double Agent: The Critic and Society* (New York: Oxford University Press, 1992).

a way that no one as gifted and complex as these four writers could ever be, of some overall directions in current academic literary criticism. What Levinson and Ross assume, many others assume now as well. Levinson and Ross, as smart and well read as they are, write a kind of rank and file criticism, a criticism that is less self-guarded than, say, Paul de Man's, and which can, accordingly, teach us more about developing consensus in the academy. As W. K. Wimsatt observes, "In academic criticism you see less genius than in some other kinds, but more deliberacy, self-consciousness, program, literalism, and repetition."[15] With these two critics we enter the realm of intellectual consolidation that Wimsatt describes.

Levinson's historical approach to Wordsworth's great self-reflective poem epitomizes a shift in the way many academic Romanticists, and many critics overall, approach their subject. Behind *Fearful Symmetry*, Northrop Frye's 1947 book on Blake, and Geoffrey Hartman's well-known essays on Keats's *Hyperion* poems and "To Autumn" (collected in 1975), for example, was the conviction that in some sense the Romantic poets were still out ahead of us.[16] Frye believed that most of us had yet to come to terms with Blake's comprehensive view of the imagination; Hartman that the sort of naturalistic humanism Keats arrives at in his last poems might still cure contemporary aspirations to transcendence. Both critics write in styles beholden to the authors they endorse, attempting to transfer voice as well as values into their own cultural situations. Late in his career, Frye could still say, "Almost everything I know, I learned from Blake."

To Levinson, as to many Romanticists now, the time for such identifications is gone, for we no longer live in a world on which the Romantic metaphors have much bearing. It is the distance between the Romantics and ourselves, the argument continues, that permits more detached and revealing readings of their poetry

---

[15] *Hateful Contraries: Studies in Literature and Criticism* (Lexington: University of Kentucky Press, 1966), p. 5.

[16] *Fearful Symmetry: A Study of William Blake* (Princeton: Princeton University Press, 1947); "Spectral Symbolism and Authorial Self in Keats's *Hyperion*" and "Poem and Ideology: A Study of Keats's 'To Autumn,'" in *The Fate of Reading and Other Essays* (Chicago: University of Chicago Press, 1975), pp. 57–73 and 124–46 respectively.

than the sort that Hartman and Frye could muster, caught as they were in the Romantic ideology. In the case of Levinson's reading of "Tintern Abbey," temporal distance allows the critic to locate the "suppression" that produces the poem's sublime intensity. What precisely is this suppression and what is the new knowledge, purchased at the expense of alienation, that enables Levinson to see into the life of the Romantic poem?

What's blocked out of "Tintern Abbey," as Levinson understands it, is material reality, history in short. On the day that Wordsworth sets his poem, July 13, 1798, the Abbey's grounds would have been full of beggars, miserable and homeless, who lived by soliciting alms from the middle-class tourists refining their sensibilities among the ruins. The air around the Abbey would probably have been darkened by smoke from charcoal fires; the noise of the town ironworks, busy casting cannons for the war with France, would have grated against Wordsworth's somber meditations. The "cottage plots" are "green to the very door" because the common lands had been enclosed some time before and the only area left for the small householder to cultivate was his tiny front garden.

Then there is the matter of the poem's full title: "Lines Composed a Few Miles Above Tintern Abbey On Revisiting the Banks of the Wye During a Tour. July 13, 1798." Levinson points out that the date would be invested with strong political implications for Wordsworth: it marks the eight-year anniversary of Wordsworth's first visit to France; it's nine years after the original Bastille Day, and five after Marat's murder. Yet these political events do not enter the poem. They are canceled, erased, suppressed, to have recourse to some terms Levinson uses in her analysis. "[W]e are bound," she says, "to see that Wordsworth's pastoral prospect is a fragile affair, artfully assembled by acts of exclusion" (p. 32).

The strange mixture of meditative calm and extreme urgency that has intrigued readers of "Tintern Abbey," and frequently been assigned to Wordsworth's only partially acknowledged intimations about his own mortality, here receives a more material explanation. To the question posed by her students, which Levinson says helped get her inquiry into Wordsworth going,

"Where is the Abbey in the poem?" the essay replies that it is
suppressed, smoothed over by the idealizing strategies of this
archetypally Romantic work. Wordsworth's suppression banishes
unpalatable truths from his conscious mind into other mental
regions. Their continuing, subterranean pressure gives the poem
its anxious intensity. "[T]he primary poetic action," Levinson
writes, "is the suppression of the social" (p. 37).

Perhaps, the essay suggests, Romantic poetry, the poetry of
the inner self, is nothing more than a middle-class effort to evade
the press of too many people, the claims of society, one's responsibility to history. Maybe critics who do not challenge this Romantic ideology simply reproduce such evasions in the present.
Like Wordsworth's, the blindness of the Romantic critics might
stand as a testament to the horrors of contemporary, exploitative
capitalism, from which they, like their admired poets, are compelled to turn away. In Levinson's analysis, the homeless people
excluded from "Tintern Abbey" become, by implication, our
homeless, and those among us who sustain the Romantic ideology
of inwardness stand indicted. Perhaps the most eloquent statement
of the position remains Walter Benjamin's: Our cultural treasures,
he observes, "have an origin which [one] cannot contemplate
without horror. They owe their existence not only to the efforts
of the great minds and talents who have created them, but also
to the anonymous toil of their contemporaries." And then the
famous aphorism: "There is no document of civilization which
is not at the same time a document of barbarism."[17]

Levinson's view that a forced turn away from unpalatable
truths lies at the center of the Romantic project, both past and
present, is one in which Marlon Ross concurs. *The Contours of
Masculine Desire*, though, takes the "repression of femininity" to
be the crucial issue. Ross's hypothesis is that "the romantic
ideology of the strong poet develops out of fear of the feminine.
But," he adds, "in attempting to assure their own sociopolitical
strength by casting out and smoothing over the feminine, romantic
poets only manage to repress the feminine, which returns with
the full force of desire in many forms" (p. 10). Just as Levinson

[17] *Illuminations*, ed. Hannah Arendt (New York: Schoken Books, 1969), p. 256.

draws upon developments in Marxist thinking to analyze the Romantics' relation to history, so Ross employs contemporary gender theory to see into the Romantics' anxious desire to repudiate femininity.

Ross's focus on the "strong poet" calls to mind Harold Bloom (the subject of the fifth chapter) and Ross is in a certain odd sense a Bloomian critic. Following Bloom, Ross reads Romantic poetry as being awash in Oedipal strife, filial rivalry, and the uninhibited worship of power. Ross's Romantics are imperialists of the aesthetic realm, modeling themselves after the military conquerors, entrepreneurs, and statesmen of their day. Throughout the book's first half, in which Ross reflects on the "construction" of the Romantic poetical character, he takes Bloom's "The Internalization of Quest Romance" and *Anxiety of Influence* quite literally, except that he condemns the creative agon that Bloom, in general, celebrates.[18] *The Contours of Masculine Desire* is a sort of *Harold Bloom Moralisé*.

Can one disagree with critics like Ross and Levinson, critics whose voices are so self-assured, and whose ethical imperatives so admirable? For what makes them impatient with the Romantic ethos is, of course, what they take to be its appalling social cost. If as Frye, and Bloom and Hartman after him have argued, Romanticism is rightly understood as the internalization of Romance, with the poet, however implicitly, taking the part of the questing knight, then what about the roles automatically conferred on those others who, because of gender or education or class, have no access to the quest? Inevitably they will be left out, suppressed as Levinson would see it; or they will be stereotyped to serve the needs of the unfolding fiction, as Ross believes women are in most Romantic work.

If Romantic poetry is essentially a displaced chivalric form endorsing Anglo-Saxon male power (making it prescient for Lewis Carroll to call his parody of "Resolution and Independence" "The White Knight's Song"), and if we still live to some degree within the Romantic ideology, then the work of demystification

---

[18] "The Internalization," in *The Ringers in the Tower: Studies in Romantic Tradition* (Chicago: University of Chicago Press, 1971), pp. 13–35; *The Anxiety of Influence: A Theory of Poetry* (New York: Oxford University Press, 1973). Both volumes will be cited in the text.

that Ross and Levinson undertake must be of crucial importance. In what better way can the professor of Romantic poetry contribute to spreading social justice? And how could one criticize the political strategies of Ross and Levinson without oneself being aptly accused of serving repressive interests?

One might, first of all, question the subtlety of Ross's reading of the Romantics', and especially Wordsworth's, conception of gender, doing so not without gratitude to Ross for insisting on the issue's importance. Keeping within the Freudian vocabulary, then, it is worth pointing out that Wordsworth's attitude to femininity is better described as a matter of ambivalence than of repression. In "The Ruined Cottage," which was probably Wordsworth's first great poem (F. R. Leavis thought it his finest overall), it's clear that some part of Wordsworth identifies passionately with Margaret, the woman who pines away and dies of grief for her missing husband. Margaret is someone who can't let go. She perishes because she will not surrender her attachment to the past, her drive to recover what Wordsworth, reflecting later on his own early bliss, would describe as "the glory and the dream." Margaret is akin to those poets Wordsworth describes in "Resolution and Independence" who begin in gladness, with a preternatural capacity for joy. But the danger is that they come – as a direct result of their early power for feeling bliss – to ruin. "We Poets in our youth begin in gladness;/But thereof come in the end despondency and madness."[19]

Such figures appear again and again in Wordsworth: think not only of Margaret, but of Lucy, of the Winander Boy, Dorothy in "Tintern Abbey," and also (looking back to chapter 1) the child of the great Ode. These figures, always women and children, are Wordsworthian images for the source of poetic power. And yet the poet also knows that a full identification with any of them would end tragically: it would mean living almost entirely without defences, as Burns and Chatterton struck Wordsworth as having done. Thus the proliferation in Wordsworth of chastening wisdom figures: Armytage in "The Ruined Cottage,"

[19] *Poems*, I:553.

the old leech-gatherer in "Resolution and Independence," the Cumberland Beggar, the discharged soldier in *The Prelude*, figures who seem so stoically self-reliant as to be nearly invulnerable.

One approach to Wordsworth would involve a careful tracing of the dialectics between his figures of passion and of restraint, for Wordsworth is movingly restless in his desire to conceive and conceive again responses to the question, "How do I go on living, defending myself against the extreme susceptibility of a figure like Margaret, but how do I continue, too, to have access to her voice, her sensibility?" For without that sensibility, what we would recognize as authentically Wordsworthian poetry would not be possible. The poetry that comes from the mouths of characters like Armytage tends to be neoclassically sententious:

> "I see around me here
> Things which you cannot see. We die, my Friend,
> Nor we alone, but that which each man loved
> And prized in his peculiar nook of earth
> Dies with him"

Armytage says to the young narrator of "The Ruined Cottage."[20] But that is only one strain of Wordsworth's voice. His major poetry lives in the dialectic between spontaneity and defence, joy and stoicism, Margaret and Armytage. To claim, as Ross does, that the feminine is repressed in Wordsworth is to blunt Wordsworth's subtlety in the interest of a contemporary cultural polemic.

Yet it is quite possible that a critic like Ross, even if he were to accept my account of Wordsworth's self-making achievement, with its *ambivalent* relations to femininity, might decide that it was still in the interest of his readers and students to criticize Wordsworth's images of women. Wordsworth allegorizes his female figures and does so all through his major work. But at what point does allegory pass into stereotype? Perhaps Romantic stereotypes do inform contemporary culture, and to the detriment of women and men both. Perhaps there are better ways of talking about gender than those the Romantics used.

[20] *Romantic Poetry and Prose*, eds. Harold Bloom and Lionel Trilling (New York: Oxford University Press, 1973), p. 132.

Yet a writer disposed to such critique needs to take into account another instance of what I've been referring to as the rule of critical compensation: to the degree that you read a text analytically, to the degree that your terminology claims to encompass it, claims to know the text better than it knows itself, to that degree you give up the possibility of being read by it. If you limit your focus to gender (as Ross and many others now largely do) and find the text culpable, then depart from it, how much that is rich and potentially invigorating will you overlook?

Wordsworth, as I see it anyway, continues to challenge us, asking, among other things, how much we have turned against our capacity for vital joy. For being "blindly with [your] blessedness at strife" is, to Wordsworth, almost everyone's lot in an age obsessed with knowledge devoid of feeling. It's the ability to be interrogated by great writing that the single-minded analytical reader sacrifices, and such a reader ought to think carefully about whether the exchange is worth it. A good deal of contemporary analytical criticism seems to me motivated, at least in part, by a fear of transferring power to major works. In this context one recalls that Narcissus's response to his many wooers before he fell in love with his image in the pool was simple and abrupt: "I'll die before I give you power over me." Some works we read; others have the capacity to read and interpret us. It's a matter of critical taste, and critical modesty, to discern the difference.

What then of Levinson's historical critique of Wordsworth and his Romantic ideology? How much heed should one pay it?

In general, Wordsworth's major lyrics emerge from times of intense inner strife, moments when whatever means of figuring the self are at the poet's disposal no longer suffice, no longer provide access to experiential joy or poetic vitality. As life goes on, and the prospect of death becomes more intense, erupting unexpectedly into the mind, it becomes necessary to rebel with more vitalizing – and effectively defensive – fictions.

Part of the genius of "Tintern Abbey" is in the way Wordsworth refigures his own self-preserving urge. It is memory in this poem that holds the childhood self at just the right distance, close enough for Wordsworth to feel its powers, distant enough so he isn't overcome by the allure. For to merge with the child (as Wordsworth, as I argued in the first chapter, does, albeit temporarily, in "Intimations") would be to dissolve every defence. So Shelley, from a Wordsworthian perspective at least, makes himself wildly vulnerable by stripping himself down permanently to pure desire. Saying that "I always go on until I am stopped and I never am stopped" is about as far from a Wordsworthian formulation as one is likely to get, as is the stunning speech that ends *Prometheus Unbound* and culminates in the resolve "To love, and bear; to hope till Hope creates/From its own wreck the thing it contemplates."[21] Shelley, in a Wordsworthian diagnosis, courts poetic extremism and experiential ruin in part because he cannot conceive for himself a humane principle of inner authority, a figure like Armytage, or "Tintern Abbey"'s memory. When Shelley arrives at major fictions of authority, they take forms like the tyrannical Jupiter, insane Count Cenci, or the horrible chariot heading the procession in *The Triumph of Life*. No Wordsworthian dialectic between desire and limit is possible in Shelley, which is part of what moves some of us about him. It's as though he were determined to write in Margaret's, or the child's, unmediated voice and suffer the consequences.

Wordsworth's movement in "Tintern Abbey" from an allegorical figure like Armytage, with his neoclassical associations (there's something of Samuel Johnson in his sensibility, at least at the beginning of the poem), to a myth of memory represents an advance in inwardness and in self-reliance. The structure of defence is now Wordsworth's own, not something that derives from an imagined teacher. Wordsworth wanted to be as upright and strong as Milton was, but with as little external support, be it theological or cultural, as possible.

It's also important that Wordsworth's new-found mode of defence works as a device for self-excavation or, more grandly, self-divination. His reliance on private memory gave him new material for poetry; it helped him both to preserve and to create. *The Prelude* is the result of Wordsworth's intuition, articulated in "Tintern Abbey," to the effect that he could use memory to write a new kind of poem and to become another sort of person

---

[21] *Shelley: Poetical Works*, ed. Thomas Hutchinson (London: Oxford University Press, 1967), p. 268.

than he had been. True, at the end of the poem Wordsworth has already begun to suspect his myth of memory. He delegates to Dorothy the role of sustaining her youthful intensity lest, in times to come, his "genial spirits . . . decay." To some, this is no doubt a confession of failure. To me it is the impressive proof of Wordsworth's tough-minded ability to turn and doubt himself, which he does more than once in "Tintern Abbey," interrogating his own process of self-renewal with all the rigor he can muster. But the turn to Dorothy, and the doubt implicit there, also convey Wordsworth's sense that no mode of self-creation and defence will work forever. Invention must in time displace what it has most lovingly and arduously made. For myself, I take Wordsworth's mode of self-remaking to be timely; I see no reason why one might not adapt it to contemporary purposes.

Levinson on the other hand makes continual reference to the distance that separates us from the Romantics, and that compels a critical, detached reading of their work. We know things, she says on a few occasions, that they did not. But what precisely they are, she doesn't say. One can, however, infer them. The shadow that she perceives falling between us and Wordsworth belongs to Karl Marx, and Levinson relies on Marx's view that history, and in particular material history, is the crucial determining force for any significant event. The historical narrative isn't, for Levinson, one among a competing or tensely collaborating group of stories; it's *the* story.

Anyone who, faced with a consequential event, doesn't develop a version of the materialist historical narrative is in the grip of ideology. Thus the standard for all writing becomes the standard of history writing. If a historian describing the Wye valley late in the eighteenth century had refused to see the pollution, the beggars, and the ruins, she would obviously have failed her craft. But is the same thing true for a poet? To Levinson all writing that isn't history, and materialist history at that, must stand accused.

Levinson doesn't lay out and defend this view, I suspect, because in the current intellectual climate it is close to indefensible. Critics now are, quite rightly, skeptical about claims to transcendence, to encompassing narratives that assume they trace the ultimate horizon of meaning. Levinson has recourse to standard and frequently criticized versions of ideology and knowledge. One thinks again of Foucault's remark, "Like it or not," ideology "always stands in virtual opposition to something else which is supposed to count as truth." And truth, in a transcendental sense, is today in bad repute – deservedly so.

To me, when Wordsworth chronicles his inner drama in "Tintern Abbey" he does not erase, or even denigrate the historical situation; he is simply absorbed in another matter, one of no greater or less *essential* importance than the material or the historical. Wordsworth's inward movement is comparable to the one effected in Freudian therapy, with the crucial difference that Wordsworth will concede to no one's terms for representing the drama of the inner self but his own. So understood, Wordsworth's poetry is, as I suggested in the first chapter, a poetry of performance and of process, unfolding throughout his great period. Every major poem rewrites the last one and, too, all of those that come before.

What I'm saying is that the inward turn of Wordsworth's poetry is part of its design, and that the allegorization of the ostensibly human figures is so as well. Wordsworth believed, as many people in the West have for some time, that severe introspection is the chief means by which the self can be transformed. Such introspection, therapeutic in its intent, may well be a prerequisite for effective action, action which can, but need not, be of a public nature. To be effective in the public world, one needs to know the difference between anger at political injustice and resentment against one's neglectful father, between the present and the past. This is perhaps something that only introspection can achieve.

Levinson's work has an oddly mixed quality about it. In one way, her criticism is oriented to the present: she asks whether developments in historiography and philosophy haven't made Wordsworth obsolete. Does Marx's system put Wordsworth completely under eclipse? But she answers that question by recourse to the past, answers it metaphysically. She seeks for "Tintern Abbey"'s origins, under the assumption that once you know where a poem comes from, you know its meaning. An

Emersonian approach is concerned with questions of use and of value. What can you do with this poem? Does it help you to use language better, to talk to yourself, to understand the uses of the world? From my point of view, Levinson would be doing something much more valuable if she asked directly whether conceiving of the self in terms akin to Wordsworth's, in our moment, the cultural present, would inevitably be conducive to political quietism, and then stayed in the present to answer, rather than retreating into a story about poetic origins.

As amusing as Carroll is in "The White Knight's Song," the poem continually betrays a fear of inwardness, a fear that Wordsworth continues, even in the present, to provoke. But why does he do so? What is it about Wordsworth's poetry that has so frequently of late made it the object of purportedly demystifying criticism? To answer I have to enlarge the sense of Wordsworth's achievement that I have offered so far. For his greatest poetry is far more than a triumph in conceptual self-reinvention, though it is that. Wordsworth's voice, which is both idiosyncratic and, in Arnold's apt term, inevitable, is also central to what he offers a reader. The voice of the poems in which Wordsworth discovers fresh self-descriptions is the evidence he offers for their renewing power. And though his voice modulates somewhat from poem to poem, one thing seems constant, at least in his best work: Wordsworth, to put it simply, will not divorce feeling and thought.

At the climax of "Tintern Abbey," for example, Wordsworth succeeds in finding a formulation for the state of being that, removed as he now is and will always be from childhood's full immersion in nature, he hopes to cultivate and cherish:

> For I have learned
> To look on nature, not as in the hour
> Of thoughtless youth; but hearing oftentimes
> The still, sad music of humanity,
> Nor harsh nor grating, though of ample power
> To chasten and subdue.[22]

The crucial phrase "still, sad music of humanity" beautifully conveys what Wordsworth has gained through his humane re-

---

[22] *Poems*, I:360.

nunciation; but with its subtle echoes and dignified but unforced fluid rhythms the phrase also allows a reader to experience for a moment the emotional state, which is both calm and slightly elevated, that attends on deciding to live one's life as much for others as for oneself.

Wordsworth always wants to be as precise as he can in describing spiritual conditions. I can't think of another major poet who is as willing to bring forward qualifications and distinctions. "Nor harsh nor grating": yet though full of such negative constructions, "Tintern Abbey" remains a passionate poem. For Wordsworth insists that along with its very impressive strength of intellectual discernment, his poetry must have the right tone of feeling. But just as criticism has largely turned away from the visual element of literary experience, it also now habitually ignores its music.

Part of what may make it difficult to appreciate Wordsworth's intellectual power is that he thinks differently from most of us. Unlike that of most literary critics, Wordsworth's thinking is not oppositional or agonistic. His mind is non-violent. He doesn't pit ideas against one another dialectically, stripping them down to pure force, to fighting weight. In fact, one might speculate that it is Wordsworth's avoidance of the dialectic that allows him to sustain emotion even in the most intricate intellectual turnings of his poetry. He's prone to let his mind wander, open to distraction and ostensible irrelevance, confident that so long as it maintains contact with his life of feeling, it will go where it needs to go to restore him. And this, I think, helps make his mind's workings so strange and so hard to assimilate to existing critical models.

Wordsworth's refusal to allow thought and feeling to split – and to me he thinks as well as almost anyone – is a powerful reproof to our contemporary culture of academic theory. To many theorists it is only the action of the mind in recoil from common experience and from the life of feeling that can produce knowledge, usually negative knowledge, that is worth having. (Recall Plato's insistence, in his assault on the poets, that the philosopher isn't prone to excess emotion – unlike a woman, unlike a child.) Theory often begins by saying "No" to what is given in common experience and what is possessed by non-intellectuals. (This negative gesture is, of course, related to the philosopher's dictum to stop and think that I, relying on Havelock and Arendt, described in the prologue.) The ethos of alienation that informs theory – that informs Ross and Levinson as much as Derrida and de Man – is one that Wordsworth would have recognized both as a tendency in himself (he describes it in *The Prelude* under the heading "Imagination and Taste, How Impaired and Restored")and as a principle that encouraged some of the worst excesses in the French Revolution. "We murder to dissect," as he put it in "The Tables Turned."

There is thus a good deal at stake in the polemic contemporary academic criticism has aimed at Wordsworth. If some of the things I have said about his achievement have been said before, it seems worth repeating them (often, as Doctor Johnson observes, we need to be reminded more than to be informed), for we have reached a point where Wordsworth's fate within Anglo-American literary culture is at issue. It is an open question whether he will, in twenty years, be part of university curriculums; or, if he is, whether he will function as anything more than a cautionary exemplar of errors recently overcome.

To me, "Tintern Abbey" remains a poem of our moment, and of the future, for the dilemma that Wordsworth dramatizes there continues in many ways to be ours: the self that achieves its freedom by skeptically regarding all established beliefs, social and religious, and making a sustaining myth about its own identity, has a vulnerable and tenuous being. Always it is in danger of being shattered by loss or suffering in that it has no generally accredited story to tell about how we'll meet again in a future life, or how later generations will be free thanks to our sacrifice. "Tintern Abbey" indicates that all there is to do when one self is ruined is to try to create another with the same flimsy materials. Any recourse in the face of crisis to an exterior certainty, be it religion, law, or history, is a betrayal of the hard earned skepticism in which Wordsworthian self-making begins. Is our own situation, honestly considered, very much different?

One may grant that critics could plausibly, on political and ethical grounds, reject the West's faith in introspection, and the

Cartesian insistence that the individual subject is the primary arbiter of reality. The critical objective, then, would be to refigure the self in more comprehensively social terms. And one could easily see such an inventive procedure beginning with a critique of Wordsworth – beginning but not ending there. One would be compelled then to offer a competing story, another truth, about how to conceive of identity and history, and let readers decide whose is better, yours or Wordsworth's. The burden of being an intellectual in a democracy is to convince people to switch terminologies, to jettison ways of talking that they've gotten used to. People ought to be asked to get rid of habitual ways of seeing and saying not because they are functions of repression, or ideological constructs, but because alternate ways will help them to live better.

Ever since "Tintern Abbey" was published, readers of many sorts have protested its intense inwardness, and for a variety of reasons. But what has been more difficult than articulate protest has been coming up with tenable alternatives to what Keats called Wordsworth's egotistical sublime. And to this failing the Marxist tradition has been particularly susceptible. Pondering the future of the human spirit under socialism, Marx offered a passing thought about someone who was a hunter in the morning, a fisherman in the afternoon, and a critical critic at night. Trotsky, a more supple mind, reportedly said that under true communism everyone would need less sleep and that sex would improve. Good enough. But what we have not had are comprehensive imaginings of a socially comprised self that is as richly persuasive, challenging, and complex as the inward being that Wordsworth unfolds.

For their part, Levinson and Ross are much less interested in telling a fresh story about gender, history, and the subject than they are in discrediting Wordsworth's (and the other Romantics' as well). And the chief means for discrediting him is to find his supposed blind spots and to insist on their own powers of discernment. Wordsworth is who he is because he suppresses history; or because he represses femininity. They know him better than he knows himself.

The power that results from finding a critical position that will fix the truth of Romantic writing once and for all is akin to the power that people have sought for some time from metaphysical systems. If the essential drive of Romantic writing is to impose "masculine hegemony" or to suppress history, or anything else for that matter, then Romanticism can come at last under the control of concepts: "Wordsworth, yes, we know what he's all about." But a more accurate way to understand Romantic writing, I think, is as striving to render experience in such a way that it cannot be assimilated to oppressive normative principles, or to those that are likely to arise in the future. Surely one can say that Wordsworth, at a certain point in his career, does stop changing, does let go of his willingness to slough off needless confinements. But the part of Wordsworth that responds to the press of events with new invention continues, as I have tried to show, to be out ahead of us. It dramatizes the need for spiritual renovation in a world from which God has departed, and gives us examples of what that renovation might entail. It urges us, gently, to try to do likewise. Then too Wordsworth's invention persists, transferred into Keats and Shelley, Emerson and Whitman, and into those critics of Romanticism who have understood that no stabilizing analysis will do Romantic work justice.

Harold Bloom's best criticism is Romantic not because it excludes female experience, or because it ignores historical pressures, but because it is speculative and surprising, and answers Romantic invention not just with philosophical stabilities (which, alas, it sometimes does) but with more invention. Wordsworth had to revise his inner relations to go on living and writing, and he mediated those relations through figures like Armytage, Margaret, the Winander Boy, and Nature: just so Bloom writes a critical poem on the shiftings of his own spiritual life in which the key mediating figures include Blake, Coleridge, Shelley, and Wordsworth (much more interesting names to give interior energies than, say, ego, super-ego, and id). Bloom, in the most valuable dimension of his work, isn't out to get Romanticism right once and for all, but to revise his relations to it (thus revising himself) and to perpetuate its energies. Bloom says that he's a comic critic who seems condemned to getting serious readings.

And Ross's seriousness, like Levinson's, is of the highest order.

Each critic has, after all, uncovered a dynamic that determines Romantic writing; each has arrived at the somber truth about what makes Wordsworth and the Romantics in general what they are. "The theory of repression," the Dutch psychoanalyst J. H. van den Berg has written, "is closely related to the thesis that there is a sense in everything, which in turn implies that everything is past and there is nothing new."[23] Applying a theory of repression to Wordsworth is an effort to relegate him to the past, to literary history. (Suppression sounds like a more nuanced diagnosis, suggesting that Wordsworth carries out his mental operations "both consciously and unawares," but Levinson is in complete possession of that latter element, that which the poet cannot know.) Once he's been brought under the rule of concepts, Wordsworth is someone who can't surprise us any more. But as Freud himself came very close to admitting, wielding the theory of repression puts the interpreter in a "Heads I win, tails you lose" situation. If the subject agrees with the interpretation, the interpreter must be right; if she disagrees, well, how could she not? Freud did give the patient an out: she could disagree calmly enough to persuade the therapist that he was mistaken. But works of art are mute, and can offer no rebuttal to the charge of repression. Other readers who would counter the charge are, naturally, repressing or suppressing matters in their own right. With one word, Ross and Levinson could dismiss the arguments I've offered thus far.

Once someone makes central use of categories like suppression, no real critical conversation is possible. What one faces then is cultural politics by fiat. And here it's worth making a distinction between Ross and Levinson on the one hand, and a New Historicist like Stephen Greenblatt (whom I will discuss in the next chapter). Greenblatt's criticism focuses on the ways that energy circulates from cultural productions into politics and social life, then back again. He claims, for example, that *King Lear* reworks material given to it by contemporary controversies over exorcism, and that the reworking has a bearing in the public

[23] *The Changing Nature of Man: Introduction to a Historical Psychology*, trans. H. F. Croes (New York: Delta, 1961), p. 176.

world.[24] *Lear* doesn't repress exorcism: that would be to swallow the subject up, make it disappear with only the most oblique traces. Accordingly, Greenblatt's text constitutes an interpretation, a story; one may construe his facts differently (many have); one may say that his facts aren't facts at all, or that important ones have been neglected (a few have). But at least one may disagree, propose another story.

A reader who claims to uncover a determining obfuscation is attempting to achieve the interpretive sublime, an act not quite transcendental but descendental, in that it seeks penetration to ultimate depths rather than contact with a deity who reigns on high. Of course it's an open question as to why, after William James, Richard Rorty, and Jacques Derrida, one can still claim godlike powers of penetration in a critical text. There is also the matter of the arbitrariness that critical descendentalism can entail: within loose boundaries, you can anoint almost any demiurge as the invisible prime mover of the poem. Levinson's history and Ross's femininity join a list of Wordsworthian repressions that already includes the precursor, sado-masochistic sex, death, the mother, and the future. What is it that could motivate such outdated and coercive approaches to a great poem? What's at stake in asserting that Wordsworth didn't know enough, or couldn't force enough through inner resistances to be a credible poet in this, a more comprehensively aware cultural moment?

It's important, I think, to see the historical critics' claim to a larger knowledge than the Romantics possessed within the tradition of critical response to Romanticism. For the charge that the Romantics did not know enough is not unfamiliar. The famous passage from Matthew Arnold's "The Function of Criticism" runs as follows:

It has long seemed to me that the burst of creative activity in our literature, through the first quarter of this century, had about it, in fact, something premature; and that from this cause its productions are doomed, most of them, in spite of the sanguine hopes which accompanied and do still accompany them, to prove hardly more lasting than the productions of far less splendid epochs. And this prematureness

[24] *Shakespearean Negotiations: The Circulation of Social Energy in Renaissance England* (Berkeley and Los Angeles: University of California Press, 1988). Henceforth cited in the text.

comes from its having proceeded without having its proper data, without sufficient materials to work with. In other words, the English poetry of the first quarter of this century, with plenty of energy, plenty of creative force, did not know enough.[25]

Did not know enough: in the Age of Freud, the critic is compelled to translate that well-known phrase, so that "did not know enough" becomes had repressed or suppressed too much. (Levinson speaks at one point of "the wisdoms [sic] of our own moment, that very wisdom Wordsworth could not, in 1798, produce" [p. 45].) The best-known inheritor of Arnold's sentiment about Romanticism was T. S. Eliot, who castigated Romantic poetry for being "fragmentary," "immature," and "chaotic," as opposed to Classical work: complete, adult, and orderly – knowledgeable as well, no doubt.

With Arnold and Eliot, as with Levinson and Ross, criticizing the Romantics for their ignorance in contrast to some stable principle of knowledge is inseparable from a desire to serve culture by proposing normative ethical and political values. I am arguing, then, that the drive to cultural stability matters as much as the values in the name of which the critical process proceeds. And Levinson and Ross are right in much the way Arnold and Eliot were in being hostile to the Romantics: no one who wishes to set a "myth of concern" (Northrop Frye's phrase) in place is going to have much use for Emerson or Shelley, or for a great deal of what Wordsworth wrote, either.

How, then, to return to the question with which I began this chapter, do writers like Levinson and Ross manage, in the interest of philosophical stability, to preserve the notion of ideology? How do they rehabilitate an antiquated concept and use it as the fulcrum for a potent criticism? The answer should by now be plain. In effect they do to Marx what Paul de Man did to Coleridge. They add Freud. With Freud's theory of repression, Marx and one of his least tenable ideas can be resuscitated. When Levinson speaks of "enabling blindness" (p. 44) she is echoing de Man, with the difference that to her it is history, rather than, as he would have it, temporality, that is being erased.

[25] *Essays in Criticism*, pp. 12–13.

But her rhetoric of blindness and insight, and her drive to disenfranchise poetry on behalf of metaphysical thought are entirely
de Manian. At times, it seems that criticism will go to any lengths
to fulfill its chief current function, the disciplining of poetry.

The description I have offered thus far may seem unfair to two
talented and learned critics who take themselves to be on the
left, not like Arnold and Eliot at all. Surely it makes a difference
to align oneself, however critically, with the tradition of Marx?
Arnold and Eliot were critics of the middle class, and overall not
displeased with that fact. But to what degree are Ross and
Levinson – and indeed most members of the cultural left writing
today – authentically Marxist? When the students who got
Levinson's critical project moving by asking her where the Abbey
was in the poem become graduate students, they may ask her
another question on the building and grounds theme: "Where
was the university in your analysis?" In other words, why do
contemporary forms of criticism that seem devoted to leftist politics
rarely address, in *practical* ways, the institutional situation from
which they arise?

In 1976, Richard Ohmann published *English in America*, a
book that viewed professors of English as a class, and reflected
on their productive function within the prevailing capitalist
economy.[26] Ohmann argues that the profession functions ideo-
logically for English professors. To him, our immersion in scholarly
writing, in various learned societies, in conferences, in the com-
pilation of bibliographies, and the production of authorized
editions serves to disguise from ourselves and others our real
social role. Our true task, Ohmann believes, is to serve capitalism.
We teach students to write clearly and to abstract the meaning
of texts, to be punctual and obedient in ways that will directly
serve the needs of the corporate world. We take pains to choose
those students who will join the elites, and to eliminate the ones
who, for whatever reason, would not fit in. All of our professional
exertions divert us from recognizing this fundamental, and rather
unglamorous, economic role.

[26] *English in America: A Radical View of the Profession* (New York: Oxford University Press).

Ohmann's argument is sometimes simplistic. For one thing, he uses the very same analytic skills that universities dispense, supposedly in the interest of capitalism, to challenge the existing system. By his own example, what's going on in freshman composition can't be all bad. Then too he employs the elementary notion of ideology-as-cover-story that's well worth getting rid of. Yet whatever its reductions, *English in America* is extremely provocative: with the leftward turn in the academy, it would seem logical to start refining Ohmann's views, and considering the practical politics he enjoins. Something comparable has been going on in the Critical Legal Studies movement, where Duncan Kennedy and others have been writing what amount to anthropological critiques of the tribal customs alive in law school and the legal profession, while offering lots of suggestions for reform.[27] But this is not happening in any dramatic way in the English departments. There have been plenty of studies of the profession published over the past ten years, but most have little to say about our relations to the economy and to society overall, and few make suggestions for practical reform.

In little of the work from the cultural left that I have read is anyone particularly worried about how as a professor of English one must be sustained by, and help sustain, a culture that's taken to be exploitative, racist, and phallogocentric. Few professors, if any, seem to be writing essays enjoining their colleagues to cease dispensing grades, or to stop sending letters of recommendation to corporations involved in global weapons sales. There is very little critical discussion on the rhetoric of recommendations, one of our major links to the world outside the classroom. Nor does anyone seem particularly interested in abolishing the hierarchies that preside in English departments, hierarchies that at times can make the Vatican look rather free-form.

There is a great deal of talk in the academy about subversive criticism, but in general that means intellectual, or ideological subversion. Anyone wishing to try out some more localized subversion might do what I suspect Oscar Wilde would were he

---

[27] See Kennedy's *Legal Education and the Reproduction of Hierarchy: A Polemic Against the System* (Cambridge, Mass.: Afar, 1983).

compelled to become a professor: stop giving grades and begin speaking almost exclusively about the sensuous pleasures to be had from literary art. By going on about pleasure, you will threaten literary study's status as a discipline based on knowledge, and thus worthy of institutional nurture; by shutting off the grades, you interfere with business. The latter will get you the dean's immediate attention; but the former, though slower to be noticed, may finally cause more consternation.

The move to left-wing criticism has, to say the least, not inclined us to look critically enough at either our motives or our methods of teaching. An important question along these lines arises out of a passage from Hannah Arendt's superb book, *Between Past and Future*. "The educators," she says there, "stand in relation to the young as representatives of a world for which they must assume responsibility although they themselves did not make it, and even though they may, secretly or openly, wish it were other than it is."[28] The notion of ideology works to absolve intellectuals from the responsibility that Arendt feels they must accept in order to introduce others to the world. For it allows one to claim a purified space: it's the others who are hemmed in by bourgeois consciousness, not me. One of the most productive kinds of tension that can arise in the classroom, I think, comes from the willingness of teachers to identify themselves, even if ambivalently, with existing social forms, and submit those forms, and implicitly themselves, to the critical attention of their students. For the teacher to join students in the freedom to doubt everything from no particular position may bring pedagogical acclaim, but it fails to convey how tough established social forms can be. Professors who partake of middle-class comforts and deride the system unqualifiedly aren't owning up to the compromises they've had to negotiate.

These reflections on contemporary pedagogy point to what, by now, is probably an obvious conclusion: the kind of left criticism that one encounters in Ross and Levinson, and all through literary studies at present, is not, in Marx's sense, political. That is, it does not concern itself with material, but with ideological issues.

[28] *Between Past and Future: Six Exercises in Political Thought* (Cleveland: World Publishing, 1963), p. 189.

Such criticism is, I think, open to the charges that Marx made in *The German Ideology* against the Young Hegelians: "Since [they] consider conceptions, thoughts, ideas, in fact all the products of consciousness, to which they attribute an independent existence, as the real chains of men . . . it is evident that the Young Hegelians have to fight only against these illusions of consciousness."[29] Inevitably there will be a philosophical or conceptual dimension to any Marxist work. But Arendt was also right to say that Marx's impact on Western thinking derived in considerable part from his reversing the standard philosophical view that held the life of the mind to be superior to the life of action. From the Marxist perspective, cultural criticism unattached to plans for material transformation, even transformation of one's immediate material surroundings, counts as nothing better than an attempt, characteristic of all idealist philosophies, to "solve the world" rather than changing it.

At the point where one turns away from practice (and even praxis), as the cultural left in America largely has, and tries to provide culture with some useful ethical and intellectual standards, then, even if the preferred terms are commonly associated with Marx, the project is far more in the spirit of Arnold. It is also close to the philosopher's project when she is determined to get a vocabulary in place that will help people to live better and that will last. Arnoldian criticism has been accurately described as the process of making literature available to the uses of culture, and that is what Ross and Levinson attempt to do. The best concise Romantic rebuttal is probably Blake's: "One Law for the Lion and Ox is Oppression."

So far I have been critical of Ross and Levinson, and of the sort of work I take them to exemplify, a criticism that uses a materially inflected version of the blindness and insight motif to contribute to the philosophical disenfranchisement of poetry. Though I hope that I have indicated a regard for their learning and intelligence, it must be plain that my disagreement with them – my wish to take the part of poetry against what I see as their

[29] P. 41.

inadequate conceptual critiques – is nearly unequivocal. Nearly.
For I do think that they, and many other critics who have been
influenced by Marx, exemplify an invaluable drive. I can describe
this enriching tendency – and challenge one of the reigning pieties
in contemporary literary studies – by contrasting *The Contours of
Masculine Desire* and *Wordsworth's Great Period Poems* with a book
that, on the face of it, appears to be committed to the defence of
poetry.

In *Wordsworth and the Enlightenment*, a book published around
the same time as Ross's and Levinson's, Alan Bewell had an
ideal chance to write criticism that both praises invention and
exemplifies the inventive drive.[30] Bewell sets out to show where
Wordsworth's poetry participates in Enlightenment anthropological discourse, and – by far the more important point – where
and how Wordsworth renews what the tradition gives him. For
Bewell, Wordsworth continually succeeds in translating what
were, in the writings of the *philosophes*, abstract case studies of
outcasts into narratives about human beings whose dignity is
comparable to the poet's and the reader's. Thus Bewell sees
Wordsworth's depiction of female isolates such as Goody Blake
and the Mad Mother as revising the Enlightenment discourse
on witchcraft, rendering former objects of persecution in sympathetic ways, and so enlarging the number of different kinds of
persons that his readers can think of as part of the human
community. And, Bewell argues, in these women Wordsworth
finds images for his own imaginative workings. Bewell's Wordsworth is alive to the issue of gender, and concerned to reform
the class politics of his day.

Bewell's book is genuinely historicist work, attempting to take
Wordsworth on his own terms and complicate our sense of his
relation to the Enlightenment. The book shows what Wordsworth
does, for example, to recast Enlightenment treatises on idiots,
on wild children and savages, on the origins of religion, on natural
history, on human attitudes toward death. In doing so, Bewell
works in a mode eloquently commended by Milan Kundera:
"Without criticism, the discoveries effected by art go unnamed

[30] *Wordsworth and the Enlightenment: Nature, Man, and Society in the Experimental Poetry* (New
Haven: Yale University Press, 1989).

and thereby remain absent from the history of art, for a work enters history and becomes *visible* there only if its discoveries, its innovations, are specified and recognized. Without the meditative background that is criticism, works become isolated gestures, ahistorical accidents, soon forgotten . . ."[31]

Bewell is a formidable scholar, as one would have to be to undertake his task. Is it ungrateful then to observe that he renders Wordsworth as too much a scholar, a servant to the logic of the next step, dutifully revising and revising? His Wordsworth offers something very much like an intellectual's critique of the Enlightenment, a carefully worked out response to its practices and values. And often what is most surprising and moving in Wordsworth disappears in Bewell's book into meticulously constructed intellectual history. For Wordsworth doesn't just put forward an alternative to Enlightenment values as a politician might put forward a reform bill; his poetry conveys the energy that could aid a reader who would transform and truly humanize the ruling assumptions of his or her own day.

The problem is commonplace among comprehensive scholars like Bewell. Frequently the labor of learning required to speak knowingly about where a writer actually departs from her context conditions the critic's mind to the belief that all mental action must take the form of gradual unfolding. The scholar has trouble conceiving of a mind that works more swiftly and intuitively. Goethe is to the point: "Thought expands but lames; action animates but narrows."

Perhaps even at its most sympathetic, historical criticism is disposed against fully recognizing imaginative achievements. There is a temptation, alive throughout Bewell's book and much more pronounced in other, less responsive historicist work, to find a context for anything apparently novel in literature, to assimilate what appears to be invention into the spirit of the age, the episteme, or some other preexisting context. Many have thought that historical criticism could function as a corrective to metaphysical approaches to literature, approaches that sought out the work's essential, or archetypal meaning. By placing the

[31] "On Criticism, Aesthetics, and Europe," *Review of Contemporary Fiction*, 9:2 (Summer 1989), p. 13.

work in its historical context and emphasizing the distinctions between its generative moment and our own, the critic might record its difference, testify to what makes the writing resist current categories.

But a difficulty arises when the historical critic finds contexts in the past – the Medieval mind, the Modernist ideology, the Enlightenment – that come to contain the text just as wholly as the ideal, trans-temporal categories supplied by, say, Northrop Frye in *Anatomy of Criticism*. Though it may be sacrilegious to say so in a climate where responsible literary-historical scholarship is venerated above most other virtuous acts, I think that such literary history often devolves into a containing system, another philosophical disenfranchisement of art.

Bewell's criticism could have been quite moving as something of an object lesson: see, it might have said to the present, how one vital spirit enlarged the moral imaginations of his contemporaries. Go then, if you can, and do likewise; or at the very least, when you see it being done around you, proclaim and, if need be, defend it. Biographies matter, Doctor Johnson said, because they show us what can be done against odds, and Bewell's criticism, revised away from its too-scholarly sense of how poetry does its work, could have achieved something comparable.

But the problem is that most scholars are even more devoted to context than Bewell, and they are all too willing to succumb to the professional tendency to create knowledge where they can: accordingly they set about assimilating everything to some prior set of texts, ideas, or power relations. One feels such studies to be wrong, but one could spend one's life refuting, say, an essay that claimed that Hamlet's great soliloquies were no more than a patchwork of existing theological, legal, and philosophical writings – and that there was really nothing new about his character.

What we want, more often, is to ask of literature what a more coldhearted Johnson, Lyndon Baines, used to ask of his political colleagues who sought preferment for the way they'd served him in the past: What have you done for me today? And, too, what kind of future, for words and for human acts, does the work in hand open up or foreclose? Questions about context are questions that, finally, reduce to the question, "What is it?" The better question to ask is, "What can one do with it?" Past and present literature matters, at least for me, when it is what Nietzsche hoped all of his painstaking philological work would be: untimely. "I cannot imagine what would be the meaning of classical philology in our own age if it is not untimely – that is, to act against the age, and, let us hope, to the benefit of a future age."[32]

The Blake that Northrop Frye brings forward in his great book, *Fearful Symmetry*, is untimely in something like this sense. Blake's prophetic intensity – his belief that the imagination must remake the world in accord with a higher image of humanity – is aimed against the traditions of eighteenth-century empiricism, classicism, and political absolutism. About these historical matters Frye is marvelously articulate. But, though Frye never needs to say as much, his 1947 version of Blake is also the antithesis of the kind of person who would succumb to fascism or become, in the next decade, a member of Riesman's lonely crowd, a thorough-going organization man. In a similar way, Hartman's Keats would teach us what we still need to know: the deep appeals of transcendence, and how we might, without reverting to a Derridean coldness, defend ourselves against it.

Levinson and Ross, whatever may be said against them, ask the right question: what have these poets to say to us in the present? They cheat, then, making use of ersatz descendental categories to answer. But their critiques, once located firmly in the present, merit serious reply. Perhaps Ross scores off Wordsworth when he criticizes his gender politics: but, by the rule of critical compensation, he loses too much in insisting on gender as the central category. No, one wants to say to Levinson, we don't need to relegate any story that doesn't base itself in history to the cultural past. There's too much in Wordsworth's self-transforming dramas that's worth preserving and transferring. Bewell, for the most part, wants to make literature an affair of the past – "a history only of departed things," as Wordsworth puts it. His criticism doesn't travel. Levinson and Ross, though they would not like it put this way, do in significant measure what Emerson commends: they "bring the past for judgment into the thousand-eyed present."[33]

---

[32] *Unmodern Observations*, trans. William Arrowsmith (New Haven: Yale University Press, 1990), p. 88.
[33] *Essays and Lectures*, ed. Joel Porte (New York: Library of America, 1983), p. 265.

Criticism, as Emerson continually indicates, ought to measure art and literature against the ways of seeing and saying implicit in our socially insinuated discourses and those that inform our various reigning intellectual systems. When art exceeds those established forms in a profitable way, we want to preserve and celebrate it. When art passes beyond the given context, we wish to expose our students to it, and write complimentary essays about it; we become, to adapt Kundera's words, the "discoverers of discovery," defenders of poetry.

It is crucial for a critic to provide a context, to know and embody his age, which is inevitably related integrally to other times. Yet to provide a context, to put art in context, is not enough. Along with the learning and instinct required to establish the contemporary setting, one must also have the imaginative sympathy to respond to new work: to work which stays vital over long periods of time, to work that, once moribund, becomes, by the press of changing events, necessary again, and to the fresh work our contemporaries produce. Academic criticism, with its love for respectable, negotiable knowledge, treasures intellectual context, but is suspicious of the power to see what Eliot called "the new (the really new) work." Eliot, in the great essay "Tradition and the Individual Talent," seems to care most about how really new work would modify our conception of past art. One might instead care how it enlarges our conceptions of ourselves, how it expands our experience by giving us new possibilities for representation and for life, both now and in the future.

Yet there seems very little place, at present, for the kind of criticism that Robert Frost was endorsing (not without self-interest) when he talked about how critics should take some pains to see "what a feat it was to turn that that way, and what a feat it was to remember that, to be reminded of that by this." As I see it, the perception of such feats is bound up with literary pleasure overall, the sort of pleasure one may find in Wordsworth's unfolding quest to go on living and go on writing. Such pleasure entails the ability to take joy in change, to accept the fact of time's inevitable modifications of who and what we are, collateral with the wish to be imaginatively out ahead of time. Such literary

pleasure, which comes down to the pleasure in trope in the largest
sense of that word, is something for which Ross and Levinson,
and alas Bewell as well, have little use.

Pleasure in all its forms has been in rather poor repute among
academic students of literature for some time, of course. In 1963,
Lionel Trilling felt compelled to publish an essay in defence of
pleasure, an essay that made particular use of Wordsworth and
Keats.[34] (Conceive the situation wherein the somber Trilling
became pleasure's most prominent advocate among the critics.)
Since that time, Foucault has forced us to ask if there is any form
of pleasure that hasn't already been codified by the normative
disciplines.[35] Even erotic pleasure, Foucault implies, has been so
extensively surveyed by the various discourses of knowledge that
it can be neither innocent nor subversive. Rather than providing
a release from the burdens of determinate self, sexual acts, of
however eccentric a sort, may serve merely to consolidate the
subject and thus reinforce power's dominion over her. A comparable suspicion of the pleasure principle seems pervasive in
academic literary criticism at present, and for a number of reasons.

The story is frequently told of how Cleanth Brooks kept the
English program at L.S.U. alive by demonstrating to the dean –
with copious use of blackboard diagrams – how the New Criticism
he had helped to devise was a coherent, cognitive discipline, not
unscientific at all. Literary studies could thus be conceived of as
a branch of knowledge, with a place among those other forms of
knowing that make up the liberal arts curriculum. To thrive as
a university discipline, the study of literature had to look as
serious as its competitors, and, if possible, more so. The current
rage to be interdisciplinary is a rage to get more terms on the
blackboard, to purloin, if possible, some respectability from the
other departments. As each hungry new generation of critics
treads its forerunners down, new terms, new abstractions, get
added to the game. And of course the quickest way to move out
ahead of one's critical progenitors is to say that they have been

---

[34] "The Fate of Pleasure," collected in *Beyond Culture* (New York: Harcourt Brace
Jovanovich, 1965), pp. 50–76.
[35] *The History of Sexuality, Volume I: An Introduction*, trans. Robert Hurley (New York:
Random House, 1978).

mystified, too soft, too idealizing in their conception of literature: thus the necessity of concepts like "ideology" and "blindness" to make short work of one's precursors.

One thing that has certainly aided this process whereby – to speak broadly – philosophy has gotten the upper hand on poetry is the disappearance of a culture of informed literary journalism. Edmund Wilson, for example, was extremely good at challenging Brooks and Company's pretensions to authority in ways that they were compelled to respect. That creditable journalistic counterweight has now all but disappeared; in its place, we have the angry, muddled responses of Hilton Kramer, Dinesh D'Souza, and David Lehman. To be maligned by one of these writers is, to a literary academic, proof that his critique is hitting home.

The makeup of the English departments has also changed significantly. Free-lance critics like Blackmur, Jarrell, and Delmore Schwartz were eventually absorbed into university literature departments, but their presence there effectively blurred the borders between the academy and the larger reading public. Now virtually all the critics in the English department hold Ph.D.s, a shift that helps set the scene for developing a professional culture well-insulated from the public, and possessing its own languages, rites, and hierarchies. Within that culture the pursuit of pure critical knowledge – even if it is what Wordsworth feared, knowledge purchased through the loss of power – can go on largely unchallenged.

What other trends might be inspiring this critical recourse to more severe abstraction (for surely it is more than a matter of institutional or professional politics), it is very difficult to say. Trilling would probably have ascribed the phenomenon to a drive for "negative transcendence." What's at stake, as he sees it, in getting beyond the pleasure principle is the hope of arriving at a position of superiority in culture, a position from which, having been liberated from every interest, one might speak with complete detachment, complete authority.[36] In a culture teeming with images that promise total bliss (a culture for which Paglia

---

[36] "The Fate of Pleasure."

is in many ways an apologist), the total repudiation of all images and all pleasures is perhaps an understandable reaction.

Then too, energies that transcend individual designs might be in play. Hegel, as I observed in the introduction, could conceive of a time when humanity would outgrow its need for art. Freud in his turn reflected on those happy few, the scientists, who had full access to the reality principle and didn't need their instruction gilded with delight. That scientific type might in time, as Philip Rieff reflected, become the norm, even as society itself grew more rational, technological, abstract in its workings.[37] Perhaps contemporary criticism with its polemic against aesthetic pleasure is merely keeping pace with culture's overall movement; or perhaps demystifying criticism is in culture's vanguard: that anyway would explain its strong attractions to talented writers like Ross and Levinson. Yet such criticism involves considerable risk. As Harold Bloom puts it in a remarkable sentence from *The Anxiety of Influence*, "The only humane virtue we can hope to teach through a more advanced study of literature than we have now is the social virtue of detachment from one's own imagination, recognizing always that such detachment made absolute destroys any individual imagination" (p. 86).

For his part, Wordsworth spoke of "the grand elementary principle of pleasure," observing that it constitutes "the native and naked dignity of man," and that it is the principle by which a person "knows, and feels, and lives, and moves."[38] In Wordsworth's poetry the principle of vital energy, of pleasure, is manifest as Lucy, and Margaret, the Winander Boy, and the child of "Tintern Abbey." Its presence, wisely mediated, has restored and invigorated readers for nearly two hundred years. Wordsworth recognized a trend toward freezing abstraction in his own cultural moment, but he did not see its triumph as inevitable, and he set his own best poetry against it. Still there was something even in Wordsworth that feared the vital presence enough to kill it off ritually time and again: "She sleeps in the calm earth,

---

[37] "The Emergence of Psychological Man," *Freud: The Mind of the Moralist* (Chicago: University of Chicago Press, 1979), pp. 329–57.

[38] The phrases are from the 1802 preface to *The Lyrical Ballads*, and appear in *Poems*, I:880.

and peace is here"; "No motion has she now, no force;/She neither hears nor sees"; "This Boy was taken from his mates, and died." At some point around 1805, he succeeded in doing away with it for good, and the sane and lifeless voice that we meet in Armytage (before telling Margaret's tale has changed him) comes on to infuse the poetry of the next forty-five years. Armytage, in his neoclassical guise, is an admirable personage: stoical, detached, dutiful, and morally beyond reproach. But by himself he is nothing like a genuine poet. Nor is he an ideal critic, either.

CHAPTER 4

Foucault Inc.

I hate the builders of dungeons in the air.   Emerson

When Michel Foucault died of illnesses stemming from AIDS in 1984 he was probably the best-known intellectual in the West. Since that time his influence has only grown. Foucault's thinking has come to inform work throughout the humanities and social sciences. In philosophy, history, political science, and the study of human sexuality, Anglo-American professors criticize and celebrate Foucault with an intensity no other figure provokes. And no discipline has grappled onto Foucault as fervently as literary studies. His thought is central to much of the most intelligent work that has come out of American English departments over the past two decades. D. A. Miller, Eve Kosofsky Sedgwick, and Stephen Greenblatt, along with the many critics who have followed Greenblatt into what he baptized New Historicism, find a chief inspiration in Foucault. It's been said that literary studies have entered the Age of Michel Foucault.

I want here to offer a compressed account of Foucault's intellectual achievement, and then to show how academic literary critics have used – and misused – his potentially renovating energies. That done, I will point to some ways in which Foucault might still get us asking profitable questions about the limits and promise of criticism, and the value of literary art. In Foucault, I find the basis for a philosophical critique of poetry that need not end in reductive disenfranchisement. Rather, Foucault helps us arrive at a contemporary version of the kinds of linguistic, conceptual, and spiritual limits that literary art, to be worthy of the name, ought to pass beyond.

One way to describe Foucault's most important work, says the American political philosopher Michael Walzer, is as an extended play on two senses of the word discipline.[1] Discipline in Foucault refers first to ways of getting people to do what's expected of them: it compels us to produce at maximum efficiency with a minimum of squirming and muttering. In its second sense, discipline signifies the intellectual disciplines, and in particular the so-called sciences of man: psychoanalysis, anthropology, criminology, sociology, cognitive psychology, and the like.

In the initial stage of his career, Foucault, broadly speaking, wrote two sorts of books, studies of physical, and of intellectual, discipline. *Madness and Civilization* and *The Birth of the Clinic* described the ways that the mad and the sick were confined, supervised, and frequently abused in the age of Enlightenment.[2] In *The Order of Things* and *The Archaeology of Knowledge* Foucault was concerned with intellectual confinement.[3] *The Order of Things* (*Les mots et les choses*), the book that, in 1966, made Foucault's Paris reputation, set forth the now well-known theory of the epistemes. One can think of an episteme as a set of assumptions and procedures that governs what qualifies as a true, and even as an understandable, statement during a given cultural period. To accrue authority in the Renaissance a writer resorted to analogy: the world was, potentially, a set of complex correspondences; to see metaphorically was to begin unlocking nature's secrets. In the Enlightenment, classification – the chart, the table, the graph – displace metaphor as the ruling procedure for establishing truth. And that procedure gives way in turn (for no reason Foucault is willing to identify; the epistemes replace one another suddenly and without discernible cause) to the penchant for genealogy, history, narrative organizations of knowledge. By the nineteenth century the analogical impulse that informed

[1] "The Lonely Politics of Michel Foucault," *The Company of Critics: Social Criticism and Political Commitment in the Twentieth Century* (New York: Basic Books, 1988), pp. 191–209.
[2] *Madness and Civilization: A History of Insanity in the Age of Reason*, trans. Richard Howard (New York: Random House, 1973); *The Birth of the Clinic: An Archaeology of Medical Perception*, trans. Alan Sheridan (New York: Random House, 1975).
[3] *The Order of Things: An Archaeology of the Human Sciences* (New York: Random House, 1973); *The Archaeology of Knowledge and the Discourse on Language*, trans. A. M. Sheridan Smith (New York: Harper and Row, 1972).

scientific thinking in the Renaissance becomes the signature of poetry, the sheerly imaginary.

Whatever the truth in Foucault's synopsis of the consecutive determining structures that circumscribe periods of intellectual activity (and I'm not alone in finding his schema too pat), *The Order of Things* put Foucault in a position to develop an analogy, latent in his work from early on, between forms of thought and forms of physical coercion. In *Discipline and Punish* Foucault succeeded in writing his two kinds of studies simultaneously. He called *Surveiller et punir* his first book: surely it is his best.

As Foucault sees it, many of our social institutions, such as schools, government agencies, and businesses, take their cues for what a person ought to be from the human norms that the intellectual disciplines dispense. But so too do the intellectual disciplines shape their views of what is normal in accord with what institutions require to function at maximum efficiency. The intellectual disciplines, which one might have thought locate and identify aspects of the self already in existence, actually do not so much find the self as, in collaboration with techniques of institutional control, help to create it.

Thus to Foucault there exists a symbiotic relation between many of the supposedly disinterested areas of intellectual inquiry that claim to seek knowledge as an end in itself and the exploitative world of getting and spending purportedly outside the university gates. For Foucault, social institutions working in concert with norm-creating intellectual disciplines now manufacture persons in something of the way that factories produce commodities. In *Les mots et les choses*, Foucault refused to speculate on why the epistemes take the shapes they do, and why they displace one another. But by thinking of truth in conjunction with power, he is able to suggest that the requirements of social control and the production of authorized norm-inducing statements shift in tandem. There is no truth, only truth/power, which is to say that the contemporary worker is the product not only of certain kinds of physical discipline, but of the many stories she is in a position to tell herself (and that others tell about her), that justify and help to fix her place in the world by formulating her identity.

Foucault's concept of discipline has some clear advantages over the Marxist notion of ideology. First, there is no truth outside the disciplines to which one might refer: there may be better ways of representing and inflecting matters, but those ways are not associated with absolute knowledge. Nor are the disciplinary circuitries repressed, the exclusive object of a professional knowledge, like de Manian blindness and insight theory: just look around, Foucault seems to say, see if this way of conceiving the relations between accredited speech and institutional life brings things into focus for you.

Granted, from one angle Foucault looks like the grandest anti-metaphysical metaphysician that the theory boom produced. His preeminent magic word, Power, is often just as all-encompassing as Derrida's presence. God, said St. Augustine, is a circle whose center is everywhere and whose circumference is nowhere: and that sounds like Foucault's Power, with the distinction that it's as consistently malevolent as Augustine's God is loving and generative. But Foucault, as I see it, shows us how to save his work from being a grand theory like Derrida's when he stops talking about Power and starts talking about lots of different disciplines. That gesture enables one to begin thinking about the relative proportion of confinement and humane benefit available in, say, this or that discourse about human sexuality, and – this by far the more important point – how one might begin talking about sex in ways that enlarge and refine human possibility.

Foucault's vision, in which all the disciplines are acting at full strength, invites modification, invites the kinds of modulated, particularized descriptions that he rarely engaged in, busy as he was offering a vision of Fate in its contemporary manifestation. In a sense, pure, uncut Foucault is no friendlier to the literary mind than Derrida. But, as I'll be going on to show, Foucault does allow for more useful revisions than any theorist we've encountered so far.

From whence, then, does the currently enforced conception of identity – of the self as an entity fixed in its range by a sequence of normative vocabularies and corresponding institutional practices – derive? Foucault's answer is that a determining source for contemporary disciplined selfhood lies in a shift in the strategies of punishment, a shift coinciding with the move from dualistic to relational social power. To put it crudely, pre-modern law punished acts; modern justice is visited upon persons. In fact, the creation of the entity called man may be in crucial ways (though surely not in all) the result of a new penal leniency in which the objective is rehabilitation, not retribution.

In the pre-Revolutionary system, it was enough to know whether the accused had committed the crime or not. The act was judged, says Foucault, not the individual. But with the advent of a new, humane jurisprudence, all that changed. The objective was to transform the guilty one from being a criminal to being a normal, productive member of society. And to rehabilitate someone, it is necessary to know him, to understand who he is, what forces made him act as he did, and to find a punishment, not only to fit the crime, but also to fit the criminal's need for reform. Punishment remained in some manner retributive, Foucault is willing to admit. But the major innovation in modern penal thinking was that prison also became a center for a certain harsh form of prescriptive therapy.

What does it mean to know the criminal? To the powers of the state it means knowing him as a type, someone amply described by narratives about the criminal character. And those narratives must come from diverse sources: medical doctors reflecting on the genetic disposition to crime and the physiology of the criminal; psychiatrists with ideas about sociopathy, and its origin in infantile experience; sociologists discoursing on the subcultural milieus that breed thieves and killers; economists with something to say about the material conditions conducive to lawlessness; historians discussing the place of the criminal in society over time; priests hearing confessions to claim souls who have been condemned in this world for salvation in the next; social workers comforting and comprehending the families left behind when the criminal goes off to prison. Foucault describes the function of the intellectual disciplines within the criminal system thus: "by solemnly inscribing offences in the field of objects susceptible of scientific knowledge, they provide the mechanisms of legal punishment with a justifiable hold not only on offences, but on individuals; not only on what they do, but also on what they are, will be, may be" (p. 18).

A key fact to note, Foucault indicates, is that even as the experts concoct theories about the criminal, they are, at the same time and often without fully noticing it, arriving at profiles – psychological, historical, medical, sociological, what have you – of those who do not break the law and go to jail. They are arriving, by different routes, at versions of the normal, socially productive citizen. For she is the person who appears as almost a residue from the manifold reflections on deviancy. Much is entailed in the juridical shift from punishing acts to punishing persons, and not the least is that it provides a source for the disciplined study of a creature called man. Thus in *Discipline and Punish* Foucault attempts to give substance to the enigmatic (and rather pretentious) observation near the close of *The Order of Things* to the effect that "man" is a recent invention.

At one point in *Discipline and Punish*, Foucault mentions that he is not simply saying that the human sciences – and thus one quite influential version of man – emerged from the prison (p. 305). Yet he is, it seems to me, saying something very close to that. The book, after all, presents itself as a "genealogy or an element in a genealogy of the modern 'soul'" (p. 29). To Foucault, the soul or self is the place in which knowledge and power meet, where "power relations give rise to a possible corpus of knowledge, and knowledge extends and reinforces the effects of this power" (p. 29). And though this happens nowhere so intensely as in the prison, disciplined reflections on the prisoner function as a matrix for more encompassing, scientifically respectable versions of human selfhood.

Two corollaries to Foucault's reflections arise here, the first concerning the prisoner, the second modern intellectual life. If what Foucault says about prison and the genesis of normative subjectivity is true, then it follows that the prisoner is, at least in some regards, our representative man. That is, prison discipline attempts to create a normal citizen from resistant material; for the prisoner is the person who could not be inducted into existing norms without strife. What most of us assumed as second nature – the limiting contours of our selves or souls – the prisoner had to be broken to accepting. Thus in the gradual, painful rehabilitation of the prisoner, one may see, as if in slow motion, an allegory for the process by which we of less resistant temperament became who we are.

Second corollary: we in the academy, and in particular those of us employed in developing reflections on mankind, operate in a tainted tradition. If the implicit mission of the human sciences is theorizing the normative, noncriminal type, the type who fits in rather passively, then one can hardly continue to describe academics as attempting to arrive at detached accounts of human behavior or at descriptions of the most humanly satisfying social arrangements. When the social scientist suggests, however indirectly, standards for human happiness based on communal renewal, or on the end of certain social imbalances, it is difficult, given the association of her discipline with enlightened penal theory, to credit her work as dispassionate, or as believably reformist in its goals. From the Foucauldian perspective, she's promulgating terminologies for self-understanding that help in nothing so much as in breeding social discipline. To Foucault, every discipline disciplines.

For him, there is a continuous relationship between the academy and the prison and not only because many of the standards for evaluation and behavior in the schools – examinations, psychological profiles, disciplined dispositions of the body – have their analogues, if not in some measure their beginnings, in prison. There is also what one might call a circulation of terms between penitentiary and professoriat. The vocabularies coined by the academy for describing deviancy and establishing remedies for it reach the prison in a number of ways. One route is through the students whom the professors train and confer credentials on. There in prison the terminologies are tried out, as in a laboratory, adopted, modified, or thrust aside, then sent back, as it were, to their place of manufacture for revision in numberless essays, reviews, dissertations, books, seminars. Something similar presumably happens with the normative terminologies that the social workers, psychiatrists, health care officials, teachers, and other helping professionals absorb during their time as students.

Those normative terms can become the conceptual limits for

the so-called clients on whom the helping professionals work. In order to qualify for benefits (federal, state, private) one must often learn to account for oneself in the language of the social scientists and their students: that is, usually, as a fixed type, generally a subject, often a victim of events. One of the reasons that respectable intellectual work can go on serving questionable social procedures, presumably, is that we academics often refuse to entertain any but high-minded views of who we are and what we do. We are loath, it sometimes seems, to ask ourselves questions about our place in larger productive systems.

In the first volume of *The History of Sexuality*, Foucault located another matrix for the contemporary subject, the subject of discipline.[4] Here Foucault argues that the proliferation of sexual discourses has been central to creating contemporary disciplinary society. It has been said that in the twentieth century an erotic life is the closest thing many people have to a spiritual life, a remark that, from a Foucauldian point of view, gives the game away almost entirely. Where there is a spiritual life there are likely to be commandments, transgressions, guilt, and penance: the priest is close at hand. But if the black-robed priest with his holy icons has, for much of the educated middle class in this century, taken a step back into the shadows, perhaps he has been succeeded by the genial therapist commending faith in the trinity of good health, steady earnings, and good normal sex.

According to Foucault, the movement from the policing of the spirit to the far subtler policing of desire began even before Freud and the culture of normative psychoanalysis.[5] For, Foucault demonstrates, the Victorians, whom we like to imagine as button-lipped on the subject of sex, actually talked compulsively on the subject, though always in the language of scientific high seriousness. The drive behind the newly burgeoning *scientia sexualis* was to describe and codify sexual life, creating multi-volume encyclopedias of human sexuality that might exhaust the variations. Anything but an age of simple repression, Foucault argues,

[4] *Volume One: An Introduction.*
[5] For a commentary on Foucault's critical relation to psychoanalysis see John Forrester's *The Seductions of Psychoanalysis: Freud, Lacan and Derrida* (Cambridge: Cambridge University Press, 1990), pp. 286–316.

the Victorian period was loud with erudite babble on the subject of sex.

The Victorian science of sex was distinctive for its focus not upon acts, but upon persons (note the correspondence with the juridical vocabularies). That is, the assumption began to take hold that a person's essential identity was established by some generalization that summarized – and in so doing at least partially eclipsed – a life's sequence of specific erotic encounters. Thus came a vast glossary of sexual types: the pedophile, the fetishist, the hysterical woman, the public school masochist. A miser was someone who had never quite taken leave of the anal-erotic stage; the compulsive talker was locked in an impossible romance with her mother's breast. Suddenly you were what you did in bed or, a sophisticated step later, what you had done in excess or insufficiently as a child. When Foucault says, provocatively enough, that homosexuality was invented in 1870, he means that around that time people began talking less about same-sex erotic acts and more about homosexual persons.

Those who worked to arrive at a scientific characterization of *the* homosexual – a labor that continues to the present day, and includes debates on such elevating topics as whether or not there exists a homosexual gene – often believed that they were contributing something to human liberation. They worked in an atmosphere of transgression: they said the unsayable; they coolly investigated what had, through fear and bigotry, been ignored since the beginnings of civilization. But to Foucault, they actually contributed to creating the homosexual self, an entity to which those who practiced same-sex sex might be expected to conform or, if they were more daring, *against which* they might establish their identities by rebelling. The homosexual is, at least potentially, another version of the inveterate criminal, someone whose self-production intensifies and reveals the general procedures for creating a well-adjusted individual.

Very well then, said Jean Genet at what he took to be the turning point of his life, they call me a thief and a homosexual, that's what I am; that's what I'll be. It's at the point of embracing an identity imposed by criminal and sexual discipline that Genet, according to Sartre, becomes a worthy figure of resistance, the existentialist par excellence.[6] And Foucault, like Sartre whose work he disliked and whose role in French culture he assumed, is also sometimes moved by the criminal and by the sexual outlaw. But his most challenging thinking on these matters goes in a different direction.

Foucault then is very much unlike his contemporary Norman Mailer, someone who also takes a strong interest in marginal figures. It's their disdain for a stifling status quo that attracts Mailer to Jack Henry Abbott and Gary Gilmore.[7] Both men frequently disgust Mailer, but he's also moved by their anti-establishment intelligence: he'd like to distill their more productively antinomian impulses to help make himself a plausible figure of opposition to suffocating conformity. When asked to condense his social criticism, Mailer has sometimes simply observed, "The shits are killing us." By "the shits" Mailer means the organization men, the WASPs, tied to efficiency, production, and the logic-of-the-next-step. Against the shits Mailer poses, with great invention and rhetorical verve, the image of himself as white negro, and as sophisticated sociopath, a man complicated and refined, but also fed by pure, unruly energies.

Foucault doesn't believe that oppositional paragons like Genet, Mailer, *the* criminal, or *the* homosexual have much promise under the contemporary dispensation, and seeing why brings us closer to an appreciation of what's fresh in his thought. "We need," says Foucault in an interview titled "Truth and Power," "to cut off the king's head; in political theory that has still to be done."[8] Foucault might have added that in theory overall, and indeed in most forms of Western thinking, an obsession with the king continues. Foucault implies that although the realities of social power have, since the effective end of European monarchy, been completely transformed, thought has not kept pace. The world of our reflective lives too often remains the world of

[6] *Saint Genet: Actor and Martyr*, trans. Bernard Frechtman (New York: Pantheon, 1963), especially pp. 17–72.

[7] Mailer wrote the introduction for Abbott's *In the Belly of the Beast* (New York: Vintage, 1982), pp. ix–xviii; Gilmore appears in *The Executioner's Song* (Boston: Little Brown, 1979).

[8] *Foucault Reader*, p. 63.

pre-revolutionary Europe and America, where the king presides as a monolithic force to be criticized, converted, deposed, or slain.

Foucault's point, ultimately, is that dialectical thinking, the movement of mind that places forces in dualistic opposition, is a philosophy of illusion. The dialectic continues as a residue of a political dispensation now obsolete. But equally illusory will be any anti-philosophy that attempts to challenge the dialectic without having first developed a historically inflected view of the contemporary relations between power and intellectual discourse.

Foucault begins *Discipline and Punish* with the well-known scene on the scaffold, the torture and execution, in 1757, of the regicide, Damiens. The scene is grisly. The condemned man's flesh is torn from his body; molten lead and boiling oil go directly into his wounds; finally he's drawn and quartered, a part of the punishment that's botched repeatedly, to horrible effect. At the end the executioners throw the trunk and severed limbs onto the fire; in four hours they are ash.

In the execution of Damiens one may discern – though Foucault never says so directly – an image of an event that would occur three and a half decades later, the guillotining of the king. For, Foucault suggests, the spectacle of violence perpetrated by the king against his enemy, in public with full ceremony and in full view, helps to make his own execution more likely. All capital crimes in the *ancien régime* qualify as crimes against the sovereign, and an execution, particularly a gaudy, prolonged exhibition like the one enacted around Damiens, concentrates the power of the king in one place, at one time. There is the king, figured by his troops, his clergy, his ministers, and there the criminal, who in a certain sense faces his monarch one to one: a pair of foes stand poised in opposition.

Such a scene allows one to imagine that the contest might go the other way. Suppose it was the rebel who triumphed, or that segment of society from which he comes. A bloody pageant that is supposed to make royal power look absolute and invulnerable actually does something closer to the reverse. It reveals an opposition, dialectical in form, whose issue might at some future point be otherwise. And for all purposes it is when Louis XVI ascends the scaffold.

Foucault isn't suggesting that a certain style of execution ought to head the list of causes for the French Revolution. In *Discipline and Punish* he is writing an illustrative fable about power, something like Nietzsche's *Genealogy of Morals* and Freud's *Group Psychology and the Analysis of the Ego*. What Foucault suggests, I think, is that the forms in which people imagine power, the stories they conceive and that seem most natural when they're thinking about the forces that compel obedience from them, aren't without consequences. Such imaginings have some part to play in how they devise their future liberation, and if they do. By manifesting itself in concentrated, directly identifiable ways, royal power demonstrated its vulnerability to direct confrontation.

But Foucault believes that when that happens, when the king's head comes off, power, which following Nietzsche he takes to be an abiding force in all consequential human affairs, exerts itself in other ways. Power, to put it crudely, moves from being an essential to a relational phenomenon. One can no longer find the center of power, or even the centers. Rather power penetrates society, permeating every personal and productive relation as mutual and self surveillance become the effective forms of social control. By means of the kind of surveillance practiced in schools, hospitals, offices, factories, and thanks to the ministrations of the so-called helping professions and the various coteries of experts on daily life, a discipline without center or source establishes itself as the order of the day.

By means of surveillance, Foucault says, disciplinary power achieves its status as a "multiple, automatic and anonymous power; for although surveillance rests on individuals, its functioning is that of a network of relations from top to bottom, but also to a certain extent from bottom to top and laterally; this network 'holds' the whole together and traverses it in its entirety with effects of power that derive from one another: supervisors, perpetually supervised" (*Discipline and Punish*, pp. 176–7). The transition to a new economy of power takes place gradually over time, as the technology of observation becomes more wide ranging, sophisticated, and effective. "Discipline," Foucault observes, "makes possible the operation of a relational power that sustains itself by its own mechanism and which, for the spectacle of public events, substitutes the uninterrupted play of calculated gazes" (p. 177).

The current dispensation of power differs from the regime it displaces in another critical way. The power of the king, or of the ruling class (for Marxism is at issue here as well), exerted itself repressively. It said no. It held down the forces of the individual or of the proletariat, until, as though following the laws of pneumatic physics, the pressures at hand exceeded the strength of repression and the boundaries burst. Foucault's view of relational power – the kind of power that informs the society of mutual surveillance; our society, supposedly – is that though it does sometimes serve a repressive function, it also works productively. "What makes power hold good," he observes in "Truth and Power," is "the fact that it doesn't only weigh on us as a force that says no, but that it traverses and produces things, it induces pleasure, forms knowledge, produces discourse. It needs to be considered as a productive network which runs through the whole social body, much more than as a negative instance whose function is repression."[9]

Why should relational power be such an effectively productive kind of power? Why should this dispensation of authority get people to perform at maximum efficiency? Presumably, one can sometimes hide from monolithic power, operate in its shadows, avoid its edicts. Centralized, unified, prone to conspicuous displays, such power cannot be everywhere at once. Or, one can meet it head on, face, challenge, and overthrow it. One cannot, however, comprehensively confront disciplinary power. Because its forces are multiple, and non-localizable, there is no place and no time at which they might all gather together – or be gathered together – to enter into mental or physical strife.

William Hazlitt was probably the first major English critic to argue that there existed a shaping relation between the revolution in France and the poetry of his contemporaries. "According to the prevailing notions," says Hazlitt in his lecture "On the Living

---

[9] *Foucault Reader*, p. 61.

Poets," "all was to be natural and new" – in politics and art alike. "Kings and queens were to be dethroned from their rank and station in legitimate tragedy and epic poetry, as they were decapitated elsewhere."[10] Hazlitt's high-spirited equation between royal decapitation and the new literary forms contains, from the Foucauldian perspective, a ring of encompassing truth. For in Foucault's fable, a good deal of what qualifies as literature and social theory after the Revolution may be understood as rehearsing, time and again, the Revolution's victory over arbitrary monarchical power. Having cut the king's head off in life, we continue to do it again, repeatedly, in theory, in poetry, in social thought, in everyday speech and reflection. From a Foucauldian perspective, dialectical thinking conceals the realities of contemporary power. It allows those still responsive to this Romantic tradition to concoct fantasies about major revolutionary confrontations.

It is here that we can touch on a paradox that arises from Foucault's thinking, but that he never, as far as I know, goes very far in exploring. On the one hand, the forces of discipline are various: they take up many angles on the individual, speak many different languages. There are a diversity of disciplines. On the other hand, the result of these disciplines is the hardening of the self into an essential identity: *the* criminal, *the* homosexual, or, more broadly, the resistant but unified self who takes dialectical thinking as second nature and conceives of herself as a strong identity that can enter into strife, or collaboration, with other fixed selves and forces.

One can legitimately resolve this difficulty, I think, by bringing forward the theory of the epistemes that arises from *Les mots et les choses*. There Foucault takes it that all of the discourses of knowledge at any given time hang together, relying on common assumptions: to put it crudely, the Classical age takes the chart to be the obvious appurtenance to knowledge, just as the age of history that follows it relies centrally on the unfolding narrative. In what one might call the age of the social sciences, the age of man, a belief in the norm as defining the human essence might

---

[10] *The Complete Works of William Hazlitt*, ed. P. P. Howe, 21 vols. (London: J. M. Dent and Sons, 1930), V:162.

be said to connect many, if not most, of the self-creating disciplines. As Hannah Arendt puts it, in the modern period the consensus takes hold that "behavior has replaced action as the foremost mode of human relationship" and that "men had become social beings and unanimously followed certain patterns of behavior, so that those who did not keep the rules could be considered to be asocial or abnormal."[11]

If the various sciences of man share a commitment to the norm, then the diversity of disciplinary languages and institutions may well be able to function to create, broadly speaking, two groups, those whose unified sense of self comes from conforming to the balance of norms, and those whose deviancy defines them (and are thus also the creations of disciplinary power): the homosexual, the state-raised criminal, the mental patient. Thus an unlocalizable and non-specific power could give rise to very local, very specific convictions about selfhood. An asymmetry arises: a coherent and unified subject can never locate a comparably fixed center of power against which to contend.

In saying as much I have tried to solve a difficulty in Foucault's thinking, for though I will have some critical things to say about Foucault, I want the most perdurable version of his achievement to be in place. Yet I am aware that the version I have offered so far may be too abstractly speculative. I'll try to remedy that now by taking a little time to put matters in more practical and experiential terms.

Perhaps you saw the advertisement: it was for Delta Airlines and it frequently ran with sports events. American soldiers dismissed from formation in pelting rain mob a telephone booth, waiting for a chance to make reservations with a Delta agent, Gayle, for their flights home. Cut to Gayle at the end of her shift. Her supervisor approaches her desk and asks, "How many calls did you get this afternoon, Gayle?" She raises her finger, one, then slumps down in her chair. Her colleen's face is exhausted, but beaming loyally. "Delta," goes the song, "we love to fly and it shows."

[11] *The Human Condition: A Study of the Central Dilemmas Facing Modern Man* (Garden City, N. Y.: Doubleday, 1959), pp. 38, 39.

But had Gayle's workaday equivalent the bad luck to book a variety of flights from only one call, she would have some explaining ahead of her. Airline reservations agents are monitored electronically, silently, at undisclosed intervals. If they don't manage to take a certain number of calls a day, and don't convert a set percentage of them into sales, their jobs are in danger. They live in a web of electronic surveillance. Because the monitoring is intermittent and because the supervisor is often hidden from view, sometimes in an office whose doorway isn't visible to the bookers on the floor, the bookers are never sure when they are being listened in on.[12]

This not knowing probably induces a good deal of speculation. Based on various clues, on gossip, maybe even on coordinated attempts to gather information, the bookers at their terminals will arrive at some ideas about management's tactics. They'll have a sense of when the supervisor is likely to be on the line. But that sense will be tentative, always prey to doubts. What if management gathers some intelligence on the bookers' lore and changes its procedures? Or what if the workers' information is simply wrong? Always there's a guessing game going on, a game in which the worker tries to psych out the company.

But however successful the effort of Gayle's experiential double to get inside the corporate mind, the corporation gets inside of hers. By playing out various scenarios with the surveillance system, the booker in effect installs the presence of the supervisor within herself, simultaneously playing two roles. She becomes her own boss. Thus real productive labor emerges from a relation that is at least in some measure speculative, fictitious.

Nor can the booker readily change her situation by confronting her supervisor and explaining a bad day's performance in sympathetic terms. It's likely that the supervisor herself is being monitored. Her interventions onto the booker's line are themselves subject to supervision. For the supervisor is easy enough to replace. Her job has been so perfectly quantified – she has specific instructions for almost every situation – that nearly anyone can do

[12] See "Cracking the Electronic Whip," by Sharon Danann, *Harper's Magazine* (August 1990), pp. 58–9.

it. One needs no more qualifications (in fact may need fewer) to do the supervisor's job than the booker's.

The supervisor, who perhaps looks to the ticketing agents like a figure of considerable power, can be more vulnerable than her charges. It takes skill to engage customers, serve them cheerfully, and not lose your temper when they become confused or unreasonable. But the supervisor may not be able to do that much; she may have been kicked upstairs after failing as a ticket seller. Thus the figure installed in the authority position by the corporation, then by the booker, is without the power that could make an encounter with her, in which the booker spoke her mind, emotionally or practically significant. The technological arrangements remove the possibility of meaningful human confrontation. Victory is always decided in advance.

Readers of *Discipline and Punish* will see the parallels between the ticket booker's plight and the situation that, in Foucault's interpretation, exists for the prisoner under observation from Bentham's bizarre device, the panopticon. Like the prisoner isolated in his cell, visible from a looming tower that may or may not actually be staffed at any given moment, the flight reservationist is induced to assume "responsibility for the constraints of power," making them play spontaneously over herself (p. 202). She's induced to internalize the power relation in which she simultaneously takes both roles, becoming, in Foucault's phrase, the principle of her own subjection.

The booker's capacity to communicate with co-workers, at least while she's on the job, is little better than that of Foucault's prisoners. Bentham designed the panoptic prison so that the convicts would be invisible to each other, and thus their most immediate and decisive relationship would be with the tower. The reservationist is surrounded by others doing the same job: there will be as many as three hundred and fifty people working in one place. But because she's compelled to maximize efficiency, contact with others is difficult (though not impossible). Like the prisoner she can be seen, sometimes without seeing her superior, but she can also be overheard. Bentham, Foucault observes in a note, abandoned the hope for acoustical monitoring because he couldn't come up with a device that would let the supervisors overhear the prisoners without themselves being heard (p. 317 n. 3).

In *Discipline and Punish* the panopticon turns none too subtly into a metaphor for surveillance society: its machinations are supposed to condense the workings of civilization overall. But the fact is that no one ever produced a panopticon. Bentham's design didn't leave the drawing board. The photos in Foucault's book of prisons that are supposed to resemble Bentham's model seem fairly far from the mark, at least to me.

Then too there are conceptual difficulties with conceiving the panopticon allegorically. It resembles both the enchanted tower of conventional romance and also the Bastille, by now an almost equally mythic locale. Both enchanted tower and Bastille connote dialectical strife and overthrow: in moments of pure triumph the questing knight and the Revolutionary crowd cast down all that the structures represent. The dialectic, which Foucault achieves some of his originality in trying to pass beyond, is inherent in both images. Then, too, informing the trope of the panopticon is the Judeo-Christian God, all-seeing, all-knowing, yet inscrutable in himself.

But with the advent of computer surveillance and what has been called an information economy, Foucault's observations about panoptic society, which seem rather tenuous when illustrated by a bizarre, never-produced prison scheme, advance in plausibility. Computer terminals, unlike isolated observation stations, can communicate swiftly with other data bases, bringing information to bear for the better management of subject groups. The locus of computer exchange has been called cyberspace, but where precisely is that? It's a world of communication and retrieval without centers, without significant material status. Cyberspace could function as an observational web that exists everywhere and nowhere, the fulfillment, perhaps, of Bentham's dream.

Computers, rightly programmed, are superior monitoring devices. The terminal at the booker's desk processes ticket purchases, but also delivers read-outs on how she spends her work time. Daily the computer provides TNCH, total number of calls handled; TATT, total average talk time; TACW, total average after-call work (the paperwork for tickets); and, most significantly, UNM, unmanned time (a particularly inapt term, since most bookers are women), the total number of minutes that the booker was away from her desk on a given shift. When these numbers stray too far below certain standards (the booker is supposed to take between 150 and 200 calls a day) disciplinary action is necessary: a sharp talking to, a letter in the file, suspension. The pay for this kind of work, even when all goes well, is somewhere around $5.50 an hour.

Note that the discipline Gayle's workaday double undergoes is both technological and discursive: that is, she's defined by the statistical read-outs that the company amply produces, as well as by the mechanisms that monitor her. She's watched and described simultaneously by the same equipment. The booker is doubly subjected, disciplined in both senses of the word. Surely Gayle's surrogate has more vocabularies to describe herself than the ones that the company dispenses. But her livelihood depends on these numbers and so they will matter a good deal.

The sources for the technology that monitors the booker will of course be various, but university departments of management technology and computer science will be among them. The circuit of power that traverses the bookers also runs through the university. If the booker, trying to explain the peculiar day when she only took one call, goes beyond her immediate supervisor and brings her case to white collar management, the terms the manager uses to describe her and her situation are likely to derive, at least in some measure, from the psychology and sociology departments. The manager may want to discuss an entity he'll call "your anger," or maybe "your resentment." Perhaps he'll *accept* the emotion (as a good therapist would), invite her to express it fully, knowing from his courses in personnel management that such expression can be cathartic. He'll deal with the emotions, not the practical grievance, and in so doing profit from the ways that psychoanalytic thinking can be adapted to what's called the real world. He'll be enhancing, by a small degree, the symbiotic relation that can exist between the academy and the world outside its walls.

But can't the booker see that no encounter with a purported

figure of authority is likely to yield satisfaction? Can't she then adopt – small enough consolation though it might be – an ironic attitude toward the whole mechanism? Yes, but it may not be easy. If Foucault's implications are true, most of the ways Gayle's double and the rest of us have for representing ourselves are informed by the dialectic, so that we're still looking for a unified superior power to blame or overcome. The stories the booker tells herself about the invisible supervisor are informed by a line of Western thought that begins at least with the Revolution, and that misconceives the reality of contemporary power, in which all observers are themselves observed. Believers in the dialectic keep waiting for a life-transforming encounter, an encounter that, Foucault explains, will never take place.

Right now about twenty-five million Americans have their work tracked electronically; ten million receive regular, computer-generated statistical evaluations. And the potential for this kind of observation is growing exponentially such that, in time, enhanced surveillance, at home and on the job, will be the price for enjoying the security civilization offers. To Foucault, I suspect, the current figures would constitute a bottom line, a literal index of the way discipline now functions. The woman, whose machine has, with a literalness Marx never imagined, become in certain regards more powerful, more autonomous than she, could serve the function that Foucault attributed to prisoners, to the mad, and to so-called sexual deviants. If the example of Gayle's working double is homelier by far than anything Foucault, who retains a residual Romantic attachment to the outlaw types, comes up with, it seems to me to hit closer to home. For who among us cannot imagine being in the booker's position? And who among us will not, in time, be more closely surveyed, more ably monitored, than we are today?

"People give and bemoan themselves," says Emerson, "but it is not half so bad with them as they say": a line that, in my view, ought to serve as the epigraph to Foucault's collected works.[13] For we might think of Foucault as something like one half of

---

[13] *Essays and Lectures*, p. 472.

Ralph Waldo Emerson. Foucault offers an intricate, persuasive, strongly felt version of the form that fate or limitation (to use the Emersonian terms) takes at our current historical juncture. Think about the forces that hem you in as being not essential, but relational, not dialectical but dispersed, Foucault tells us, and see how much that way of thinking clarifies your experience.

Karl Marx, says Edmund Wilson in a memorable passage in *To the Finland Station*, didn't understand America because he couldn't conceive a country where there were real encounters between owners and workers, bourgeois and proletariat: "He had no key for appreciating the realities of a society in which men are really to some degree at liberty to make friends with one another indiscriminately or indiscriminately to bawl one another out." In the age that Wilson was describing, when class lines were more firmly drawn, maybe you got some satisfaction out of hollering at the boss or, as Wilson says later, upping the ante, "socking him in the jaw."[14] But with authority attenuated to the point of disappearance in the contemporary, complexly interconnected institution, there's often no one worth hollering at, much less cracking in the jaw. Knowing as much, and knowing why, won't solve Gayle's problems but, difficult as the Foucauldian view might be to assimilate, it could at least clarify her situation, giving her a new sense of where she stands.

Then too Foucault asks one to stop conceiving of intellectual activity as automatically being a world apart from the spheres of exploitative power and see then how various puzzling phenomena begin making more sense. The willingness of government and major corporations to fund university research activities and to tolerate, albeit with a little grumbling, purportedly subversive inquiry is altogether less baffling when you take the double sense of discipline seriously. For those who contribute to the analytical disciplines, especially in the so-called sciences of man, do important social work. Believers in their own freedom, they are, Foucault suggests, minor lords of limit, people whose collective effect is not to be underestimated.

To the graduate student in English who is continually chastised

[14] *To the Finland Station: A Study in the Writing and Acting of History* (Garden City, N. Y.: Doubleday, 1940), pp. 324, 325.

for writing criticism in the experiential, non-professional mode, the mode of Pater, Woolf, Hazlitt, Ruskin, Wilde, and in fact of Edmund Wilson, what Foucault has to say about disciplines will not be welcome news, but it may help clear up a few perplexities. To refuse analytical terminologies is to refuse to contribute to truth in its current form, and to join issue with those who do. It is to behave unprofessionally, to repudiate the discipline. And for this intellectual luxury there's some tax.

Yet we turn to a visionary writer – and Foucault aspires to that status – not just to clarify the contours of our current limits, but also to learn ways of overcoming them. Starting out with Emerson, I want to offer a few examples of how writers in the past have taken up the renovating challenge that Foucault, alas, turns away from. Attending to these writers may give us some clues about how we might move from Foucault's anatomy of contemporary fate to an account of future freedom.

Emerson, in great essays like "Fate" and "Experience," would teach us about the forces against which we have to contend in order to do or say something that is indelibly our own and to live with some energy, spontaneity, and joy. His extraordinary toughness lies in his ability to show in detail how we are often most limited, most imprisoned, by those things that we love, and love truly. Our friends, our children, our husbands and wives, the societies in which we take our ease, the books we read and reread, the natural scenes that delight us, foreign travel, even past achievements about which we're justly proud tend, as Emerson says in "Circles," "to solidify and hem in the life."[15] To Emerson, the battle with inertia entails revising, or in some cases even dissolving, love in the interest of self-renewal. Love is often ruin: Emerson's status as a revolutionary moralist is inseparable from this disturbingly amoral insight.

Similarly in William Blake's work there is a strong attempt to rename and redescribe fate.[16] Like Foucault, he is an implacable enemy of the stable self; the Selfhood, for Blake, is the repository

---

[15] *Essays and Lectures*, p. 404.
[16] Steven Marcus draws a parallel, though of a different sort, between Blake and Foucault in "Madness, Literature, and Society," *Representations: Essays on Literature and Society* (New York: Random House, 1975), pp. 137–60.

of the moralistic virtues: possessiveness, conformity, calculation, prudence, timidity, acquisitiveness. The Selfhood cherishes its own stability, for every break in continuity threatens the possessions – spouse, home, wealth, material goods – on which its supposed happiness relies. Pleasure is the Selfhood's most immediate enemy, for pleasure induces a letting go, a melting, however temporary, of defences – and the Selfhood, to switch for a moment to Freud's terms, is an ego composed exclusively of defence mechanisms.

But the greater enemy of the Selfhood is genius. For the visionary insists upon a life of continuous effort aimed toward enlarging and so transforming the self. Genius demands that we see more and see more deeply. Blake charges us to apprehend multiple realities, seeing from the perspective of other people, but also animals, birds, and vegetation. He has a shaman's hunger for various experience.

Blake's moral gamble in his brief epic *Milton* is that he can change his readers' sense of what evil is. For the educated eighteenth-century man or woman, evil is likely, Blake believes, to be epitomized in a figure like Milton's Satan. Satan, as Milton conceives him, is a character of tragic dimension, equally capable of action and of suffering. He's radiant with pride and energy, defiant, deceitful, eloquent, brave, self-serving. In his epic, Blake corrects Milton's version of evil: in *Milton* Satan isn't a fiery Homeric hero in the mode of Achilles, rather he's a blandly supreme administrator. He's a late eighteenth-century man of sensibility capable of bursting into tears at any moment. He seems to have only fond wishes for Palamabron, Blake's stand-in in the poem, and it takes a while to see that beyond Satan's sweet exterior there's an obsessive creature bent on repressing every vital instinct he encounters.

Evil won't come at you on flaming wings any more, Blake tells his readers, but rather as the small-minded, punctilious gentleman official with a high regard for himself and his own probity. Yet make no mistake, such figures are the enemy of art and joy, which they smother quietly, with cavils, slander, and responsible criticism. The climax of the poem comes when Blake can own to his investment in such a figure and say with Milton, "I in my

Selfhood am that Satan; I am that Evil One!"[17] By anatomizing himself, and his own commitment to the currently reigning form of self-enclosure, Blake invites us to turn and do the same for ourselves.

Like Foucault and unlike Emerson, Blake is a historicist: he would teach us that fate changes its guise as social forms shift, that what was rightly anathema a century ago may be what's most needed now. So Satanic energy, Blake shows in *The Marriage of Heaven and Hell*, must serve as at least a temporary antidote for passive, inert forces of angelic respectability that hem in life – at present. Similarly Hannah Arendt in her most controversial book, *Eichmann in Jerusalem*, redescribes contemporary evil (somewhat in line with Blake) as banal. "The longer one listened to him," Arendt observes of the war criminal Adolf Eichmann, "the more obvious it became that his inability to speak was closely connected with an inability to *think*, namely, to think from the standpoint of somebody else. No communication was possible with him, not because he lied but because he was surrounded by the most reliable of all safeguards against the words and the presence of others, and hence against reality as such."[18] So Arendt invites us to see Eichmann, and numerous other good Germans, not as raving beasts, but as vapid, dull, cowed men and women. She challenges our sense of evil, our sense of limit.

Arendt, Blake, and Emerson are all, like Foucault, consequential allegorists, with pressing images of evil or fate to disseminate. Yet they differ from Foucault in a critical way. Arendt spent the last years of her life writing the three volume *Life of the Mind*. The objective of that work was to describe the kind of thought that can make a person as close to Eichmann's opposite as possible. Is there anything we can learn from the major philosophers, Arendt seems to be asking, that we could broadly dispense (for education is her perpetual theme), to guarantee that our students would not turn into banal, killing conformists? If Arendt never answers this question to her satisfaction (she died before the trilogy was completed), her attempt seems to me consistently admirable, worthy of our study and of further intellectual elaboration.

[17] *Milton by William Blake*, ed. Kay Parkhurst Easson and Roger R. Easson (Boulder, Colo.: Shambhala Press in Association with Random House, 1978), p. 81.
[18] P. 49.

For his part, Blake, through the self-anatomizing, self-purging process that is *Milton*, comes to an understanding of what qualities in himself and others might defeat Satan in mental fight. He speaks at the end of the poem about casting off rational demonstration in favor of faith; of eschewing memory to rely on inspiration; about battling the reductionists, Hobbes and Locke; and – this perhaps most important of all – about braving the charge of madness, not being turned back when it's cast at him and his work. Perhaps the lines in which Blake makes his ultimate profession are too high-pitched. Maybe they're too close to the ranting style to which Satan rises after Palamabron exposes him for what he is. The style of mind that Satan possesses, harsh and grating, is at enmity with the feminine mildness that Blake aspires to, both for Milton, his character, and for himself: self-proclaiming Blake is at least in some part self-undermined.

So too Emerson's skepticism about every stay and prop sometimes takes on a mannered air. There's occasionally something too cozy in the perpetual turnings of his mind: they smack more of a politely choreographed dance than of a chancy athletic performance where if your grace fails you're likely to be humiliated or hurt. His puns become too easy, as when in "Self-Reliance" he refers to the loquacious ineffectual denizens of the drawing-room, his friends and sometimes himself, as "parlour soldiers."[19] He's capable at times of minting the kind of platitudes that will feed commercials for sneakers and stereo gear many years down the line. On the other side of the equation, he's capable, in "Experience," of growing cold beyond human belief about the death of his dear child, Waldo. Yet he and Blake and, in my opinion, Arendt, are major writers in part because having laid out the current sorry human condition in memorable language, they move to invent ways to shift the ground of fate, ways that are humanly difficult and costly enough to fit the dire situations they've described.

There are any number of cogent objections to Foucault's work. Though I consider him foremost a visionary moralist and mythmaker, part of his authority comes from his supposed status as a historian. H. C. Erik Midelfort has shown, with considerable

---

[19] *Essays and Lectures*, p. 275.

subtlety and restraint, how riddled with errors is Foucault's first consequential book, *Madness and Civilization*.[20] The nadir comes when Foucault offers the ship of fools, a boat loaded with a town's madmen and women and sent adrift, not as the legend it apparently was, but as historical fact. *Discipline and Punish*, the book of Foucault's that I think will be read into the twenty-first century, is more accurate, but historians have complained, with some justice, that the survey of judgment and discipline is too narrow for the large claims the book makes about the genesis of the modern soul.

Discipline and Punish asks us to see an intensified image for the workings of other contemporary institutions in the prison protocols that it describes. I do see those parallels (though with qualifications I will get to soon), and it seems just, given the book's factual accuracy, to extend Foucault's work into alternate spheres and see how well it might apply. In other words, talking about Gayle's working double in terms derived from *Discipline and Punish* seems reasonable and potentially illuminating.

There is, though, what I take to be a major difficulty in Foucault's conception of norms. Surely rigidly conceived and cruelly enforced norms do present dangers. But Foucault never pauses to discriminate between different kinds of norms, different kinds of disciplines: some presumably are more destructive than others. And, too, some are more susceptible to revision. Nor has Foucault anything to say about how a generous and compassionate individual might, despite social pressure, apply norms humanely. Having some empirical information about the ways that memory tends to atrophy in old age – and the ways that it does not – can give rise to stereotyping: it can help create what Blake and Foucault abhor, fixed selfhood. But such information might also help one to treat an aging parent more humanely, modifying expectations without being patronizing. The engendering of norms, a social scientist would say with at least some truth, encourages one to understand more and to judge less. A psychoanalyst who had even a measure of the tough-mindedness and

[20] "Madness and Civilization in Early Modern Europe: A Reappraisal of Michel Foucault," in *After the Reformation, Essays in Honor of J. H. Hexter*, ed. Barbara C. Malament (Philadelphia: University of Pennsylvania Press, 1980), pp. 247–65.

compassion that Freud at his best showed – and there are plenty of such therapists – wouldn't stand by tranquilly while a personnel expert used analytic technique to deflect a subordinate's just complaints.

But compassion and understanding may at times be techniques of discipline, all the more dangerous for their humane appeal. "Pity would be no more," says Blake, in many ways Foucault's original, "if we did not make somebody Poor."[21] It is, for example, difficult to deny that there is something reductively normative about the theory of the Oedipal complex, the basis of much psychoanalytical thinking. To say that all of our life stories are at best elaborations on one eternal story strikes hard at the sense of human diversity that literature affirms. For why would we need the great variety of novels and poems if they all reduced to one master tale in the end?

And when the personnel officer, fresh from university management courses, allows the employee to vent her anger, the thinking behind his gesture is that in all of us there's a residue of anger at our fathers for their Oedipal prohibition, and that such anger transfers itself onto contemporary figures of authority. But – and here is the important point – it is a rage that is fundamentally regressive: it belongs to the past. Thus the manager is right to invite the worker into a cathartic expression: the rage isn't his affair. As discomfited as a first-rate psychoanalyst would be at the manager's tawdry reduction of his techniques, the analyst would, I believe, have to admit that the manager was not operating entirely outside Freudian terrain.

Perhaps a more important rebuttal to Foucault lies in the fact that every day people resist normative generalizations about themselves, no matter how respectable the figure who propounds them, and how august his affiliations. There's always a tension operative between official versions and popular or individual accounts. This tension comes through in jokes, slang, popular art, and the overall Anglo-American distaste for expertise in every form. De Tocqueville, someone whose sense of democratic life in many ways accords with Foucault's (the epigraph about

[21] "The Human Abstract," *Blake, Complete Writings*, ed. Geoffrey Keynes (London: Oxford University Press, 1966), p. 217.

dungeons in the air is from Emerson's response to *Democracy in America*), said that in America everyone can say what he likes, but everyone ends up saying the same thing. I would counter this with a fine observation of David Bromwich's to the effect that America would be a lot more like the country de Tocqueville described and prophesied if Emerson had never come along.[22] Emerson planted the seeds for a culture that's insouciant, eccentric, and unpredictable, and if that culture hasn't been entirely realized, one still senses its promise in most of the American art that matters. One can in fact divide much of American culture into passionate continuation of Emerson, or vehement protest against him and everything he stood for.

Emerson matters so much because, like Blake and Arendt, he has a strong conception not just of fate but of potential freedom. And it is on this point that one touches the sullen depths of Foucault's work. Though his diagnosis of current civilization *at its worst*, once it is refined, qualified, deprived of its unequivocal, overheated force, seems to me one of the very best we have, Foucault refuses to offer transforming alternatives. He has said that to imagine utopian possibilities is to support the current disciplinary dispensation, and yet if one does not look for utopia any longer, one does look for some impulse toward renewal, some contemporary equivalent to Blake's prophecy, Emerson's self-assaulting self-reliance, Arendt's worldly thinking. This has been said before about Foucault, but it needs to be insisted upon.[23] Foucault's refusal to go further, to risk his authority by coming up with renovating alternatives, testifies to self-serving timidity.

And yet it is also an opportunity and one well suited, I believe, to the needs of contemporary literary criticism. Foucault himself took only a peripheral interest in literature. He is generally respectful and intrigued, particularly in *Les mots et les choses*. At no consequential point in his work does he associate the literary

---

[22] *A Choice of Inheritance: Self and Community from Edmund Burke to Robert Frost* (Cambridge: Harvard University Press, 1989), p. 148.

[23] My view of Foucault's pessimism is in line with two fine critiques of his work, Edward Said's "Foucault and the Imagination of Power," *Foucault: A Critical Reader*, pp. 149–55, and Frank Lentricchia's more comprehensive piece in *Ariel and the Police: Michel Foucault, William James, Wallace Stevens* (Madison: University of Wisconsin Press, 1988), pp. 29–102.

with the disciplines. But Foucault need not be, as Harold Bloom said he is, massively irrelevant to the study of literature.

Foucault's work invites us to face in two directions, toward our own institutional practice and to the relation of poems, plays, and novels to the disciplines that surround us in the university and in society at large. Is criticism a disciplinary practice, in Foucault's sense of the term? Yes, sometimes, and here readers will recognize, if they have not before, that this book's first chapter, on Coleridge and de Man, and its third, on contemporary versions of Marx, take some cues from Foucault. There I tried to show the disciplinary uses of the unconscious: I pointed out how recourse to it as a sort of critical god-term – whether what is purportedly repressed is material history or death – enhances the professional cartel of literary studies, though at a cost. For generating methods for describing texts, we also teach others and ourselves to describe persons. And there are few critical modes more conducive to a culture of mutual surveillance than those that rely on images of blindness and insight, or repression and disclosure.

One might take this Foucauldian inquiry about the disciplinary dimensions of criticism in a number of different directions. Given the attention I paid to him, it will be worthwhile here to consider the case of Derrida. Though Derrida and Foucault have squabbled over a number of things, most notably about how to read Descartes, it seems that the most pregnant Foucauldian critique of Derrida would be, to put it rather brusquely, that he's still interested in cutting off the king's head. He wants to do away with logocentrism, belief in the one, so as to free us from arbitrary, monolithic authority, a form of authority that, to Foucault, has been out of play for a long time. And what does Derrida use to displace logocentrism? The most common positive image in his work is that of the text, the ever-expanding web, an image that reproduces the current form that power takes. Derrida's textual web and power's web might thus be mutually reinforcing. Derrida seeks freedom in the form, or anti-form, that to Foucault best figures our current mode of confinement.[24]

Foucault's thinking also helps one see how Derrida's theory of

---

[24] For some related remarks about Derrida see Slavoj Žižek's *Tarrying with the Negative: Kant, Hegel, and the Critique of Ideology* (Durham, N. C.: Duke University Press, 1993), pp. 216–19.

the text meshes with another set of contemporary developments, apparently far from the provinces of humanistic study. A good deal of the current work in business management theory conceives of itself as revolutionary, putting forward as it does a fresh philosophy of corporate organization. The new wisdom dictates that the "pyramid structure" of management, the design in which a manager works on a level with other managers, with a single controlling supervisor above, is now obsolete. The old hierarchical mode doesn't take into account the multiple functions and associations that the new executive must sustain. In the pyramid system, the manager is too dependent on the approval and veto power of his superior; he hasn't enough freedom to act quickly, independently, and at his own discretion.

The change – which is taking place on a level that someone like Gayle, the airline booker, never sees – is undoubtedly a major one: John Naisbitt's best-seller, *Megatrends*, asserts that one of the ten (naturally, ten) major transformations in company organization over the next few decades will be the shift "from hierarchies to networking."[25] Naisbitt's book sold hugely in the business community, but most of it simply reduces for easy consumption ideas that had been around in the major MBA programs for some time. Naisbitt prophesies networking with flat assurance: "In the future, institutions will be organized according to a management system based on a networking model. Systems will be designed to provide both lateral and horizontal, even multi-directional and overlapping, linkages."[26]

In his influential study, *Images of Organization*, Gareth Morgan, a far more sophisticated thinker than Naisbitt, voices preference for metaphors of organization that stress "flux and transformation."[27] But it's in Morgan's textbook, *Creative Organization Theory*, that literary critics would, I suspect, find the most to surprise them. Not many pages prior to tracing the development from "bureaucracies to networks," Morgan inserts a quotation from Nietzsche designed to move the thoughts of MBA students toward the future: "What is truth? A moving army of metaphors, metonymies, and anthropomorphisms, in short a summa of human relationships that are being poetically and rhetorically sublimated,

[25] *Megatrends: Ten New Directions Transforming Our Lives* (New York: Warner, 1982).
[26] *Megatrends*, p. 198.   [27] London: Sage, 1986.

transposed . . . and beautified . . ." The reader will be familiar with the rest.[28]

Now a Foucauldian critique of textualism doesn't necessarily cook up a conspiracy theory. It's not that at the 1966 conference on the Sciences of Man a secret seminar convened in which the deconstructors signed a devil's pact with a few captains of industry. The Foucauldian critic, interested in forms of corporate discipline, is simply impatient with the textualists' claims to avant-garde status. Must it be the case that the latest form of academic apostasy is out ahead of all other cultural discourses?

Let us push the matter a bit further. In an information economy, the thinking goes, what's crucial is the ability to make contact with a wide spectrum – or better, a large, perhaps unending web – of persons who can provide key expertise and necessary data. The manager must be versatile, assuming a number of roles, contributing to a span of projects, always flexible and on the move. Networking, by doing away with simple hierarchy, refocuses the manager's loyalties: where there was a simple role, now there are many interlocking tasks; where there was one boss, now there are numerous associates involved.

In order to thrive in this new corporate environment, the manager must be someone rather unlike the successful manager of the past. And – the Foucauldian case might go – one of the best means for making over one's character to meet the new corporate demands would be by exposure to Derrida's method of reading. It too is a form of networking, emphasizing the ongoing, perhaps interminable creation of linkages, alliances, associations, without telos, without the prospect of termination. For all tasks branch out into others in corporate networking; every successful operation generates fresh resources to be deployed. In some measure this has been the case since the advent of capitalism, but the rise of the global market and developments in information technology allow for – in fact, require – investment to go on at an unprecedented rate of speed. For this kind of ceaseless and independent unfolding, Derrida's kind of reading provides a means of correct training.

But Derridean reading may be helpful in creating a new

[28] London: Sage, p. 22.

managerial type in yet another way. Part of what's at stake in the shift from the conventional corporate structure that puts a single supervisor over a subordinate may be a shift in established ways of conceiving authority. Hegel, Nietzsche, and Freud all imagined crucial relations with authority in binary terms: think of Hegel's master, Nietzsche's teacher, Freud's primal father. Spiritual health would consist in arriving at the point where one had stabilized relations with this superior person, and with his various surrogates, both inside oneself and out. And this intense relation is often a productive one: the passion it generates helps us to get our work done. We want to please, thwart, or surprise the patriarch.

Imagine Derridean reading, then, as a mode of therapeutic instruction that helps a person brought up in the old dispensation to move into a new relation to authority, one more suited to current modes of production. (The king's head is off; it has been for a long time.) The student taught to read by a disciple of Derrida will learn how to resist the claims any single author or authority makes on her. For Derrida repeatedly shows how the author's attempts to dominate language are undone by the figurative energies of words. Deconstruction demonstrates how the intentions of a single authority dissolve into network, text, writing. An education composed of such reading might help a student to dislodge her sense of authority as naturally enforced in binary relations (my father and I, the author and I, the boss and I) and get her ready to function within a network of relations where power works less crudely. (She'll be able to think of herself as a willing subject manipulating the systems that intersect human objects like Gayle.) What the Foucauldian critic might say is that Derridean reading, rather than being the death knell of all civilized values, etc., etc., may be very good preparation for a bright economic future.

But Foucauldian critique need not yield exclusively harsh news. To suggest as much, we might turn from Derridean radicalism to a purportedly old-fashioned and conservative approach, the New Criticism. Consider the language of Brooks, Wimsatt, and Martz from Foucault's perspective. Their terms, Foucault helps one to see, were implicitly ethical and self-fashioning. The New Critics didn't just teach students to recognize tension, irony, ambiguity, and organic form, they taught them to cultivate qualities in their own characters that would be in line with what was most valuable in poems. The well-wrought student of Cleanth Brooks would be able to tolerate a fair amount of unresolved tension in life. He'd be able to suspend himself in uncertainties, mysteries, doubts, to cite a phrase of Keats's that meant something to many of the New Critics. The student, like the accomplished poet and his poems, was supposed to be mature. Surely there's something of the '50s organization man in this model: someone reserved, well-contained, hyper-masculine (no Shelley allowed). But one ought not to write off this kind of teaching too quickly. When the members of the Frankfurt School conducted experiments to define the "authoritarian personality," they found that such persons had little or no tolerance for the kind of suspended belief that the New Critics cultivated.[29] A comprehensive Foucauldian analysis of the supposedly retrograde New Critics might yield more than a few surprises.

But what of the other direction Foucault's ideas might tend, toward the study of literary works themselves? There is no need to speculate here, for the New Historicists, led by the gifted and energetic Stephen Greenblatt, have been working hard to apply Foucault to the reading of literature, and with the overall result that literature is revealed as another among the disciplines, as a force for social conformity. The foremost exhibit has been Shakespeare, who according to Doctor Johnson is the most humane and disinterested writer we have. Are Greenblatt and his followers right? Have they used Foucault to reveal the coercive dimension of apparently exalting work? Should literature be written off as one among the disciplines? Let us see.

What is new, one might begin by asking, about the literary critical movement that springs from the later work of Foucault and that finds Stephen Greenblatt at its head?[30] What is new about New Historicism?

---

[29] Theodor Adorno, et al., *The Authoritarian Personality* (New York: Harper, 1950), pp. 461–4.

[30] Much has been written about Greenblatt. The pieces I have found most useful are William Kerrigan's "Individualism, Historicism, and New Styles of Overreaching," *Philosophy and Literature*, 13:1 (April, 1989), pp. 115–26 and Gordon Braden's "Greenblatt's Trajectory," *Raritan*, 13:1 (1993), pp. 139–50.

Greenblatt and his many followers press an apparent paradox of traditional literary historicism until it reveals itself as a mere contradiction. That contradiction comes clear when we consider Hippolyte Taine's monumental work of nineteenth-century historicism, the two volume *History of English Literature*. To know the literary work, Taine insists, you must know the nature of its creator, and Taine excels at freehand portraiture. Edmund Wilson, America's last major historicist critic, remembered himself as a young man walking the streets of New York and reciting below his breath Taine's description of Swift, standing in the great hall of Dublin University to be examined for the bachelor's degree. "A poor scholar, odd, awkward, with hard blue eyes, an orphan, friendless, poorly supported by the charity of an uncle, having failed once before to take his degree on account of his ignorance of logic, [he] had come up again without having condescended to read logic . . . He was asked how he could reason well without rules; he replied that he did reason pretty well without them."[31]

Almost all of Taine's authors have violently singular personalities – they radiate their natures as unequivocally as characters out of Saul Bellow or Martin Amis – and the personalities, as Taine sees it, determine the works. Yet the works he examines are always superbly representative summaries of the spirit of the age: they express everything in perfect balance. So from one perspective, the works, like their creators, are idiosyncratic; yet Taine also insists on the power of great writing fully to summarize the cultural moment, to be representative, not eccentric. On this view, Balzac, who dies calling out upon the characters of his *Comédie Humaine*, fades into universal light. It's this crossing of the bar into a space of transcendent generality that New Historicists like Greenblatt are prone to resist.

The grand organicism, derived in part from a rather simplistic construction of Hegel, that underwrote Taine's mode of historicism was too palpably theological to survive all the way through twentieth-century literary study. In time, the carefully cultivated garden – or the poet's green thought of that green enclosure –

---

[31] Trans. H. Van Laun, 2 vols. (New York: Henry Holt and Company, 1879), II:116.

became a reigning emblem for the well-made poem, as the New Critics taught their students to be content with microcosms. Part of the genius of New Historicism has been to recognize that after the deconstructive critique of totalizing thought and the unanimous sign, one could return to literary history and see the commerce between text and historical context not in terms of reflection or progressive dialectic, but of circulation, exchange, transformation, and transvaluation. New Historicists like Greenblatt understand that while a culture may tend toward total cohesion, the actual situation is always a dynamic one, in which numberless discourses, energies, and desires circulate, ceaselessly inflecting and reinflecting each other. The artist's work doesn't summarize any particular configuration of forces: a text isn't, as Taine would have it, a culturally expressive whole. Rather texts enter into the exchange of energies and metamorphoses of forms occurring among all cultural languages. "Eternity" may be, as Blake's proverb says, "in love with the productions of time," but those productions, rightly read, resist timeless categories.

Consequential literary texts, according to Greenblatt and his followers, tend to be the most sophisticated disciplinary devices that a culture produces, but this is so because they don't function in the mode of the standard disciplines. Literary works continually reveal the existing structures of coercion, and in fact challenge those structures with liberating alternatives. But the challenge is inevitably reabsorbed into the larger disciplinary patterns that are then culturally active. Literature, according to Greenblatt, is a sort of Foucauldian discipline to the second degree.

I want to focus on Greenblatt's "Invisible Bullets," from *Shakespearean Negotiations*, an essay that considers the sequence of plays featuring Prince Hal (who becomes Henry V). Greenblatt has expressed some doubts about the methodological dimension of the article; he seems to think it too pat. But I take it up here because, however schematic, it's a brilliant piece of work and too because it's been the most influential of the New Historicist essays. It's the mold from which much of the work by younger historical critics has emerged.

"Invisible Bullets" gets briskly to its point, which is to read the plays as forms of anthropological discourse. The chapter – without needing to say as much – relies upon the reverse effect of a boom in mythography, the boom initiated by Lévi-Strauss and his followers in the 1950s. Lévi-Strauss took pains to demonstrate that myths participated in a systematic order, possessed a grammar, and functioned, like the configurations of paint on the faces of the Amazonian natives, to balance and beautify contradictions. From there it was not difficult to grasp the analogies between myth and metaphysics, and to stigmatize metaphysics, as Derrida does, as the white man's mythology. At the moment this analogy is apprehended, conventional anthropological writing reveals its double-sided effect: it enforces terms upon so-called primitive cultures, and also works to focus the Western gaze away from its own peculiar tribalisms. Enter Roland Barthes with the conceit of seeing the French petite bourgeoisie as a tribe in its own right, replete with peculiar ceremonies, protocols, and a bizarre little portfolio of myths. Barthes takes himself as a sort of Parisian fieldworker, though (as the second chapter indicated) without the complex sense of connection to his subjects that Lévi-Strauss sustained for the Nambikwara.

But something more follows, and here Foucault and Greenblatt come in: one begins to realize how pervasive the discipline of anthropology is and has been within Western culture itself, how it has been employed as a means of knowing such indwelling alien tribes as the lower classes, delinquents, the poor, children, and women. Foucault, presumably, might have done with anthropology something very close to what he did to the discipline of humane jurisprudence and to the enlightened study of human sexuality. The surprise of "Invisible Bullets" is how persuasively Greenblatt can show Shakespeare's plays to be dramatizing the anthropological function, and doing so in something of the same ways as two more quotidian productions of the time, Thomas Harriot's *A Brief and True Report of the New Found Land of Virginia* (1588) and Thomas Harman's pamphlet *A Caveat for Common Cursitors* (1566). The first treats social customs among the Algonquians of Virginia, the second among the criminal poor of Elizabethan London.

Prince Hal, in good anthropological fashion, is a devoted learner of foreign tongues: after his sojourn in Eastcheap, he can "drink with any tinker in his own language." The lower classes are, to Hal, a separate but unequal nation. Their voices, Greenblatt observes, exist within the order of the plays much as do the voices of the French, of the Welshman Fluellen, the Irishman Macmorris, and the Scotsman Jamy, those stereotypical "puppets jerked on the strings of their own absurd accents" (p. 57), as Greenblatt says in a characteristically fine turn of phrase. The potentially subversive voices, says Greenblatt, arise "within the affirmations of order; they are powerfully registered, but they do not undermine that order. Indeed, as the example of Harman – so much cruder than Shakespeare – suggests, the order is neither possible nor fully convincing without both the presence and perception of betrayal" (p. 52).

Harman and Harriot too devote themselves to learning languages, compiling glossaries, but of the London underclass and of the native Virginians: it is their anthropological practice that alerts Greenblatt to the techniques of domination that he takes to be operating in Shakespeare's three plays. The alien languages in each case represent alternative ways of life and the possibility of breaking up monolithic order in the interest of human variety; rather than avoiding those refractory possibilities, Harman and Harriot, and supposedly Shakespeare too, dramatize them, thus containing potentially rebellious forces.

In Harriot's analysis, which reveals the Algonquian religion to be a means of social control, there lies an implicit indictment of the Anglican faith along exactly the same lines. Yet the Machiavellian reading of the alien culture, Greenblatt argues, serves to reaffirm, not threaten, the dominant one, as though the potential subversion were exorcised by being discovered in a culture so markedly different from England's. In fact, the English faith does go to work in the New World, often quite directly, as a means of social control over the natives. The threat of divine retribution by the invaders' God continually brings the tribes back into line. But this Machiavellian use of religion, clear as it may be to us, seems invisible to the perpetrators themselves. As Greenblatt summarizes matters: "English power in the first Virginia colony *depends* upon the registering and even the production of potentially unsettling perspectives" (p. 37) – as well as their forced reabsorption back into binding social arrangements. And so, Greenblatt feels, it goes throughout *The Henriad*. In the darkening progress of those plays – in which Greenblatt seems to see an allegory for the evolution of the West – power works inexorably to generate and then to contain potentially subversive energies.

Here Greenblatt's debt to Foucault becomes palpable. To Foucault of course society generates criminals in order to affirm itself by protecting the middle class from the created threat. And too those criminal figures who appear to be the most threatening to society actually are constituted, through discipline, so as to illustrate norms inversely: one supposedly measures oneself, instinctively, on a scale where the delinquent inhabits an extreme position. The common criminal, like the pervert, is a subversive presence that serves behavioral order. Greenblatt's Foucauldian theme, worked subtly through a number of instances, is power's capacity to reaffirm itself by appropriating resistant energies.

What I find surprising is Greenblatt's determination to see Shakespeare as an unwitting victim of the subversion and containment plot. "The ideological strategies that fashion Shakespeare's history plays," he observes, "are no more Shakespeare's invention than the historical narratives on which he based his plots. As we shall see from Harriot's *Brief and True Report*, in the discourse of authority a powerful logic governs the relation between orthodoxy and subversion" (p. 23). Greenblatt does show rather persuasively that some such logic operates in Harriot and Harman. But it need not follow, as Greenblatt soon insists it does, that because such limits bind these two they also bind Shakespeare. Might it not be that Shakespeare's plays work to illuminate the operations of power that Greenblatt, cued by Foucault, identifies?

Greenblatt is determined – or so it seems to me – to think otherwise. He observes that the "apparent subversion of the monarch's glorification has led some critics since Hazlitt to view the panegyric [of King Henry] as bitterly ironic or to argue, more plausibly, that Shakespeare's depiction of Henry V is radically ambiguous. But in the light of Harriot's *Brief and True Report*, we may suggest that the subversive doubts the play continually awakens originate paradoxically in an effort [on Shakespeare's part presumably] to intensify the power of the king and his war" (pp. 62-3). But the fact that one Thomas Harriot conceives matters in such and such a way is thin proof that Shakespeare does too. Greenblatt's observation relies on a theory of ideology which insists that everyone in a given age concurred on a set of major assumptions. To this view a key difference between a writer of genius and a common hack like Harman is that the former is a more articulate and comprehensive source for abiding unexamined prejudices.

In truth it would not have been difficult for Greenblatt to credit Shakespeare with dramatizing the subversion/containment dynamic, of placing it theatrically in the foreground, so that, among other things, members of his audience might better detect it in the likes of Harriot and Harman. Accordingly Shakespeare could be summoned as an ally in a cultural struggle, in which Foucault also might play a part, to recognize and respond to an intricate stratagem for human domination.[32] Letting Shakespeare offer the terms in which we comprehend Harman would, I'm inclined to think, be at least as likely a procedure as assuming that Harman and Shakespeare, because they lived in the same period, must be enclosed by identical limits.

Unlike Foucault and Greenblatt, though, Shakespeare is more than an analyst of disciplinary ruses; he also exemplifies alternatives. But the possibilities that Shakespeare offers in this regard are, in Greenblatt's constructions of the plays, unusually difficult to detect. Greenblatt assumes that Hal is the central figure of the plays, and that the audience identifies with him. Hal's language learning and powers of improvisation all are understood as working to feed his will to power, his wish to be able to manipulate everyone he encounters. And with this diagnosis of Hal I fully concur. Yet, as Nabokov remarked, if you're going to identify

---

[32] A similar dynamic seems to be in effect in another brilliant New Historicist essay, D. A. Miller's "Discipline in Different Voices," which appears in *The Novel and the Police* (Berkeley and Los Angeles: University of California Press, 1988), pp. 58–106. A good deal of Miller's critique of Victorian discipline is launched against Dickens; it finds the author in complicity with various forms of surveillance and quiet domination. But, as I see it, the most substantial part of the critique simply takes Dickens's own indictment of the Chancery system and casts it in Foucault's idiom.

with anyone in a literary work, you might try identifying with the author, or at least conceiving what it would be like to go through the process of composition as he did. So Helen Vendler says that when a poem seems to her freighted with significance, but resistant, opaque, she finds that the best thing to do is copy it over in longhand, imagining how it was to get from one line to another, what it was like to arrive at such and such an invention.

In the Henry plays the great improviser of dialects is not Hal but Shakespeare himself: an observation so commonplace that in our drive for a higher sophistication we are likely to forget it. Hal's lexical mobility is contained within Shakespeare's; in Hal we have an image of a young man who uses his skills in mimicry for self-advancement and self-protection: he despoils the rich verbal possibilities he comes in contact with. But that despoiling is a subject of the play, not an unquestioned ideal. We can feel this because we are continually asked to contrast Hal's exploitative play-making with Falstaff's richer, more generous, and more vulnerable exercises in the same medium. Falstaff's desire for pleasure and largess, though not itself an untainted drive, provides an alternative against which to measure Hal's compulsive scheming. Hal, in other words, isn't a full image for the playwright proper, and Falstaff proves it.

The power to move through idioms and identities, the ability for which Shakespeare has long been justly celebrated (not least by Keats in the Negative Capability letter) may stand as a plausible alternative to disciplinary urges, urges to consolidate other selves by knowing them, knowing their languages. Shakespeare teaches us how to draw on different aspects of ourselves, different indwelling voices, to create a coherent variety and richness that represent an alternative to monolithic official versions. And this, I believe, is one of the things literature does overall, opening us up to the manifold voices and vocabularies we contain or may borrow, giving us access not just to this or that idiom but to intricacies of tone, valences of hyperbole, irony, wit, and density that aren't easily disciplined. Discipline often depends on our willingness to answer back seriously, to echo its monotone: Shakespeare teaches play, not play in the baroque, self-regarding Derridean mode, not unconditioned play, but play that weaves itself into and through the various sciences of man, the varieties of official cultural experience, making them the elements of our game, if only temporarily.[33]

Granted this is a playing with words, not with institutional structures, but anyone who wishes to escape words – and I think the frustrated, weary tone of much contemporary literary criticism derives in part from a dull rage at living among shadowy types and not real presences – must find another field of endeavor. Yet who knows what transforming acts linguistic renovation may precipitate? Perhaps we'll try to make ourselves worthy of our best verbal inventions. "Falstaff," says Harold Bloom, "is passionate, and challenges us not to bore him, if he is to deign to represent us."[34]

Why then does Greenblatt choose an adversarial relation with an imaginative writer who may well be his own best ally? Why does it seem necessary that one use Foucault *on* literature rather than testing the notion that literature provides resources for an anti-disciplinary critique? A moment of methodological reflection by Greenblatt offers some valuable clues. Greenblatt believes that when one sees the play of orthodoxy and subversion at work, then the contingency of power, its transitoriness and potential instability, is revealed. But – and here is the important point – that revelation is available not to the contemporary perceiver, who is necessarily blind to the process, but to the observer–analyst distanced in time. Thus Greenblatt's twice-made profession that "There is subversion, no end of subversion, only not for us" (pp. 39, 65). His implication is that we live, blinded, within our own peculiar ratios of subversion and containment, much as the Elizabethans did in theirs. The allusion to Kafka ("there is hope, no end of hope"), gives the idea a certain vatic resonance, as well as associating it with the kind of easy pessimism characteristic of Foucault.

Yet the idea itself is one we have learned to associate with

---

[33] As Richard Poirier puts it,

> [T]hough troping involves only words, it might also, as an activity, make us less easily intimidated by them, by terminologies inherited from the historical past or currently employed in the directives of public policy. It might like any art prevent a society from "becoming too assertively, too hopelessly, itself," as Kenneth Burke phrased the possibility some sixty years ago in *Counter-Statement*. (*Poetry and Pragmatism* [Cambridge: Harvard University Press, 1992], p. 129.)

[34] *Ruin the Sacred Truths: Poetry and Belief from the Bible to the Present* (Cambridge: Harvard University Press, 1989), p. 87.

something else: for, thinking back to the first and third chapters, we can recognize Greenblatt's profession as a displaced version of Paul de Man's blindness and insight dynamic. "The insight exists," de Man wrote in his essay on Derrida, "only for a reader in the privileged position of being able to observe the blindness as a phenomenon in its own right."[35] And it is only the observer, distanced in time, who, according to Greenblatt, can apprehend the ratios of containment and subversion, of blindness and insight, active in cultural productions. Greenblatt sees one's immersion within certain historically fixed forms of discourse as being as epistemologically confining as de Man saw the attachments of various twentieth-century critics to the ideology of the symbol, organicism, the centered self, and the aesthetic of the beautiful to be. Similarly, Marjorie Levinson achieves her interpretive sublime when she identifies the Romantic ideology as the force that suppresses historical truth: she combines Marx with de Man. What Greenblatt gives us in "Invisible Bullets," and what his disciples most assiduously take up, is a historically inflected version of de Man's central trope for dramatic irony, blindness and insight.

This de Manian gesture arises in some rather unexpected places, and among critics who are too accomplished to be thought of as anyone's disciples. The central argument of Eve Kosofsky Sedgwick's brilliant *Epistemology of the Closet* declares that we are all, inevitably, caught between essentializing and universalizing ideas about sexual identity.[36] (That is, between the notion that people are by nature bisexual, and that they're born with an inalienable disposition to one or another kind of object choice.) As Sedgwick sees it, we're suspended between metonymy (we could go any number of ways) and metaphor (we are what we are), a most de Manian state to be in, and one without exit. Similarly, at the end of *The Novel and the Police*, D. A. Miller would demonstrate how Dickens's characters (and perhaps, by implication, ourselves as well) are left trapped between liberal and carceral identities, a condition not unlike de Manian undecidability. Like Greenblatt, these two impressive critics begin with Foucault, and end up, alas, with Paul de Man.

[35] *Blindness and Insight*, p. 106.
[36] Berkeley and Los Angeles: University of California Press, 1990.

The genealogy I offered in the first chapter associated de Man's blindness and insight method with Coleridge, with Freud, and also with the need disciplinary literary studies has for a form of intellectual authority broadly negotiable in current academic life. When Greenblatt chooses to find in Shakespeare a victim – and not a self-aware analyst – of subversion and containment, he works, drawing on Foucault, to do something that Foucault puts one in a position to identify and challenge: he disciplines literature. He renders literature susceptible to the languages of anthropology, history, political science, and, above all (recall Freud's central place here), psychoanalysis. De Man (and I use de Man here to signify the disciplinary imperative of academic literary criticism at its most sophisticated and attractive) working as it were through Greenblatt, succeeds in diverting Foucault's critique of the disciplines away from a most promising object, literary criticism as it is practiced within academic institutions, and instead toward literature itself.

I am not denying that literature should be interrogated to disclose its disciplinary affiliations – that seems to me a most promising route. I am saying that most literary criticism now begins by assuming that the questions that ought to be its chief matter for debate – questions about the relations between literature and various socially insinuated languages – are already resolved. Criticism now often assumes that the correct procedure exclusively entails the application of various vocabularies, often social-scientific in provenance, to the works at hand. Whereas the objective ought also to involve discovering the resistances that literature offers to being encompassed by this or that generalizing terminology.

Greenblatt's capitulation to de Man allows him to take some institutional high ground; and, perhaps equally important, it provides something of a rationale for the illusions of powerlessness that so dog contemporary academics. For, presumably, whatever implicit challenges to the established order lie hidden within Greenblatt's text, they are not discernible to the reader in the present. This is too bad, because a good deal of Greenblatt's force is allegorical: implicitly he asks us to look for contemporary situations that resemble those he finds in the Renaissance: I took it, wrongly Greenblatt would be compelled to assure me, that his stories about Harman and Harriot taught me a good deal about the ways in which contemporary anthropology functions to direct and refine society's attempts to keep the underclasses in line. The great German historicist critic Arnold Hauser said that the only justification for the historical study of art was that it might lead to a better comprehension of one's own moment. "What else could it be?" he cheerfully asks.[37] By this standard, "Invisible Bullets," and the other chapters in *Shakespearean Negotiations* on *Lear* and the Elizabethan politics of exorcism, on sexual identity in the comedies, and on romance and the generation of anxiety would, given Greenblatt's overt commitment to a historical version of de Man's blindness and insight model, have to count as empty expenses of spirit.

Perhaps Greenblatt's epistemological gloom arises out of a bad conscience at how much *Shakespearean Negotiations* is actually using the past to ponder, by analogy, our current situation. For it is the postulate of classical historicism, put forward by, among others, Erich Auerbach, that every epoch must be understood as absolutely alien from the present, "as incomparable and unique, as animated by inner forces and in a constant state of development."[38] And it was upon this capacity to negate the present that the traditional historicist's authority supposedly rested. Greenblatt's authority, on the other hand, is to a certain degree that of the poet, or the maker of metaphor, who finds similarity in difference, or perspective by incongruity, to use Kenneth Burke's phrase. When Greenblatt discusses the oppression of native peoples, women, and the poor by the application of anthropological techniques, by medical practices that seek to normalize sexuality, by religious and aesthetic devices to manipulate anxiety, and by official onslaughts in the name of progress against popular belief and popular culture, he's asking us to draw analogies with things as they are today.

To evoke these sorts of analogies the critic has to have the integrity to keep his sense of the present dilemma from determining his construction of the past. And here lies the source of much of the productive tension in *Shakespearean Negotiations*. The essay on

[37] *The Social History of Art*, trans. Stanley Godman, 4 vols. (New York: Vintage, 1951), IV:3.
[38] *Mimesis*, p. 444.

the comedies, for example, "Fiction and Friction," never acquires the large resonance that the three other pieces do, and simply because here Greenblatt won't contort his findings about the Renaissance to suit his current allegiances. In fact, Greenblatt's practice doesn't need to fall under de Man's disabling shadow. Little actually separates Greenblatt from the genuine critical art of attempting, with all the inevitable difficulties, to bring the past to life in the present.

Where *Shakespearean Negotiations* runs shallow is in its polemic against "conventional" notions of Shakespeare's genius, and the assumption, so feebly argued, that Shakespeare was by necessity a servant, not an anatomizer, of existing power. Greenblatt is out to disrupt the idea that the plays emanate from a "numinous literary authority," working in splendid isolation, without the pressures of literary influence or social force. This will be a hard view to displace, but for the reason that it isn't current to begin with: almost none of Greenblatt's readers hold it. One may believe everything that Greenblatt does about the social energies released and appropriated by every significant work, and about the contingent rather than universal values those works put into action, and still see Shakespeare's as a power of mind that is unique. In Greenblatt's assault on Shakespeare's genius, one may discern (as one may with Sigmund Freud, who having borrowed many of his best notions from Shakespeare went on to try to show that Shakespeare hadn't written the plays, that the Earl of Oxford had, that Bacon had, that we had no idea who had, etc.) a certain uneasiness lest the dynamics of power he claims to discover operating among the Elizabethans might already have been understood by another, and an Elizabethan at that.

But the most important point is this: Greenblatt's brilliant work – particularly his creation of an effective critical technique to inspire numerous disciples – has had the effect of blunting the challenge against the disciplines that literature offers. This challenge is present in all literature that matters, and yet right now there seems little or no profit in saying as much, at least for a university critic. Literature's power to struggle against false limits is something that Harold Bloom, to whom the next chapter turns, once understood superbly well. In a fine passage from *The Ringers in the Tower*, he points out how Romantic poetry gestures toward enhanced freedom by resisting easy conceptualization, resisting discipline: "The great enemy of poetry in the Romantic tradition," Bloom writes, "has never been reason, but rather those premature modes of conceptualization that masquerade as final accounts of reason in every age. It is not reason that menaces the shaping spirit, but the high priests of rationalization, the great men with the compasses who have marked out circumferences, from Descartes, Bacon, Newton, and Locke down to subtler limiters of the imaginative horizon in Hegel, Marx, Freud, and their various revisionist disciples. Romanticism . . . is a revolt not against orderly creation, but against compulsion, against conditioning, against all unnecessary limitation that presents itself as being necessary" (323–4).

CHAPTER 5

Under the influence

Harold Bloom, one of the most gifted, original, and provocative literary critics in the Western tradition, is often as acute about his own work as he is about others'. In an interview published in 1987 Bloom told Imre Salusinszky that "Although I can write, and probably will write, my dear – if I live – another thirty-five books, I am reconciled to the fact that to my dying day and beyond I will be regarded as the author of one book: *The Anxiety of Influence*."[1] Bloom is surely on target; when his name comes up, people think first of his theory of influence anxiety. Yet on its publication in 1973 *The Anxiety of Influence* was accorded anything but a gracious reception. "Harold Bloom had an idea," mocked one reader, "then it had him."

But Bloom has apparently enjoyed the last laugh. Borrowing some lines from William James, Bloom notes that response to *The Anxiety*'s thesis has passed through three stages. Granted people began by calling it absurd; in time, though, academic critics claimed that the book was completely obvious and that they'd known it all along; then finally the last phase: Bloom's antagonists started saying that they'd come up with the celebrated idea of influence anxiety themselves. In doing so they presumably indulged in the kind of fantasy that Bloom's book seeks to debunk, the wish to be your precursor's great original, to father your own father.

There is something to Bloom's hyperbolical account of *The Anxiety*'s reception. For his theory of poetic influence, in which the new poet enters into Oedipal struggle with a precursor, and

---

[1] *Criticism in Society*, p. 49.

in which poetry arises not from generosity of spirit and the urge to multiply sweetness and shed light, but from bitter strife and self-deception, has become, though often in displaced forms, an article of critical faith among many members of the contemporary academy. Male poets engage in symbolic parricide to bring themselves to painful birth; female poets must thwart the phallocentric tradition; modernism conquers Romanticism; postmodernism smashes high culture to curiously reflecting shards: art clears a space for itself by maiming, sometimes murdering, past art. Whether they concocted the notion themselves or learned it from Harold Bloom, critics today know that writers are at everlasting internecine war.

It's too bad that Bloom is so right about how *The Anxiety of Influence* has taken hold. *The Anxiety* is anything but a bad book, but its central ideas, rendered icily abstract (and not without help from Bloom), have worked to diminish the scope of contemporary criticism. In the pages to come I will try to identify what's most delimiting in Bloom as well as to make contact with the more vital tendencies in his work. For if Foucault, despite his remarkable inadequacies, may be our moment's most acute prophet of fate, Bloom at his best dramatizes literary freedom and power.

I shall approach *The Anxiety of Influence* by way of an essay that Paul de Man accurately sees as its point of departure, "The Internalization of Quest Romance," published in Bloom's 1971 collection, *The Ringers in the Tower*.[2] The essay is something of a *tour de force*, capping off more than a decade's brilliant defence of the Romantic poets. In *Shelley's Mythmaking*, *The Visionary Company*, *Blake's Apocalypse*, and a range of essays, Bloom struggled against the New Critical devaluation of the Romantics inspired by T. S. Eliot.[3] The Shelley book, published before Bloom was thirty, was an especially spirited affront to presiding academic pieties. Not only did he champion Shelley, the poet that Eliot and his minions had written off as a perpetual adolescent, but Bloom

[2] *Blindness and Insight*, p. 275.
[3] *Shelley's Mythmaking* (New Haven: Yale University Press, 1959); *The Visionary Company: A Reading of English Romantic Poetry* (Ithaca: Cornell University Press, 1971); *Blake's Apocalypse: A Study in Poetic Argument* (Garden City, N. Y.: Doubleday, 1963).

made his case by recourse to a Jewish theologian, Martin Buber. In the anti-Semitic atmosphere of 1950s American academia, this was almost too much to be borne. Almost: Bloom's unusual powers won him success despite his controversial ideas. The members of Yale's "secular clergy" (Bloom's latter-day name for them) tenured and promoted him, making him one of the youngest full professors at Yale. By the time he wrote "The Internalization," Bloom was both an academic pariah and a considerable success.

The essay is an effort – and as effective a one as I know – to arrive at a comprehensive view of English Romantic poetry, to discover what the major writers held in common. But "The Internalization" is more than a brilliant work of synthesis; in it Bloom also attempts to take his critical findings and *do* something with them that might bear on current experience, both his own and his readers'. It is probably Bloom's finest essay, which is saying a great deal.

The essay's title indicates an overall view, derived at least in some measure from Northrop Frye, that the Romanticism of Blake, Wordsworth, and the rest grows out of a literary form, chivalric or quest romance. Frye notes that traditional romance takes place in the world of realized human nature, by which he means that the outward scenes through which the questing knight wends reflect his inner condition and perhaps the reader's. The wasteland Galahad traverses is a state of nature, but also a soul state. In Romanticism, as Bloom has it, the tension between inner and outer largely drops away, and the poet explores the life of the spirit or psyche, taking it as the primary arbiter of experience. Though there is reference in Bloom's essay to the revolutionary energies that invest Romanticism, political motives are finally subordinated to literary origins: quest romance is understood as more central to the genesis of Romanticism than the revolutionary drive.

In his second book, *The Visionary Company*, Bloom regards the poetry of all the major Romantics from a Blakean perspective. In doing so he successfully reveals the visionary longings that inspire even such apparently naturalistic poets as Keats and Wordsworth. *Visionary Company* is a sprawling book, Bloom's *Four*

Zoas, if you like, as compared to "The Internalization," his brief epic on the order of *Milton*. All of the Romantics, Bloom argues in the essay, pass through phases akin to what Blake called States. There are three such phases (with various permutations): the Promethean, the Purgatorial, and the final phase, achieved only by Wordsworth and Blake, that of the Imagination or Real Man, a designation that comes from a letter Blake wrote when he was near death.

"Prometheus," writes Bloom, "is the poet-as-hero in the first stage of his quest, marked by a deep involvement in political, social, and literary revolution, and a direct, even satirical attack on the institutional orthodoxies of European and English society, including historically oriented Christianity, and the neoclassic literary and intellectual tradition, particularly in its Enlightenment phase" (p. 22). Bloom associates Prometheus with the figures Blake calls Orc and Rintrah, figures who rebel against repressive moralities of all sorts. In this connection, Bloom is thinking of the Shelley who wrote *Prometheus Unbound*, Wordsworth and Coleridge during their period of revolutionary enthusiasm, Keats's *Endymion* (a genial enough Prometheanism), and of course the Blake who declared his prophetic majority by writing *The Marriage of Heaven and Hell*.

Yet this Promethean phase tends to dissolve because, to put it in Blake's notation, Orc, the proponent of total revolution, inevitably grows fanatical – for *all* must be changed and *now*. Orc becomes obsessed with his vision of liberty and, seeking to impose it on all, he hardens into Urizen, the tyrant. Urizen, one might say, is the Blakean equivalent of Freud's sadistic super-ego, with the distinction that Blake's figure is the precipitate of particular cultural circumstances, not an unchanging eternal form. At the close of the Promethean phase there supervenes the state in which Bloom is most interested, and in which "The Internalization" and *The Anxiety of Influence* themselves might be said to take place, the purgatorial state. Bloom hasn't much to say about the final state called Imagination, other than that it is defined by a mysterious, and to me rather mystical, activity called "ongoing creation," but with the purgatorial condition he is fascinated. Part of "The Internalization"'s strength lies in showing how common and how central versions of purgatory are among the major Romantics.

Shelley and Keats, Bloom points out, both culminate their poetic lives with purgatorial poems, *The Triumph of Life* and *The Fall of Hyperion*. In *The Fall* Keats finds himself in front of a giant form, the goddess Moneta, who harshly interrogates the poet, drawing him away from his earlier sensuous poetry and toward a naturalistic humanism both tough-minded and generous. His weaknesses are, presumably, being refined away in the face of Moneta's questioning – their encounter is not unlike a harsh psychoanalytical exchange – until Keats becomes one of those for whom "the miseries of the world/Are misery, and will not let them rest." Shelley's purgatory seems less susceptible to transformation. His tutelary figure, Rousseau, recalls his intoxication by the enigmatic figure he calls the Shape All Light, a trope for idealized nature, and perhaps too an image for Rousseau's (and Shelley's) attraction to destructive narcissism.

Bloom can point to the period of despondency that Wordsworth chronicles in *The Prelude*, the period where the poet became the victim of abstract analysis, murdering to dissect. There is also Coleridge's incapacity to overcome his orthodox censor and emerge as the poet he only fleetingly depicts at the end of "Kubla Khan." The Man from Porlock; Sara who inhibits Coleridge's sensuous musings in "The Eolian Harp"; the silence that freezes the poet's epic fantasy in "Dejection": these are among Coleridge's images for the purgatorial inquisitor. The archetype for purgatorial contention, at least in Bloom's mind, is Blake's strivings with the Idiot Questioner ("Who is always questioning but never capable of answering ... Who publishes doubt & calls it knowledge"); with Satan from *Milton*; and with a figure that we'll encounter again at a key point in Bloom, the Covering Cherub.

And what about Byron? Byron never fits effectively into Bloom's mental cosmos, perhaps because he engages the three states simultaneously. From the beginning of his career Byron is a fierce enemy of all repressive orthodoxy, especially sexual orthodoxy. And if ongoing creation is the standard for entering the Imagination phase, which of the Romantics was more fertile than he? As to the Purgatorial state, Byron took most all of life to be something of a wasteland, inadequate to the scope of human desires – though to admit as much, without some flourish of wit to protest against the charade's sponsors (whoever they might be), would be beneath contempt.

Carping this way about Byron misses one of Bloom's deeper points, a point movingly if indirectly made in "The Internaliz-ation." To Bloom, poets achieve lasting value because of their spiritual strength and ambition, their power to change internally. A poet isn't someone who can speak with effortless beauty, or who's never lost for a rhyme. The words come second, records of unparalleled inner experience. Engaging all phases at once, Byron, great as he is, doesn't grow. He would have been skeptical about Bloom's standards, granted, but Bloom, valuing like Emerson not meter but a meter-making – and self-making – argument, is consistent in being dubious about Lord Byron.

For Bloom, at least early in his career, poetic quests matter because they are human quests. Thus the experiential stakes that he insists upon in a passage from the opening of the essay: "[W]hat, for men without belief and even without credulity, is the spiritual form of romance? How can a poet's (or any man's) life be one of continuous allegory (as Keats thought Shakespeare's must have been) in a reductive universe of death, a separated realm of atomized meanings, each discrete from the next? Though all men are questers, even the least, what is the relevance of quest in a gray world of continuities and homogenized enterprises? Or, in Wordsworth's own terms, which are valid for every major Romantic, what knowledge might yet be purchased except by the loss of power" (p. 18)?

A world of continuities and homogenized enterprises: this is an unusually social reference for Bloom; it could, in fact, come out of Adorno. The representatives of that fallen world make themselves manifest in the poetry of the Romantics, often though not always in the Purgatorial phase: Coleridge's Man from Porlock; Shelley's Jupiter; Blake's Satan; Keats's Identity, or habitual self; the figure that Wordsworth, with the dialectical awareness I tried to describe in chapter 3, calls Armytage and the Cumberland Beggar. This perception of the anti-type, the Romantic version of the deadening super-ego, culminates in the narrowed version of limit or fate that, in *The Anxiety of Influence*, Bloom will call the precursor.

Bloom's insight about the pervasiveness of the Romantic Purgatorial phase, in which poetry and the poet go on trial, though considerable in itself is not the major achievement of "The Internalization of Quest Romance." For having created what is after all a myth of Romantic myth, drawing a pattern out of the major writers' work (albeit with some trimming here and there), Bloom begins to put the myth into action.

"The Internalization of Quest Romance" is one of those Romantic works that attempts to perform what it describes. The essay describes a certain kind of Romantic quest, then dramatizes a contemporary version of that quest, the success of which the reader is left to judge. Similarly, Emerson's "Self-Reliance" both proposes a way of becoming original – trust your own thoughts more than others', no matter how august – and presents the results of that self-trust in its unconstrained, surprising, and novel perceptions. "The Internalization," fixing as it does on the Purgatorial stage of the quest, is itself something of a purgatorial essay. It submits its myth of Romantic myth to trial; it begins to defend the poetry it has both found and made. Bloom very much wants to embrace his Romantic myth, affirming that there is something close to absolute value in the secularly spiritual quest, even in this world of gray continuities and homogenous enterprises. And yet a complex of ideas that are neither properly Romantic, nor dully conventional, prevents him from doing so unequivocally.

One way to break down the antagonistic Selfhood, with all its selfish virtues, Bloom speculates, is through a Shelleyan dialectic of love. In "The Defence of Poetry" Shelley describes "a going out of our own nature and an identification of ourselves with the beautiful which exists in thought, action, or person, not our own."[4] Such an act dovetails well enough with Blake's fulminations against possessiveness, be it erotic, material, or imperial, and with the opening out to Eros that Keats dramatizes at the end of "Ode to Psyche," as well as echoing Wordsworth's notion

---

[4] *Shelley's Prose, or The Trumpet of a Prophecy*, ed. David Lee Clark (Albuquerque: University of New Mexico Press, 1954), pp. 282–3.

about the love of nature leading by degrees to the love of mankind. But Bloom feels a resistance to such a faith: his mind is divided.

For there is another potent doctrine that concedes love to be a going out of ourselves, but asserts that the motives for that outward motion are egotistical. A strong narcissism, says Sigmund Freud, is a safeguard against neuroses, but conversely, after a certain point, we must rid ourselves of internalized erotic energy, and fall in love so as not to fall ill. Freud's thinking is a form of erotic reductionism, Bloom is aware, but it is a more subtle and inflected reductionism than virtually any other. What impresses Bloom about Freud is his power to qualify his strictures convincingly. On the face of it, it is a vulgar simplification to say that mature love always reproduces Oedipal attachments. But having said as much, Freud goes on to show, with considerable subtlety and tact, how the healthy individual, or the one who has had some measure of mental freedom restored through therapy, can swerve away from that fate, if only by a few degrees.

Qualifications like this give Freud's view of erotic life, infinitely more severe than Shelley's, a plausibility that Bloom cannot discount. A *thoroughgoing* erotic reductionist like Schopenhauer would be easy enough to dismiss, but Freud, as Bloom reads him, rings true to some aspects of common experience. Freud provides a tough-minded version of lowest common denominator life. The Reality Principle that is comprised by Freud's thought may be a dull goddess, as Bloom remarks, but she does not strain credulity or precipitate the despair that can come from excessive expectations. And too she endorses toleration and measured hope, qualities not always in oversupply: "If [Freud's] myth of love is so sparse, rather less than a creative Word, it is still open both to analytic modification and to a full acceptance of everything that can come out of the psyche" (p. 26).

What Bloom does, then, is to take Freud as his Covering Cherub, or Figure of Identity. As Satan to Milton/Blake in Blake's brief epic, so Freud to Bloom. And the choice is a brilliant one. In a later essay (also among Bloom's best) that carries the lugubrious title "The Sorrows of Facticity," Bloom describes Freud as providing many of the intellectual and spiritual limits to our current lives: "Our culture in all of its most frozen aspects,"

Bloom says there, "has been created by its literalization of anterior tropes."[5] Or, as Frost puts it, "Great is he who imposes the metaphor." And no one has imposed more of them, Bloom observes, than Sigmund Freud.[6] Certain elements in culture urge us "to literalize all of Freud, so that we walk about now assuming we are uneasy triads of id, ego, and superego, and mingled drives of Eros and Thanatos. It takes an effort to remember that the Freudian agencies and drives are tropes, and not actual entities or real instances of human life. This is the tribute we pay to Freud, and I mean 'tribute' in more than one sense. We pay tribute to Freud involuntarily, as we do to all the powerful mythologies and idealisms that together constitute our historicized dungeon of facticity" (pp. 406-7). Freud, in short, builds his dungeons not in the air (à la Emerson's de Tocqueville), but in, and of, the human spirit. Whether Freud is the culturally pervasive archon that Bloom takes him to be, he certainly provides as comprehensive a map of experience as the Romantics do, even when viewed collectively, and it is a very different, much more darkly pragmatic map.

So in "The Internalization," Bloom achieves a great deal, concocting a myth of Romantic myth, and generating, in his image of Freud, that myth's resistant Selfhood. One might say that he is poised to use the Romantics to confront the disciplined culture of psychoanalysis (to merge the terms of Foucault and Philip Rieff). Yet the essay never becomes the ground for Blake-style mental fight. Bloom limits himself to writing a Freudian gloss on his composite Romantic quest: the Romantics say such and such, Freud says thus and so. Deep comparison and judgment never occur. In the eloquent closing lines of the piece, Bloom acknowledges as much: "The man prophesied by the Romantics is a central man who is always in the process of becoming his own begetter, and though his major poems perhaps have been written, he as yet has not fleshed out his prophecy, nor proved the final form of his love" (p. 35).

---

[5] *Poetics of Influence*, ed. John Hollander (New Haven: Schwab, 1988), p. 407. Henceforth cited in the text. The essay first appeared in *Raritan*, 3:3 (1984), pp. 1-20.

[6] For my own view of Freud's continuing cultural centrality see *Towards Reading Freud*, especially pp. 3-23.

The word "proved" is something of a crossroads. It leads outward to experience, enjoining readers to put the Romantic quest on trial in their lives. Poetry must prove itself on the pulse, as Keats said. But proving can also be a quasi-legal affair. One can, as it were, put poetry on trial. One can submit its claims to the most plausible forms of philosophical skepticism currently available, and see what remains intact after the refining fires, purgatorial fires, have done their worst. One can, in short, rise fully to defend the poetry that one loves.

Years after its publication, *The Anxiety of Influence* remains a strange and invigorating book. Composed of six essays, with prose poems at beginning and end, an introductory overview, and an inter-chapter on "Antithetical Criticism," *The Anxiety* bursts academic bonds, soliciting comparison with such odd, brilliant, uncategorizable works as Nietzsche's *Birth of Tragedy*, Freud's *Beyond the Pleasure Principle*, and Blake's *Marriage of Heaven and Hell*. Each of Bloom's chapters takes up a "revisionary ratio," a particular strategy poets use to read, or as Bloom likes to say, "misread," and rewrite their precursors.

Poetic misreading and revision are always a losing game. The poet is compelled to substantially repeat his great original: his own contribution is small. He struggles to deceive his readers, and also himself, as to how much in his work is actually new. A revisionary ratio is a tried and true way of lying. The poet, in Bloom's gloomy view, has as much chance to swerve away from his precursor as Freud's Oedipal son does to differ substantially from what his father has made of him. The son, Freud shrewdly observes, inherits not his father's ego, but the exacting, impersonal (and substantially unconscious) super-ego, which his father inherited in his turn. The possibilities for revision are very modest: many years of therapy can adjust the pressures brought to bear by the father, but not very much.

One may think that becoming a poet means joining another culture, an immortal freemasonry of intellect, as Keats had it. In the realm of such a culture, one chooses one's influences and ascends to a new sphere of values, leaving Oedipally charged family life and the society of getting and spending behind. Not so, Bloom insists: the life of poetry simply reproduces the Gothic romance from which one hoped to flee. The Oedipal complex transfers itself to the imaginative regions, where son vies with father for muse, rather than mother, and inevitably loses.

A theorist of influence is compelled to speak persuasively about the work that has affected his own, and Bloom cites Nietzsche's reflections on guilt and indebtedness in *Genealogy of Morals*, Walter Jackson Bate's broodings on the burden of the past and English poetry, and also – a touch resentfully, for Bloom intensely dislikes his modernism, conservatism, and anti-Semitism – T. S. Eliot and his "Tradition and the Individual Talent." Yet the major tutelary spirit here is Freud. The theory of the Oedipal complex is chiefly what underwrites Bloom's theory of poetic influence.

Thus Bloom, true to the promise of "The Internalization," brings Freud and the poets into extended contact. But the nature of that contact is, for a reader fresh from the great essay, rather surprising. For no obvious debate or contention takes place in *The Anxiety of Influence*. Bloom never actually stages a dialectical encounter between Freud and the poets. He never draws out their different ways of imagining critical aspects of experience and compares them. Rather Bloom seems to assume that Freud is right and applies his Oedipal terminology at every possible point. The poets receive no chance for rebuttal. It seems that Bloom has switched allegiances and that suddenly Freud, with a dose of Nietzsche added, has taken over the intellectual and spiritual allegiances not long ago reserved for the visionary company. Has Bloom actually gone over to the figure that, in "The Internalization," he equated with the Covering Cherub?

Bloom might easily have pitted the Romantics against Freud. Freud, like most of the Romantics, was an intense student of Shakespeare and Milton, and one could write a very good book comparing what the Romantics took from Shakespeare (speaking broadly, a sense of how large and complex human character might be or become; a Romantic poet, one might say, strives to make himself into someone worth including in one of Shakespeare's plays) with what Freud seems to have taken (again broadly, cues for many of his theories – bisexuality, Oedipal struggle, the strife between eros and civilization – theories that claim to show the tight boundaries of what character can be).

But there are other modes of comparison, too. Bloom's former mentor, Blake, offers a substantial rebuttal to the Oedipal theory. In Blake the sadistic father imago is often named Urizen, a figure associated with authoritarian Christianity, reductive empiricism, neoclassical canons of aesthetic taste, and the perpetuation of an unjust social order. He contains elements of Locke, Voltaire, Joshua Reynolds, and a number of political tyrants, living and dead. That is, Urizen embodies what Blake construes as the most authoritarian elements in a particular cultural and historical moment. Urizen is not an eternal figure, phylogenetically conveyed; he's the concentrated image for a specific, grotesque cultural configuration.

Change that configuration, conceptually and materially, and Urizen diminishes, perhaps he begins to evolve into Los, the creative force that forges civilization in the image of mankind's best hopes. (For Los requires some measure of what Urizen possesses in excess, discipline.) Blake invites one to see the Freudian super-ego, and thus the Oedipal father, as a trope for what's most confining in contemporary culture, rather than as an accurate figure for mankind's inevitable destiny. If the Oedipal complex is a powerful, but historically contingent fable about fate, then one can hardly base a binding, trans-temporal theory of poetry, or a theory of life (*The Anxiety*'s epigraph from Wallace Stevens equates the two), upon it. There is nothing easy about adjudicating between Blake and Freud on this issue, for there is much one can say in behalf of the psychoanalytic view. My point is that the kind of dialectical contention foreshadowed in "The Internalization" is absent from Bloom's book. He seems to go over to Freud and leave it at that: the Romantics enter into a Purgatorial phase, but there's no discernible exit.

When one describes Bloom's book abstractly it can sound like a formalist piece of work. There are six phases that define poetic careers, as well as characterizing the trajectory of fully accomplished poems. Though the revisionary ratios have peculiar names – clinamen, tessera, kenosis, daemonization, askesis, apophrades – Bloom claims that they possess a general applicability. And this claim is not altogether unlike the one Aristotle makes when in *The Poetics*, the founding text for formalist criticism in the West, he tries to isolate the elements that compose a successful tragedy. Aristotle's anatomy is teasingly ambiguous. He means to praise Sophocles as a great artist. At the same time, his presumption that he can isolate a set of defining characteristics for tragedy – offering a recipe for concocting good plays – implies that he has brought poetry comprehensively under the control of categorizing philosophy.

But if Bloom's approach is in some measure a formalism (something he would emphatically dislike hearing) it's much more aggressively skeptical than Aristotle's. For, borrowing from Freud and Nietzsche, Bloom makes charges against poetry that, while they grow out of Plato's, are yet fiercer. Bloom's poets are liars. They deceive us about their originality, about the newness and the value of what they say. In this Bloom and Plato concur. But Bloom's poets are also self-deceivers, victims of the unconscious and of the Oedipal complex, which they succeed not in over-coming, but in taking to what one might call the second degree. They suffer at the hands of their natural fathers, and of their poetic fathers, too.

"Oedipus, blind, was on the path to oracular godhood, and the strong poets have followed him by transforming their blindness towards their precursors into the revisionary insights of their own work" (p. 10). This eloquent sentence comes at the beginning of Bloom's book and comprises an acknowledgment of Paul de Man's blindness and insight theory, a device about which I have already had a good deal to say. Bloom's Oedipal reading of the poets would seem to fall in line with many, if not most, of de Man's procedures, though Bloom is much more willing than de Man to align himself with Freud. Accordingly, we must bring back once more our observations about blindness and insight thinking: about how, claiming knowledge that no one can ever disprove, and that no one is disposed to contend against, it grasps for the critic an unearned position of superiority over the text at hand; how it disenfranchises poetry, denigrates the author; how it leads to institutional ascendancy for the discipline and cultural authority for the intellectual guild; how it contributes to the development of a society devoted to discipline in which each one of us is in a position to know others better than we know ourselves, so that it is our duty, as well as our right, to engage in ongoing mutual observation and diagnosis.

The Anxiety's aggression against currently practicing poets has

often been noted. It says to them, recalling Socrates's discussion
with hapless Ion, that they don't know who they are or what
they're doing. In fact, as poetry becomes more thoroughly popu-
lated by the ghosts of past figures, it comes closer to being criticism,
which is always a *self-aware* texture of references. Bloom's description of his own book as "a severe poem" (p. 13) suggests
that eventually poetry must become more self-conscious about
its servitude to the past, evolving into an affair of allusion and
cross-reference. Poetry must collapse, in short, into critical writing.
So Hegel taught that what was most timely and consequential
in art would eventually be taken up into philosophical knowledge.

   Should one, then, list Bloom's *Anxiety of Influence* with the
influential corpus of works that joins in what I, following Danto,
want to call the philosophical disenfranchisement of art? Does
the book do what Plato, Kant, and Hegel and many others tend
to do: discredit poetry (however subtly) in favor of another mode
of thought that, whatever its resemblance to the work of the
poets, seeks a different kind of authority, a stronger claim on our
beliefs? If so, it might be worth asking how Bloom went from
being one of poetry's most consequential defenders, fighting its
battles against historical scholars, modernists, New Critics, against
all comers really, to being one of its most resourceful antagonists,
a latter-day fusion of Plato and Freud.

But is the description I have so far offered of Bloom's book really
a just one? For surely by reducing it to a system I am missing
much of what is appealing, indeed energizing, about the book.
The Anxiety of Influence is a stunningly eloquent, passionate performance. The book is written in the inventive style of Shelley's
"Defence of Poetry" and Emerson's "The Poet." Bloom's dire
news about the oncoming demise of poetry releases an inventive
force that is high Romantic in its provenance. Exuberance, says
Blake, is beauty and Bloom's is an exuberant book. Blake wanted
to wrest aesthetic authority from the neoclassical apologists for
balance, decorum and, indirectly, political quietism. So Bloom,
it would seem, wants to speak about poetry in indecorous ways,
ways that, no matter what the overt message, perpetuate Romantic energies by transferring them into the present.

Here is Bloom in a notorious passage equating Satan with the modern poet:

Why call Satan a modern poet? Because he shadows forth gigantically a trouble at the core of Milton and of Pope, a sorrow that purifies by isolation in Collins and Gray, in Smart and in Cowper, emerging fully to stand clear in Wordsworth, who is the exemplary Modern Poet, the Poet proper. The incarnation of the Poetic Character in Satan begins when Milton's story truly begins, with the Incarnation of God's Son and Satan's rejection of *that* incarnation. Modern poetry begins in two declarations of Satan: "We know no time when we were not as now" and "To be weak is miserable, doing or suffering."(p. 20)

To speak in such exalted language of beginnings and incarnations is to be a Romantic myth-maker in one's own right; to choose Satan as a representative figure is to follow Blake and Shelley. And of course Bloom means, with his defiant, rebellious book, to identify himself with Satan and his iconoclastic daring, much as Shelley and Blake did. Years after the publication of *The Anxiety*, Bloom observes that he takes a recent reference to himself as the Satan of contemporary criticism to be a compliment, though whether it was so intended he can't say.[7]

The passage about Satan as modern poet puts one of Bloom's most remarkable qualities in focus. It demonstrates his capacity to capture the energies infusing the writing he admires and bring them alive in the present. He doesn't usually do this by making metaphors, or with grand, flowering sentences. Rather he seeks for ideas that are fresh and – at least to him – deeply true, but that do not need a great deal of qualification. Bloom finds an analogy between Satan and the modern poet, and conveys it to you, straight on. Bloom's style – when he's at his best – works as a form of salutary transference, bringing the past into the present. There are many ways to achieve such transference; Bloom has invented but one. Yet it's incumbent on critics who want to defend poetry to try, even if only partial success is possible, to find a style that will convey energy as well as thought.

Orwell criticized H. G. Wells for being too sane to understand the modern world. Bloom's high style and extravagantly specu-

---

[7] "The Art of Criticism," pp. 230–1.

latively disposition arise from his view that most academic critics
of literature, and of Romanticism in particular, are far too sane,
too buttoned-up, to represent the great artists in the present.
For his part, Bloom seems committed to making contact with
poetic force and to conveying it in the accelerating flights and
prophetic urgency of his writing. And it is just here that we
arrive at one of the chief riddles of *The Anxiety of Influence*. Pre-
suming to teach us that Romanticism is a dying order of mind
and spirit, it is composed with a visionary daring that can only
be described as High Romantic. The kind of beautiful exuberance
with which Bloom writes is far out of keeping with what he has,
in fundamental terms, to impart.

To this difficulty a possible solution presents itself. There's a
particular kind of mind that assumes that the most unpalatable
truth must be the essential truth, and proceeds from there. A
votary of this doctrine, which has been called the reductive fallacy,
fears deception above almost everything else, and in particular
fears being taken completely unawares. So he prepares himself
by thinking the worst and then too by expressing it – with the
sad result that he sometimes tells others how to bring his ruin.
Yet saying the worst, when it is done with some measure of
ironic distance, with an awareness of what one is about, can be
salutary for interpreting both literature and life. It gives you
access to your most firmly held values and beliefs, those commitments that survive after fierce analytic scrutiny.

I make these remarks about the reductive fallacy (which
adroitly used need be no more fallacious than the pathetic fallacy,
without which some great lyric poetry would not exist) because
they lead to a way in which one might resolve the apparent
disparity between the argument and the style of Bloom's book.
Is it possible that *The Anxiety* is a very tough-minded defence of
poetry in which, if only by implication, some invaluable essence
is left intact after the corrosives have been applied? Perhaps
rather than defending against Freud outright, Bloom is applying
him at full strength, letting him, along with Nietzsche, Eliot,
and Bate, say the worst in order, at last, to discover what remains.

In his extremely intelligent review of *The Anxiety of Influence*,
Geoffrey Hartman observes that "Bloom's resolute pessimism
... is the shade from which he sees beauties that many of his

contemporaries overlook."[8] Beauties may not be quite the right word. What Bloom is very good at discerning is the precise way in which consequential poets differ fruitfully from the writers who have come before. Bloom is excellent at describing what's most singular about Wordsworth, what we would have lost if he had never become a poet. Though Bloom likes to describe those qualities as if they were fallings off from some former plenitude, a less demanding reader of poetry – someone who had invested less in poetry to begin with, someone who hadn't once seen it as a means to salvation – is likely to be more satisfied with them. Yet such moments, memorable as they are, do not seem to me to be central enough to the book's argumentative thrust to explain the gap between style and theme.

One might also account for the disparity by recourse to Bloom's last revisionary ratio, apophrades. In apophrades the poet achieves a triumph over the precursor. So ably has the living writer read and revised his forebear that certain passages in the precursor sound as though they had been influenced by the later poet. One hears ghostly echoes of Ashbery in lines by Wallace Stevens; Shelley's *Cenci* seems coauthored by the Browning of *The Ring and the Book*. It may be that Bloom now inflects the poets with his own voice, so that it sounds as though Shelley and Blake are Bloom's ephebes.

Milton, one might say, achieves something like what I am describing, and on the largest possible scale. All of the pagan poets he draws on in *Paradise Lost* contribute, without ever having been aware of it, to one great truth, the truth of Christianity. A hedgehog to foxes, Milton knows something so consequential that it changes the meaning of everything the Classical authors knew, and makes their poetry Milton's property. He can reread them and make them mean as they should have. So he can sound like Virgil and Ovid when he's so disposed, and yet sound all the more like himself.

Does Bloom have a comparable secret about the Romantics? Does knowing that rather than trying, say, to redescribe, and in so doing perhaps to remake, consciousness they were actually engaged in an Oedipal war with each other and with past poets

---

[8] *The Fate of Reading*, p. 42.

give Bloom access to their voices? Is he appropriating their styles ironically as Milton did Homer's? For it is possible that the tone of this book is mocking, that Bloom, bitterly disillusioned by the poets for not being what he took them to be, is writing their elegy in the tone of an ode to joy. This is not a sweet possibility, but the book does warn us never to overestimate anyone's motives for creation.

Yet if this is why Bloom writes as he does, I don't think he's justified, and for reasons that the reader, by now, will not find unfamiliar. The process of poetic creation Bloom claims to disclose takes place in the unconscious, the region beyond debate and discussion. Bloom has recourse to a god-term to account for Romantic genesis. This is a principle with which one cannot argue. Milton has recourse to God, granted. But at least one can see the encounter – or collision – between Christian and pagan values in his poem. One can argue with his appropriations for they occur in full daylight; one can judge Milton's transformations as less striking and vital than his sources, and one can say why. No discovery that is beyond argument should, in a secular sphere, license the sort of triumphal irony that, though it is not pleasant to think so, may inform Bloom's style.

Thus the fact remains that Bloom's most influential book is a high Romantic work about the demise of Romanticism. The two energies in the book, the force infusing the demystifying argument, and the gusto in the style and form, never make persuasive contact with each other, at least as I see it. When someone like Marlon Ross isolates Bloom's ideas from their mode of presentation and criticizes them, one would like to say that he has missed half of Bloom; he has missed what is least assimilable to academic norms. But when I am asked precisely why Bloom's method of presentation ought to temper the way one handles *The Anxiety* conceptually, I can come up with no good answer. It is tempting, in other words, to see the book as a great defence of poetry, in which the defender plays the temporary role of prosecuting attorney, making adroit use of the reductive fallacy, the better to secure for his side the freedom and relative autonomy it deserves. Bloom's style would be the evidence, then, for the final judgment, the judgment to the effect that when Freud and his temporary allies have done their work, "though much is taken, much abides." But try as I might, I cannot find the middle term, the extenuating testimony, either direct or implied, that justifies so appealing a verdict.

So to use Bloom's theory about influence anxiety, as much of the literary critical profession has (whether they claim to have invented it themselves or not), without reference to its mode of presentation, is not, I am sad to say, a distortion. Once you accept Bloom's idea that the poets are in combat with each other, then one's own hostility toward poetry – a hostility that may owe in part to the philosophical origins of literary criticism – becomes natural and justifiable. A good critic is always skeptical about literature: she must be, in some measure, a philosopher of poetry. Yet to follow Bloom in *The Anxiety* into assuming that agon is the way of the poetic world, and that a group of revisionary ratios defines all consequential poetry in a way that poets themselves cannot apprehend, brings one closer to a sense of calm control. It induces you to surrender the dialectic between poetry and philosophy that helps to make criticism a consequential form of writing.

Yet so far I have avoided a major question about Bloom's analytical disenfranchisement of the poets: does it reflect important truths about the experience of reading Romantic poetry in the present? Is it so?

One might here offer another version of poetic genesis as a counter-myth to Bloom's, a myth adapted from Keats's poems and letters. Keats is fascinated, sometimes ravished, by past poetry, in particular romance. But as much as Keats loves romance, it must change: he is determined that poetry evolve and that it should have a place in what he called the Grand March of Intellect. And, too, poetry should temper the Enlightenment's rigid ideas about progress, turn the march into a more pleasing ramble. To Keats poetry ought to give pleasure, yet ably defend itself against rational skepticism.

Keats loves major elements of Milton and Wordsworth – poets Bloom would call his precursors – but he sees that they do not quite meet the needs of the historical present. When he renews their work, it is not because he wishes to overcome their influence on him and achieve the first place among poets, so much as that he wants to make what matters in their work responsive to his own historical moment. (In this Keatsian view Milton's own antagonistic approach to his pagan predecessors would be anomalous, not representative.) Just so, a contemporary poet, like Amy Clampitt or James Merrill, who writes in a recognizably Keatsian idiom isn't necessarily competing with Keats. They are not trying to evade or surpass Keats, but to write as he would if he were alive in the present, taking into account the various structures of resistance and receptivity, the events that surround them here and now. It may even be true that by writing in Keats's mode in the present, a poet like Clampitt allows readers to see why Keats still has a bearing. She brings into the foreground those elements in Keats that continue to live. Thus poets rejuvenate – rather than attack – their influences.

Sometimes it's true that poets sound too much like their precursors, but that means simply that they aren't taking into account the second figure in the dialectic of poetic creation, the cultural present. A poet in that predicament needs to put down his Keats and pick up the newspaper, or flip on CNN, or read some Donald Davidson or Hilary Putnam to see what the most gifted contemporary philosophers are up to. Often poets do go through a phase of sounding like their precursors, but it's better described as being anachronistic than succumbing to influence anxiety. And for most poets who matter, this anachronistic phase doesn't last long, for no one really wants to hear it. Thus in *Animal Crackers*, Chico: "I tell you what I do: I play you one of my own compositions by Victor Herbert"; Groucho: "Make it short."

Bloom's theory of poetic genesis is oddly neoclassical in its sense of novelty. It presumes there is some stable field of poetic figures and stories. The first-comers partake opulently, and the following generations take their places until the time – the present, alas – when only scraps remain on the table. But to a Keatsian eye, changes in cultural and material history give fresh opportunities, enlarge the range of stories one can tell. In this myth, poets are not opposed so much to each other as to the dull versions of the reality principle against which their language contends.

This abbreviated Keatsian story about poetic origins appeals to me in large part because it matches up much better with my sense of poetry's promise and performance – the sense this book has been trying to defend – than does Bloom's saturnine epic. Keats's ideas about poetic genesis can work as something of a critical fiction, as they did in our discussion of "Kubla Khan" in chapter 3, to summarize a lot of satisfying experiences reading literature. But in another sense, I think that one should distrust Bloom and Keats about equally. For the Keatsian story can slide from being a story about results to a story, like Bloom's, about origins.

Asking where poetry comes from is another way of asking what it *is* and what it means. In my view, all literal inquiries into the origins of art are eminently disposable. To claim to penetrate to the beginnings of art betrays a naked quest for ascendancy over the work at hand. It's as though, seeing an extraordinary athlete in action, we began hypothesizing about her genetic makeup, the kinds of parents and grandparents she must have had to do what she does. The question to ask of an unusual achievement is not where does it come from, but "What good is it?" What values does it affirm or create? What new possibilities for human achievement does it open? What new possibilities for speech, or body movement, or sight does it discover? And what bearing have those possibilities on established forms?

But it is also true that when they are put forward by thinkers of Bloom's breadth and seriousness, stories about origins have another kind of weight. Thus one might look at *The Anxiety of Influence* as a work like Freud's *Group Psychology* or Nietzsche's *Genealogy of Morals*. Both of these books are difficult to accept as transcriptions of events; it's hard to believe literally in the primal herd or in the band of natural aristocrats. Yet the books are, in effect, fables about the present. They offer a *figurative* answer to the question, What must the past have been like for the present to be as it is? What beginnings could have brought us to our current sorry condition?

So one might try to read Bloom's book figuratively. How does this story, extravagant as it is, about poetic genesis after Milton reflect on the experience of reading Romantic poetry in the cultural present? What is Bloom trying to convey, allegorically, about the value of the work he once loved? For surely *The Anxiety of Influence* is a story about disillusionment, a story about lost love. Once the Romantics were all in all to Bloom; now they have failed him and they need to be driven out and interred beneath a Freudian monument. For what gives the book its authentic purgatorial intensity is that Bloom is turning against an aspect of himself. In Freudian terms, he is submitting Romanticism to the work of melancholia, the psychic labor by which aspects of the lost love are brought up into the psyche then banished, done away with, we may go so far as to say (Freud does) slain.[9]

But what precisely is it about the Romantics that has let Bloom down? Why has this love proved inadequate? The question matters because given the spiritual and intellectual resources Bloom has, his sense that a certain kind of poetry fails at a particular cultural moment ought, perhaps, to be our own.

Bloom observes that one of the main reasons that poetry matters is that it teaches you how to talk to yourself.[10] Not to others, but to yourself. Bloom, as the extraordinary essay "Agon: Revisionism and Critical Personality" repeatedly asserts, is interested in poetry for what he can do with it, and for what it can do for him.[11] His criticism, he observes, is as personal as lyric poetry: it's overheard. It's not something to be argued with, but to be reread or cast aside. Thus poetry lets you down when it no longer precipitates rich internal monologue and exchange. (There is no method but yourself, Bloom is fond of saying.) And here, I think, in Bloom's conception of poetry's value, one makes contact with the great drawback, but also the great and moving strength of Bloom's criticism, both in *The Anxiety of Influence* and in the books that come after.

"What is the aboriginal Self, on which a universal reliance may be grounded?" asks Emerson in "Self-Reliance." Then cheerfully throws up his hands. To him the self is "the last fact behind which analysis cannot go."[12] Bloom's sense of the self is

---

[9] See *Towards Reading Freud*, pp. 125–153, for reflections on melancholia.
[10] *Ruin the Sacred Truths*, p. 131.
[11] *Agon: Towards a Theory of Revisionism* (New York: Oxford University Press, 1982), pp. 16–51.   [12] *Essays and Lectures*, pp. 268, 269.

similarly mysterious: like Emerson who sees the self as being most alive when it departs from former commitments to initiate a new and vital mode of expression or of life, Bloom's true self is an ambivalent exertion of spirit against the past: the self as force not substance. The Bloomian self is intensely private, inward, unavailable to prolonged, continuous analysis.

And yet this conception of the self, I believe, is antithetical to a good deal of the promise infusing the Romantic poetry that Bloom, from *Shelley's Mythmaking* to *The Ringers in the Tower*, so memorably defended. While Bloom was writing "The Internalization," another interpretation of Romanticism was evolving in America. A much more diffuse, experiential, uncontained renewal of Romantic ideas gathered momentum and took off. In "A New Romanticism? Another Decadence?" the sour and self-divided essay that closes *The Ringers in the Tower*, Bloom takes stock of the new cultural movement: "A cheap apocalyptic intensity is in the air, and its electronic magnification appears to have overwhelmed taste, and not in music alone" (p. 339).

Lionel Trilling supposedly descried the '60s as modernism in the streets, but surely it was closer to public Romanticism. For much of what mattered in the '60s took a form not unrelated to Bloom's vision of Romantic Prometheanism. There was the attack on straitened, hypocritically applied sexual mores, on institutional religion, on a corrupt, war-mongering government. People often believed that the first step in political liberation would have to be the liberation of the senses; so a drive for political change became intertwined with a drive to learn humane ways of experiencing pleasure. In such an education, as Herbert Marcuse, following Schiller, insisted, art had to be central.[13] So in the '60s, as in the Romantic period, many sought to erase the lines between culture and politics, between private and public. Political change and aesthetic innovation were conceived as being inseparable, a notion that would have been congenial enough to Blake and Shelley, and perhaps even to Byron.

In "A New Romanticism? Another Decadence?" Bloom denigrates the culture springing up around him in part because it

---

[13] See especially Marcuse's *Eros and Civilization: A Philosophical Inquiry into Freud* (Boston: Beacon Press, 1955).

strikes him as a mere repetition. "Romanticism," Bloom writes, "insisted upon the autonomy of the individual, upon his freedom from traditions and conventions that had ceased to liberate form from chaos, and that instead had become mere stifling or blocking agents. In some clear sense, our current New Left is itself part of Romantic tradition, its rebelliousness ironically repeating a past creative outburst in a manner that could be judged a bit unoriginal" (p. 344). What saved the integrity of the first Romantic movement, Bloom says, is that it was a relatively highbrow phenomenon. High Romanticism was not diffused to the point of vulgarization.

But the truth is that the major Romantics desperately wanted to be vulgarized, to be popular, to be read. Blake, as difficult as he is, thirsted to be understood; Shelley, who seems to have been largely incapable of jealousy, coveted his friend Lord Byron's massive readership. The first wave of Romantics, it is well to remember, were, as Bloom teaches, great spiritual questers, the descendants of Milton, out looking for individual salvation, though in this world. But they also represented themselves as, and sometimes aspired to be, charismatic figures, men who glowed with unearthly erotic commanding light. In the third chapter I mentioned Coleridge's poet with flashing eyes and flowing hair: think also of Byron's extraordinary celebrity image, of Shelley's hermaphroditic persona, of Blake's eloquently muscled self-projections in the engravings. Even dour Wordsworth shows a golden light on his childhood self, the repository of beauty and undiluted love.

Many of the poets saw no necessary division between the most exalted spiritual quest and the drive to achieve popular acclaim, public charisma. And if M. H. Abrams is right about the fact that Wordsworth eventually internalized his revolutionary hopes, what he says does not apply to Blake and Shelley, who attempted all through their careers to speak simultaneously of public and private renewal. In *Prometheus Unbound* Shelley is talking about a revolution in consciousness, but he is also describing our attractions to arbitrary political rule and the way to overcome it. The best rock musicians in the '60s shared that willingness to engage simultaneously in personal and political renewal and to pursue complex subjects in hopes of attaining fame and the love of a mass audience.

It would take a lengthy critical exposition to persuade most academic readers that '60s rock culture attained anything consequential. Yet it seems to me that Bob Dylan's very idiosyncratic blend of American folk music and surreal visionary lyrics is one of the major artistic accomplishments of this century. The Rolling Stones may never achieve the grandeur of Blake, but they very much resemble him and perpetuate, if imperfectly, the angry grating protest one finds in "London" with songs like "Street Fighting Man" and "Jumpin' Jack Flash." In The Beatles one encounters an updated version of the pastoral – though it is often an urban comic pastoral – that Wordsworth wrote. Of course, it is the hard-edged Rolling Stones that, even in their early work, strike one now as contemporary; the Beatles sing about a Beulah world that never came true.[14]

Before dismissing these suggestions about '60s Romanticism too quickly, one might entertain the idea that a good deal of the severity informing literary study in the '70s and '80s derives from a need to repudiate the supposed excess of the '60s, thus to insure disciplinary seriousness and academic cultural authority. Maybe the price that my generation paid for its professorial credentials was turning against the '60s view that thought had to be a form of sensuous pleasure if it was to matter. (The vehement turn against Wordsworth's blending of feeling and thought that I described in chapter 3 might be an aspect of this repudiation: the battle over Wordsworth would accordingly be, in part, a battle about the '60s legacy.) Some day soon, a cultural historian may write a persuasive book gathering together an apparent diversity of phenomena from the past two decades' TV, film, literature, visual art, news media, business, advertising *and* humanistic study, and redescribe it all in terms of a drive to bury the late '60s for good.

My hypothesis *here* is simply that Bloom withdraws his energies from the Romantics – and with only the pretense of mental

---

[14] It would be worthwhile, but too much a diversion here, to draw some distinctions between the popular art that the Beatles and Stones created and the Presley, Guns 'n Roses, Madonna-style product described in chapter 2.

fight, the pretense provided by style – at the point where another reading, a reading that is populist, youthful, pleasure-seeking, immediately political, comes into play. Yet it is perhaps not quite fair to call this an alternative reading, for it is the view of Romanticism that Bloom affirms when he endorses Blake, and Frye's great book on Blake, which he learned much of by heart. It's alive in *The Ringers in the Tower* when Bloom talks about resisting gray continuities and homogenized enterprises, and rebelling "against compulsion, against conditioning, against all unnecessary limitation that presents itself as being necessary" (p. 324). Suddenly a huge segment of the populace had embraced Blake's – and Bloom's – iconoclastic wisdom, and Bloom does not like it.

Bloom, in the early work, which I persist in seeing as his best, dreamt a certain dream of poetry, and woke to find it true. By then telling a new fable about where Romantic poetry comes from, Bloom offers an implicit explanation of what he takes to be the contemporary fallen situation. Both '60s culture and Romantic poetry begin in mystified self-love, in Narcissus, not Prometheus. And Bloom becomes the authoritative voice (not unlike the intervening voice in Ovid, Milton, Freud, and Lacan that I described in "Polemics Against Presence"), speaking longingly about a cleansing neoclassicism, a counterweight to current Romantic energies. I can only say about Bloom's vastly influential influence book what it's often necessary to say about the rock songs that came out at the same time: the music is splendid, but the lyrics are all wrong.

One's reading of Romanticism in the present will be inseparable from how one regards the cultural and political shifts in the American '60s. I think that most of my contemporaries in the academy have, as part of the price of entrance, turned against that legacy, becoming culture's analysts and critics, rather than bringing to bear past and present energies that might revitalize the current scene. Contemporary left-wing criticism often follows the Romantics in equating private and political life, but it does so to issue prohibitions and offer high-minded moral judgments. There is enough judgment in this world and more, one wishes to say. What's needed is what the poets can help forge: visions of enlarged future possibility and the energy necessary to make them real.

Bloom's insistence on the personal self's priority delimits his range of response to the poets he loves. When we look at Bloom's story about the death of Romanticism allegorically – purge it of its descendental maneuvers – it reveals itself as what Northrop Frye would call an anxiety structure, an obsessive defence of the currently presiding myths of concern. Think of what a major event it would have been if Bloom had, in the early '70s, published the book that "The Internalization" seemed to presage. Imagine if he could, with his capacity to be simultaneously forceful and complex, have seen his way to using Freud to purge the Romantics, and their latter-day descendants, of their idealizations, and used the poets to undo the facile pessimism, the anxiety to take possession of the lowest-common-denominator version of experience, that sometimes mars Freud's work. The book might have been a grand piece of cultural criticism, and at a moment that badly needed it.

Yet what Bloom did write remains an invaluable book. Granted his sense of poetic influence seems unduly narrow: for poets receive inspiration from myriad places, including popular forms of art and entertainment. Their vocabulary, at least since the onset of modernism, can draw from nearly every register of society. (One thinks of Pound's pleasure in getting the word Frigidaire into a poem.) A writer today can feed on movies, TV, pop music, scholarship, journalism, as well as from that too-readily-discredited source, day-to-day experience.

Yet there is a kind of writing that is as tied to reading as Bloom claims poetry to be, that draws its key terms from established masters, and that grows and shifts by introducing other charged terms that must contend against those currently in place. I am of course describing a kind of composition that I think *The Anxiety of Influence* accounts for better than any other, literary criticism.

For what is institutional criticism, at least from one perspective, but the revision of one's predecessors, an ambivalent war against their vocabularies and values? Fiction, poetry, and drama are much more permeable to multiple cultural influences than an academic form can be. If you're a fiction writer, Melville and Dickens don't decide whether your book will be published, or if you will be read, or if you'll continue in your vocation. In academia you write for other writers, write, in a certain sense, for your precursors, or for their representatives. They stand above you as inhibiting/enabling forces in the way that Bloom's mighty dead supposedly do to the living poets. The fact that poets and novelists have an audience of readers whom they try to please gives them another court of appeal, introduces another constituency to judge their work. They're not just talking to their predecessors.

Bloom's view of inter-generational strife is much better fitted to the academy where the elders sit in judgment, and where their presence actually inhibits, distorts, but sometimes too inspires what the tyro says. A graduate student looking to understand the mysteries of academic professionalism could do worse than consult *The Anxiety of Influence*. The revisionary ratios, each one representing a degree more self-determination for the poet, might, a bit rudely, be called the six steps on the road of critical success: six ways, that is, to recast one's predecessors, yet to keep within the sphere of their comprehension and, potentially, recognition and accord.

Bloom's theory of influence suggests that what feels like Satanic rebellion to the ephebe, and looks like fiery insurrection to various guardians of public morality in government and journalism, may actually be much closer to inspired accommodation. In Bloom, the precursor – the senior – always wins. With Bloom's help, we can see that the new-fledged deconstructors of the late '70s and '80s who despised New Criticism for its attraction to organic form actually reproduced many of the New Critics' most treasured values. The deconstructors affirmed close reading and established canonical texts, much as did their precursors. If they refused to resolve the paradoxes they found, they were perhaps indulging a moderate temperamental difference, a clinamen if you like. Their quarrel, like the quarrels Bloom's poets sustain, was a family affair.

Similarly when the recently emergent critical generation affirms thematic expressions of social difference and excoriates white male standards of value, it is manifest, from a Bloomian vantage, that they are frequently taking Jacques Derrida, whom they commonly deride as an effete textualist, rather literally. His *différance* informs current versions of social difference, as his concept of logocentrism invests images of the social authority we all want to repudiate.

Such continuities exist between apparently warring forces not for metaphysical reasons, not, that is, because the mighty precursors wrestle so well. Rather, the fact that critical rebellion is more continuous with the maligned past than anyone is likely to admit, and that change tends to take place corporately, with an entire generation moving at once, attests to the fact that the institutional structure in which we do our work is, if often flexible, at certain points very tough. At the point of academic promotion, the professorial ephebe comes into harsh contact with some precursors, who are, alas for the romance, not much more than the senior members of the department. The precursors want to see novelty (but not too much) and continuity (not apparent, but real).

Genuine rebellion is hard in this context. It is difficult, in the universe Bloom describes, to be a maverick, to write in a distinctive style, to care about what others find undignified. And it may be even harder to commit oneself to *preserving* literary values that have been in circulation for some time. For to thrive one must present the appearance of rebellion. *The Anxiety of Influence* shows, among many other things, why insisting on intellectual progress in the humanities, on the kind of knowledge accumulation that takes place (purportedly) in the sciences, must compel false discoveries, false progress, compulsory factitious rebellion based on professional necessity rather than on renewing insight. On one level Bloom's book is about nothing more glamorous than institutional strife. It's about the apparent independence you enjoy, and the actual concessions you're called on to make, in academic criticism.

Yet though one may be called, one is not compelled. There's a risk here of proceeding too much in the manner of Foucault, and of seeing the academic system as an entirely rigid disciplinary structure. Reading Bloom against the grain this way, one might be tempted to believe that the professor is produced by the intellectual system just as Foucault's criminal is by the system of justice. But to find counter evidence, one need look no further than Harold Bloom, whose marvelous early work on the Romantics really is unexpected, humane, brilliant, *and* rebellious. (The difference between Bloom and the New Critics is a lot larger than clinamen or any revisionary ratio can express.) Or, one may look at the later work, the marvelous volumes of experiential criticism, *Agon, Ruin the Sacred Truths*, and *The American Religion*, written after Bloom had distanced himself from, though not forsworn, his influence theory.[15]

The Anxiety of Influence, with its indirect but telling reflections on *tendencies* toward intellectual discipline, might give us some hints about how to restructure the system to produce more people who remind us of Harold Bloom. One way to do that would be to open up the Ph.D. process a little, allowing anyone who could write a good book of literary criticism, and could speak well about major works, to join our number. No classes required, no residency needed. Walk in, pay a fee for the readers' time, get your degree, if you deserve it. Doing so might begin to loosen the grip of institutional propriety on critical work, might cause a decline in the number of philosophers of literature populating the English departments, and give a few poet–philosophers a chance.

For the truth is – Bloom helps us see – that we in literary studies are in the university under some false premises. It may be that only half of what we ought to do, the conceptual part, is teachable. Our attraction to metaphor, genius, the incommensurable, the weird, places us at odds with our colleagues in other departments. Rather than begging and borrowing our intellectual apparatuses from them, we ought to declare amicable war, letting them know that the literature department is where their ideas come not to be applied mechanically, but to be tested against potent structures of imagination that have survived much tougher scrutiny than they can, in all likelihood, provide. The best works that we teach will shrug off their finest theories, and too show

---

[15] *The American Religion: The Emergence of the Post-Christian Nation* (N. Y.: Simon and Schuster, 1992).

our colleagues why they might think twice about promulgating their models in the world outside the university gates. The literature department ought to be where the disciplines go to die. Or at least be made more flexible, modest, and humane.

But *The Anxiety of Influence* does more than provide a dystopian genealogy for institutional criticism that can remind us, inversely, of our better options. Though the book is not itself the inspired dialectical work of revision one might have hoped, it does help place the revisionary urge at the center of *criticism*, where I think it belongs. Critics often begin by falling in love with reading. They start out, as Bloom puts it, reading in order to be flooded. They want to be completely taken over by the writings that matter to them.

Sustained over too long a period these first loves can be debilitating. They harden into unexamined idealizations, reliance on which can lead to grief. Read and believe any poet unequivocally – use her terms without a second thought – and you court trouble, if only because the passage of time will turn various elements, even the finest, to irrelevance. So it's necessary to turn against former loves and interrogate them, find out their limits and strengths. Bloom expresses this well: "The idealizations of poets and poetry do not serve the spirit. Instead, they weaken the spirit by investing value in a context that cannot sustain value, in itself. Perhaps no context can, and yet it seems no surprise that poetry should entice so many of its readers into illusions."[16] Granted, yet where I depart from Bloom is in the summary, one might even say programmatic, way he withdraws his investments from the poets.

Critical revision ought to be a more tempered, a more qualified process than the melodramatic, all or nothing mode Bloom employs in *The Anxiety of Influence*. In learning to revise our relations to the art we have loved we acquire the resources for one of life's most difficult tasks. For we are compelled not just to love our husbands and wives, our parents and children and friends, but also to turn and interpret them. Indeed we must interpret ourselves, despite our own self-love. If we don't perform

[16] *Agon*, p. 50.

such interpretations, we won't be able to help others or ourselves to navigate experience. We'll be victims of the kind of unexamined idealizations that Bloom describes. So those who care about us read us in turn. This kind of interpretation, even at its most sensitive, does violence to abiding love. In the study of literature one has the chance to acquire the intellectual pitch, the subtle balance that is necessary to enact such vital interpretations. In the act Bloom calls literary revisionism we may learn something about how to interpret and change ourselves and those we care most about – and to do so with the least unnecessary pain.

Reading and teaching literature entail the ability to turn partially against what we love in its interest and our own. In this gesture lies some of the pain and pleasure of teaching. For we continually scrutinize works we deeply value, the books that have changed our lives. The process must go on slowly and in meticulous detail if it is to arrive at valuable appraisals. But it is a hard process, and it is no wonder that we often wish to suspend it by employing a theory that lets us decide the encounter with literature in advance.

But who is this self that interprets and for whom? (A question that's been left hanging since the Prologue.) What trope for the self, in other words, provides the context within which the work is to be measured? What is the inner principle of reality empowered to resist and endorse a given work? The intensity of Bloom's voice, his power to transfer the energies of great literature into the present when he's defending it (and even when he's not), seem a marvelous example of the passion the revisionary activity can provoke. Yet the range of reference is small: the critical context or self is intensely inward, in sight of solipsism.

How different is Bloom in this regard from a great liberal social critic like Lionel Trilling. Trilling's voice has none of the battle joy that radiates from Bloom's. He is slow, circumspect, lugubrious. He reminds one of Virgil's Aeneas, or Tennyson's King Arthur, wearily sustaining civilized values in the face of pressing barbarism. Trilling's imagined constituency is so large that to cover it he attenuates his identity: he is all character, no personality. As R. P. Blackmur said, Trilling had a mind "never entirely his own." It was a mind "always deliberately to some extent what he understands to be the mind of society, and also a mind always deliberately to some extent the mind of the old European society taken as corrective and as prophecy."[17]

Must it cost as much as it did Trilling to be a critic who embodied and sought to reform social values? For if exuberance is beauty, Trilling is plain. Yet he is, as I see it, a noble writer, and not least for what he seems to have sacrificed to sustain his comprehensive designs. Bloom's gusto arises in part because he cares not at all for any constituency that doesn't resemble him to begin with. No consideration – no effort at broadening his audience – slows him down. Could one fuse Bloom's exuberance with Trilling's breadth? Are the ways of the social critic, in the mode of Arnold (whom Bloom despises), and a deeply inward critic, a contemporary gnostic like Bloom, completely separated? I think not. And I can answer this question and bring much of what I have said in this book into sharper focus by returning for a moment to the work that *The Anxiety of Influence* might have been had it entered the mental fight "The Internalization" seemed to enjoin. What if *The Anxiety* were the defence of poetry it gave promise of being?

Bloom observes that the beginnings of *The Anxiety of Influence* were in a dream, a nightmare actually, that featured a creature called the Covering Cherub. And indeed, in the journal fragment from which the book took form, that figure has the central place.[18] As *The Anxiety* unfolds, the Cherub evolves into the precursor, but in the opening chapter on clinamen, the chapter that derives from Bloom's notebook entry, the Cherub has a much broader, more socially inclusive identity. Bloom describes the Cherub as his emblem for the anxiety that blocks creativeness. "He is that something that makes men victims and not poets, a demon of discursiveness and shady continuities, a pseudo-exegete who makes writings into Scriptures" (p. 35).

The Cherub makes past writings feel as though they were fixed, eternal, and unalterably true. "The Covering Cherub then is a demon of continuity; his baleful charm imprisons the present

---

[17] *The Lion and the Honeycomb* (New York: Harcourt, Brace and Company, 1955), p. 34.
[18] *Poetics of Influence*, pp. 77–99.

in the past, and reduces a world of differences into a grayness of uniformity. The identity of past and present is at one with the essential identity of all objects. This is Milton's 'universe of death' and with it poetry cannot live, for poetry must leap, it must locate itself in a discontinuous universe, and it must make that universe (as Blake did) if it cannot find one. Discontinuity is freedom. Prophets and advanced analysts alike proclaim discontinuity" (p. 39).

These splendid lines are anachronistic; they recall what Bloom calls his "Romantic humanism." Their hopefulness has little to do with the larger argumentative thrust of *The Anxiety*. Yet they make contact with a major dimension of art. Poetry strives to outdistance the universe of death, to surpass all of the socially insinuated languages, the ways of saying and seeing, that imprison us in outmoded assumptions. We go to literary art to find ways of talking not just to ourselves, but to others; we seek alternatives to stiflingly normative idioms. Poetry that matters is at perpetual enmity with what Foucault – and on this point Bloom comes quite close to a figure he has described as massively irrelevant to the study of literature – has suggested we call disciplines. For Foucault there will be cherubim, no single monarchical Cherub: the dialectic is dead. But the process of strong rewriting may be Bloomian, if ingloriously piecemeal.

Bloom's remarks on the Covering Cherub return us to "The Internalization" and the deep perception that the poets who matter can profitably be seen in opposition not primarily to each other, but to the languages in which "a gray world of continuities and homogenized enterprises" would legitimate itself. True poetry does not produce ideologies, or give us access to the Truth, rather it provides alternatives to habitual ways of thinking. It enlarges the stock of available reality, as Blackmur put it, by offering a verbal alternative to fixed assumptions about what the realities are.

Granted much of what calls itself poetry and advanced analysis is itself part of the universe of death or the disciplines; granted too that, given the passage of time and shifts in material life, poetry from the past, even work that was once greatly consequential, may eventually become a blocking agent, an ally of the Cherub. Critics may expend energies identifying texts gone cartilaginous, but the better alternative is to find and endorse those works that have changed their lives and might change the lives of others. As those new works take their place, the old are likely to fade and disappear from the cultural mind. The critic is a discoverer of discoveries, even discoveries that took place hundreds of years before she was born. And those discoveries may enter into mental fight with existing forms, struggling against them, much as Bloom says the poet struggles against his precursor.

So had Bloom written the defence of Romanticism that "The Internalization" seems to announce, he would have written against the disciplinary Cherub (who at times is accurately figured as Sigmund Freud), and written not only from his own limited and fascinating selfhood, but from a self in the liminal zone between the social and the personal, the public and the private.

The critics who matter have developed characters: that is, they themselves at least partially embody and comprehend presiding version of the reality principle. We read them in some measure because their sense of fate or limitation is so strong. William Hazlitt, a great cultural critic who hated tyranny, himself understood – and understood because he possessed – the hunger for being dominated that he saw fouling political life around him. Writing toward the end of the Enlightenment, Samuel Johnson, who said that the first step toward greatness is to be honest, honestly entertained the religious doubts that many of his contemporaries felt, but were unwilling to unfold. So Virginia Woolf records unflinchingly, in her literary and social criticism, the multiple inhibitions, both publicly administered and inwardly contrived, against a woman's entering cultural life on equal terms.

But as well as having a strong sense of fate or limit, these critics all had extraordinary powers of response. They were sensitive to literary works that broke through debilitating established forms and promised human renovation. Johnson celebrates the poet's capacity to "give us something that is new" and finds it in the furthest corners of literature; Hazlitt wagers that the sublime powers of speech that common men and women can begin to acquire from Shakespeare will more than compensate for the absolutist prejudices infusing the plays; Woolf assumes, and rightly I think, that the power to invent artistically is always in some measure a resource for those who need to reinvent their social identities.

These figures incarnate central forms of limitation – and know it – but they also know gestures toward freedom when they see them. Bloom, especially in his earlier works, knows freedom well, but the context he provides is impoverished: it sometimes seems little more than a matter of his particular personality. Foucault, on the other hand, develops an extraordinary image for contemporary, fallen versions of the reality principle, the disciplines: yet he will not risk his authority by offering ideas about freedom. One wonders if it might not be possible to fuse the two tendencies, Bloom's vitality and Foucault's social sense, until you got someone both exuberant and broadly engaged: a Bloom who understands how much like other people he actually is; a Foucault who likes to laugh: Socrates playing on the flute.

I have said that this is in some sense a Foucauldian book: that is, it has used Foucault's ideas about the disciplines to describe the institutional effects of certain forms of contemporary theoretical criticism. We found the Freudian blindness and insight motif, with all its disciplinary force, not only in de Man, but also (with qualifications) active in Derrida, working at near industrial strength in Levinson and Ross, entering quite needlessly in Greenblatt, and alas at the core of Bloom's most widely read book. But descendentalism is more than a mode of critical discipline. It also has social ramifications, promoting as it does forms of control that rely on subtle surveillance, on the expert's power to know his clients and charges better than they know themselves.

But if this has been a Foucauldian book, it has also, I hope, come out of Bloom. For it is Bloom who, at least early in his career, is attuned to poetry's capacity to breed excess, to open possibilities for expression and life that extend beyond the world of homogenized enterprises that we often inhabit. Whatever power this volume might have to find in Wordsworth, Coleridge, and Shakespeare, in Emerson and Blake, that which exceeds discipline (both institutional and social), and to transfer that force into the present, receives impetus from Bloom – and from those like him: Johnson, Hazlitt, Emerson, Woolf, Richard Poirier. This book, at least as I apprehend it, has attempted to merge versions of freedom and fate, Bloom and Foucault. Though it surely has not touched the standard of Nietzsche's flute playing Socrates, the interfusion of Apollo and Dionysus, I hope I have gestured effectively toward such an ideal, albeit in contemporary guise.

Of course to talk schematically about a philosopher–poet who personifies a desirable criticism is, in Emerson's phrase, a "poor external way of speaking." Johnson, Hazlitt, and Woolf became who they did as critics not with a recipe, but through an introspection so severe that it revealed their potentially determining circumstances. Their strength lay in the fact that such introspection, which perhaps placed them in contact with the worst aspects of their cultures and themselves, didn't make them despondent, didn't kill their capacity for literary pleasure. So Coleridge, in "Dejection," speaks of being taken over by his analytic temper: "Till that which suits a part infects the whole,/ And now is almost grown the habit of my soul" (92–3). To this point, I think, much of academic literary criticism has now come.

But it need not stay there. There is enough great literary art, present and past, to justify our turning away from exclusive commitment to disenfranchising theory. And opportunities are ever new in that time's passage will demand that fresh works be discovered or reinterpreted to feed the present's and future's imagined needs.

This book began with a brief look at the quarrel between the philosophers and the poets, and with the contention that Plato's view has recently been augmented by material and conceptual developments, and now stands largely preeminent in Anglo-American literary studies. What we now call literary theory in many ways comes out of Plato's polemic against poetry. The book has not argued for doing away with theory per se; rather it has maintained that the function of literary criticism is not merely to apply theory to great works and leave it at that, but to allow for, in fact to create, rejoinders on behalf of relevant works, to say, thinking of Leavis, "Yes, but." Rather than banishing theory, one wants the best possible theories in place to challenge poetry. Thus the book has measured major literary art against what I take to be some of the most impressive critiques theory can muster.

One of the difficulties repeatedly met is that some theories just don't allow for rebuttal. De Man's blindness and insight model and Bloom's ideas about influence depend on Freud's theory of the unconscious. They appeal to a descendental principle, a god-term. One can point out this reliance; one can arrive at a notion of what the theorists offer once they've been purged of their other-worldly longings, then let a dialogue begin. Without a theory of the unconscious, Bloom's *Anxiety of Influence* still has a great deal to say about criticism, and I have tried to respond. De Man, however, offers little more than a model that empowers himself, other critics who operate in his mode, and the institution of literary study – though at considerable cost – and alas does little more.

The recent wave of historical criticism came on with the expressed purpose of doing away with the metaphysical longings that, it was said, underwrote theory. It is disappointing, then, to see the theory of repression crop up in Ross, of suppression in Levinson, and in Bewell intimations of a now rather general drive to bury poetic work in contextualizing detail. Historically inflected discourses of origins have the tendency, much like Bloom's, to reduce to questions about meaning and identity. Once we know the cultural context from which the poem emerges, we know the poem. But *knowing* the poem is not the object of criticism; rather one wants to use the poem, apply it to the current context to see what it might help us do and say. The historical critics have tried to solve the world; the object, first, is to reimagine it.

The challenge to poetry that we located in Jacques Derrida derives, surprisingly perhaps, not from some liminal space between poetry and philosophy, but from the metaphysical tradition that Derrida presumes to displace. His polemic against presence takes the metaphysical suspicion about appearances to a second degree, doubting not merely visual perceptions, but words that yield images. Derrida gives us a verbal iconoclasm. To evaluate Derrida's potent challenge to literature, I applied an Emersonian law of compensation: What is gained and what lost if you read as Derrida dictates? The answer was, in simple terms, that though there is great merit in being suspicious about visual fascination and its tendency to devolve into fanaticism, Derrida's pervasive ethos of *différance* is not an adequate response. We lose too much pleasure and vitality when we turn away from all vision and join the ascetic priesthood of Derridean deconstruction. Rather than having a philosophical policy of zero tolerance for presence, it is better, I think, to adjudicate cases one by one. Criticism that interrogates particular works at given points in time allows for more flexibility in response to the energizing, but potentially deceiving, claims of sight.

In Foucault, as frustrating as he can be, full of pomp and self-protective grand pronouncements, I found a philosophical critique that one might profitably apply in the present. His theory of the disciplines (not of Power) offers a challenge to literature. He makes us ask how much the poems we love can contribute to the creation of normal, productive, terminally-numbed subjects. And too he offers a meeting place where the verbal actions that are literary art can encounter, and perhaps overcome, the disciplinary language that hems current modes of subjectivity in. But Foucault, even in revised form, is not by himself sufficient. In "Invisible Bullets," Greenblatt, guided by *Discipline and Punish*, displays extraordinary sensitivity to the disciplinary designs active in Shakespeare. But he is utterly without Bloom's power to delight in enfranchising figures like Falstaff. Bloom's own reflections on Shakespeare close exuberantly, with the warning that if we bore Falstaff, he will not deign to represent us. But what forces acting on and in us make us as likely to bore Falstaff as we are? Why do we need *him* here and now?

Thus it should be clear that I have not written against theory or negative critique as such. I think, for instance, that those who challenge literature using terms such as race, class, gender, and sexuality ought to press their claims as hard as they can. I do not – and cannot, given my own critique of contextualizing urges in historical criticism – write these challenges off by suggesting that such and such a poet's attitude is dated, and that that ought to be an end to it. If Milton is a misogynist – in the terms of the present, in *your* terms – then say so. But it is important not to stop there. One must turn and try to say what one can still learn from Milton, what in his work continues to live. Shall we deprive ourselves of contact with Milton's vast imaginative synthesis, his eloquence, his learning, his depiction of that great rebel Satan because we don't like the way he renders Eve? One is bound to be *ambivalent* about Milton as one ought to be about virtually every writer. But perhaps ambivalence does not dispense the energy that criticism requires. Maybe only simple love or simple denunciation will do now to rally the necessary powers.

My largest concern in writing this book, of course, is that having set out a plan for defending poetry – with defence inevitably involving some harsh, even assaultive questioning – my own rebuttals on behalf of the poets will have been inadequate. My remarks about transferential critical style and metaphor making, as well as about philosophical tough-mindedness, may invite a kind of scrutiny that this book will be unable to bear. Anyone who wishes to argue for the power of poetry to resist assimilation to fixed terminologies ought, one might imagine, to write in a prose that sometimes traffics effectively with the poetic, and that is, if not prophetic out and out, at least not readily assimilable to institutional norms. The possibilities for failure in this kind of criticism are large. But perhaps it is also true that for the knowing analytical critic, success is too likely, maybe inevitable. Let me close then by returning to the book's beginning, to Wordsworth's "Intimations" ode, and adducing a potent advocate for the kind of criticism, the kind of failure, I have in mind.

Despite his line about the road of excess leading to the palace of wisdom (a line which may be ironic), it wasn't Wordsworth's broodings on the soul's prior life and the imperial palace whence we come that moved William Blake when he read "Intimations." Rather, as Crabb Robinson reported, the lines at the end of the fourth stanza brought him to tears. The sequence begins: "But there's a Tree, of many, one,/A single field which I have looked upon,/Both of them speak of something that is gone" (51–3). I imagine that Blake was overcome by the sheer, appalling naturalness of that tree. In English poetry before Wordsworth, "a Tree, of many, one" would have had to be associated with the tree of the knowledge of good and evil, and with the cross on which Christ was crucified. It surely would have been in anything

Blake wrote. Now the tree was devoid of every mythical and systemic association. Blake, as I imagine it, wept for Wordsworth for being someone living in the world, if only for moments at a time, without any kind of religious or philosophical consolations. He wept in compassion, but also in intense admiration, a kind of admiration that contemporary criticism ought not to be ashamed to emulate, however difficult it is to express.

The image of the solitary tree, submitted to Wordsworth's naturalizing gaze, challenged Blake, just as the child in "Intimations," whose vitality is an affront to existing social arrangements, did Coleridge. And both continue to challenge us: they defy our smug Freudian reductions about childhood, our allegiances to systematic thought, our recourse to religious consolation. These images offer us better ways of talking, cast as they are in a language at odds with the discourse of deadening truth, of discipline. And too they gesture toward better ways of conducting life. The power to challenge established ways of seeing and saying things in the interest of something potentially better, and to do so memorably, makes a poem like "Intimations" worth teaching and studying. Such power ought to make a poem canonical, at least for now.

Index